Advanced Introduction to Mental Health Law

Elgar Advanced Introductions are stimulating and thoughtful introductions to major fields in the social sciences and law, expertly written by the world's leading scholars. Designed to be accessible yet rigorous, they offer concise and lucid surveys of the substantive and policy issues associated with discrete subject areas.

The aims of the series are two-fold: to pinpoint essential principles of a particular field, and to offer insights that stimulate critical thinking. By distilling the vast and often technical corpus of information on the subject into a concise and meaningful form, the books serve as accessible introductions for undergraduate and graduate students coming to the subject for the first time. Importantly, they also develop well-informed, nuanced critiques of the field that will challenge and extend the understanding of advanced students, scholars and policy-makers.

For a full list of titles in the series please see the back of the book. Recent titles in the series include:

Advanced Introduction to

Mental Health Law

MICHAEL L. PERLIN

Professor Emeritus of Law, New York Law School, USA

Elgar Advanced Introductions

 Edward **Elgar**
PUBLISHING

Cheltenham, UK • Northampton, MA, USA

Published by
Edward Elgar Publishing Limited
The Lypiatts
15 Lansdown Road
Cheltenham
Glos GL50 2JA
UK

Edward Elgar Publishing, Inc.
William Pratt House
9 Dewey Court
Northampton
Massachusetts 01060
USA

A catalogue record for this book
is available from the British Library

Library of Congress Control Number: 2020950914

This book is available electronically on *Elgar Advanced Introductions: Law*
www.advancedintros.com

Printed on elemental chlorine free (ECF)
recycled paper containing 30% Post-Consumer Waste

ISBN 978 1 78990 390 4 (cased)
ISBN 978 1 78990 392 8 (paperback)
ISBN 978 1 78990 391 1 (eBook)

Typeset by Servis Filmsetting Ltd, Stockport, Cheshire
Printed and bound in the USA

To Linda, for a lifetime of joy and laughter and smiles and love and happiness.

To Alex and Liz (and to Sam), and to Julie and Ben (and to Sophie), with my love to all of my expanding family. You all make me happier (and luckier) than I could ever have imagined.

Contents

About the author

Michael L. Perlin is Professor of Law Emeritus at New York Law School (NYLS), where he was director of NYLS's Online Mental Disability Law Program, and director of NYLS's International Mental Disability Law Reform Project in its Justice Action Center. He is co-founder of Mental Disability Law and Policy Associates, and is currently Adjunct Professor of Law, Emory University School of Law, and Instructor, Loyola University New Orleans, Department of Criminology and Justice. He has written 33 books and nearly 300 articles on all aspects of mental disability law. He has litigated at every court level from police court to the US Supreme Court, and has done advocacy work on every continent. He is the honorary life president of the International Society for Therapeutic Jurisprudence and a member of that society's current Board of Trustees.

He is also a member of the Lawrence Township (NJ) Community Concert Band and the board of directors of the Washington Crossing (NJ) Audubon Society.

Acknowledgements

This book draws on my treatise, MENTAL DISABILITY LAW: CIVIL AND CRIMINAL (3d ed. 2016) (2019 update) (Lexis-Nexis), co-authored with Professor Heather Ellis Cucolo.

It also draws on my articles, *"Who Will Judge the Many When the Game is Through?": Considering the Profound Differences between Mental Health Courts and "Traditional" Involuntary Civil Commitment Courts*, 41 SEATTLE U. L. REV. 937 (2018) (the source of portions of Chapter 7) and *"I Expected It to Happen/I Knew He'd Lost Control": The Impact of PTSD on Criminal Sentencing after the Promulgation of DSM-5*, [2015] UTAH L. REV. 881 (the source of portions of Chapter 10), and my book chapter, *The Insanity Defense: Nine Myths That Will Not Go Away*, in THE INSANITY DEFENSE: MULTIDISCIPLINARY VIEWS ON ITS HISTORY, TRENDS, AND CONTROVERSIES 3 (Mark D. White ed., 2017) (Praeger) (the source of one portion of Chapter 9).

1 Introduction to the *Advanced Introduction to Mental Health Law*

1.1 Historical roots

The importance of mental disability law—as a specialty of practice and as a subject of scholarship—has exploded. Mental disability issues permeate much of the general practice of law, civil and criminal, public and private, statutory and decisional, domestic and international.[1] It is crucial that practicing lawyers—and mental health professionals, as well—have some sense of the quiet revolutions that have taken place in courtrooms and in legislatures over the past near half-century.[2]

But there is nothing truly new. The relationship between law and mental health was considered in early Roman law, in Justinian's codes and in the Qing code of China.[3] Thus, even though the constitutional "right to treatment" concept is less than 50 years old,[4] questions as to the adequacy of institutional treatment date to the Middle Ages.[5] The origins of the concept of a "right to refuse treatment" can be found in Blackstone.[6] Notwithstanding these early references and

---

1 Also, the ratification of the United Nations' Convention on the Rights of Persons with Disabilities (CRPD) will exponentially increase the significance of this area of law. See, e.g., MICHAEL L. PERLIN, INTERNATIONAL HUMAN RIGHTS AND MENTAL DISABILITY LAW: WHEN THE SILENCED ARE HEARD (2011). See *infra* 7.3.

2 See MICHAEL L. PERLIN AND HEATHER ELLIS CUCOLO, MENTAL DISABILITY LAW: CIVIL AND CRIMINAL ch. 1 (3d ed. 2016) (2019 update).

3 See JUDITH S. NEAMAN, SUGGESTION OF THE DEVIL: THE ORIGINS OF MADNESS 67–110 (1975); William P. Alford and Chien-Chang Wu, *Qing China and the Legal Treatment of Mental Infirmity: A Preliminary Sketch in Tribute to Professor William C. Jones*, 2 WASH. U. GLOBAL STUD. L. REV. 187 (2003). Similarly, the sources of state responsibility for persons with mental disabilities are based largely on common-law traditions of the thirteenth century as codified in 3 BLACKSTONE, COMMENTARIES 427 (1783). See *infra* 4.2.1.

4 See, e.g., Michael L. Perlin, *"Abandoned Love": The Impact of* Wyatt v. Stickney *on the Intersection between International Human Rights and Domestic Mental Disability Law*, 35 LAW & PSYCHOL. REV. 137 (2011). See *infra* Chapter 5.

5 See generally MICHEL FOUCAULT, MADNESS AND CIVILIZATION: A HISTORY OF INSANITY IN THE AGE OF REASON (1973).

6 See 1 BLACKSTONE, *supra* note 3, at 128, as discussed in RAOUL BERGER, GOVERNMENT

considerations, a substantial body of "mental disability law" has only emerged in the past half-century.

Just over 40 years ago, Bruce Ennis, one of the primary architects of the litigation strategies that led to many of the developments discussed here, observed: "The rapidity and the extent of this change in judicial attitudes are astonishing, and, to my knowledge, unprecedented. In no other area of the law of which I am aware has so much changed, so fast."[7] Since Ennis wrote this, legal change has continued unabated, although, strikingly, mainstream attitudes toward disability continue to lag behind legal developments.[8]

In every state and in most other nations, statutory schemes regulate the care and treatment of institutionalized persons with mental disabilities, and govern the extent to which such a person's civil rights could be limited because of disability. Although for many years, these statutes were largely ignored, the emergence of a combination of social, political, clinical and judicial factors resulted in a subsequent "explosion"[9] of litigation and legislation in all aspects of mental disability law.

1.2   Social and political factors

Consider the wide range of social, political and cultural factors that have had a significant impact on developments in this area of the law, dating back to the 1960s, when the Warren Court's embrace of liberal judicial activism led many minority groups to come to seek vindication of their civil rights in the federal courts. This reality prodded the "civil rights revolution" to include persons with mental disabilities as a marginalized (often invisible) class when revelations of substandard and dangerous living conditions in state facilities for persons with

---

BY JUDICIARY: THE TRANSFORMATION OF THE FOURTEENTH AMENDMENT 20–36 (1977).

7 Bruce Ennis, *Judicial Involvement in the Public Practice of Psychiatry*, in LAW AND THE MENTAL HEALTH PROFESSIONS: FRICTION AT THE INTERFACE 5, 5 (Walter E. Barton and Charlotte J. Sanborn eds., 1978).

8 Elizabeth Emens, *Framing Disability*, [2012] U. ILL. L. REV. 1383.

9 See, e.g., John La Fond, *An Examination of the Purposes of Involuntary Civil Commitment*, 30 BUFF. L. REV. 499 (1981); Michael L. Perlin, *"Things Have Changed": Looking at Non-Institutional Mental Disability Law through the Sanism Filter*, 46 N.Y.L. SCH. L. REV. 535 (2002–03).

mental disabilities first sensitized a "stunned nation" to the plight of such institutionalized persons.[10]

Importantly, by the early 1970s, the US Supreme Court began to focus on many aspects of the law affecting persons with mental disabilities; this focus—perhaps a "fascination"—served as an impetus for many of the subsequent developments in this area, making it nearly impossible for the "outside world" to ignore questions of discrimination against persons with mental disabilities.[11]

Important changes both in clinical treatment and in social policy led simultaneously to the recognition that mental disability cannot be seen as a monolithic all-or-nothing condition.[12] Also, an organized, coherent mental disability bar developed, resulting in proliferating case law.[13] The difference between case law developments in states where there is such an organized bar and those states in which there is no such bar is startling.[14]

1.3   Criminal law developments

There have also been important parallel developments in all areas of criminal law and procedure as they apply to persons with mental disabilities. Many of these developments flow from use of the vividness

---

10 Michael L. Perlin, "*Chimes of Freedom*": *International Human Rights and Institutional Mental Disability Law*, 21 N.Y.L. SCH. J. INT'L & COMPAR. L. 423, 424–25 (2002).

11 See generally Michael L. Perlin, *The ADA and Persons with Mental Disabilities: Can Sanist Attitudes Be Undone?* 8 J. L. & HEALTH 15 (1993–94).

12 See, e.g., Aaron Dhir, *Human Rights Treaty Drafting through the Lens of Mental Disability: The Proposed International Convention on Protection and Promotion of the Rights and Dignity of Persons with Disabilities*, 41 STAN. J. INT'L L. 181 (2005).

13 See generally Michael L. Perlin, "*I Might Need a Good Lawyer, Could Be Your Funeral, My Trial*": *A Global Perspective on the Right to Counsel in Civil Commitment Cases, and Its Implications for Clinical Legal Education*, 28 WASH. U. J. L. & SOC'L POL'Y 241, 246–49 (2008).

14 See, e.g., Michael L. Perlin, "*You Have Discussed Lepers and Crooks*": *Sanism in Clinical Teaching*, 9 CLINICAL L. REV. 683, 708–09 (2003):

> A contrast between the development of case law in Virginia and Minnesota is especially instructive. Notwithstanding the fact that Virginia's population is approximately 15% greater than Minnesota's, Virginia had only two published litigated civil cases on questions of mental hospitalization during the decade from 1976 to 1986, while Minnesota had at least 101 such cases in the same period. Significantly, Minnesota has a tradition of providing vigorous counsel to persons with mental disabilities, while Virginia does not.

heuristic[15] embedded in the "public outrage"[16] at the acquittal on insanity grounds of an attempted presidential assassin nearly 40 years ago, and outrage at the *use* of the defense in other high-profile, media-friendly cases. All of this has led to a reexamination of the role of responsibility as an exculpatory defense in criminal law,[17] with many states drastically limiting or abolishing the defense altogether. At the same time, although the Supreme Court has not chosen to modify the substantive standard for competency to stand trial in the 60 years since it decided *Dusky v. United States*,[18] it has returned to the topic of *collateral* competency issues multiple times, focusing on questions of competency to plead guilty,[19] to waive counsel,[20] and to be executed.[21] It has also reconsidered frequently the question of whether the execution of a person with intellectual disabilities violates the Eighth Amendment,[22] and has weighed the right of persons with mental disabilities to independent expert evaluations in death penalty cases.[23] In short, the related questions remain of great significance to the Court.

---

15 The vividness heuristic teaches us: "One single vivid, memorable case overwhelms mountains of abstract, colorless data upon which rational choices should be made." See Michael L. Perlin, *"The Borderline Which Separated You from Me": The Insanity Defense, the Authoritarian Spirit, the Fear of Faking, and the Culture of Punishment*, 82 IOWA L. REV. 1375, 1417 (1997).

16 See Michael L. Perlin, *Unpacking the Myths: The Symbolism Mythology of Insanity Defense Jurisprudence*, 40 CASE W. RES. L. REV. 599, 686 (1989–90).

17 See, e.g., Kahler v. Kansas, 140 S. Ct. 1021 (2020) (abolition of the traditional insanity defense does not violate the due process clause), discussed *infra* Chapter 9.

18 362 U.S. 402 (1960). See *infra* Chapter 8.

19 Godinez v. Moran, 509 U.S. 389 (1993). See *infra* Chapter 8. See, e.g., Michael L. Perlin, *"Dignity Was the First to Leave": Godinez v. Moran, Colin Ferguson, and the Trial of Mentally Disabled Criminal Defendants*, 14 BEHAV. SCI. & L. 61 (1996).

20 Indiana v. Edwards, 554 U.S. 164 (2008). See *infra* Chapter 8.

21 Panetti v. Quarterman, 551 U.S. 930 (2007). See *infra* Chapter 11. See, e.g., Michael L. Perlin, *"Good and Bad, I Defined These Terms, Quite Clear No Doubt Somehow": Neuroimaging and Competency to be Executed after Panetti*, 28 BEHAV. SCI. & L. 671 (2010).

22 E.g., Atkins v. Virginia, 536 U.S. 304 (2002). See *infra* Chapter 11. This work will use "mental retardation" when it quotes or discusses contextually a case that used that now-obsolete terminology.

23 Ake v. Oklahoma, 470 U.S. 68 (1985); McWilliams v. Dunn, 137 S. Ct. 1790 (2017). See *infra* Chapter 10. See, e.g., Michael L. Perlin, *"Deceived Me into Thinking/I Had Something to Protect": A Therapeutic Jurisprudence Analysis of When Multiple Experts Are Necessary in Cases in which Fact-Finders Rely on Heuristic Reasoning and "Ordinary Common Sense,"* 13 L.J. SOC'L JUST. 88 (2020).

1.4   Backlashes

Of course, there are always backlashes. The extension of the civil rights revolution to this population has resulted in calls for more restrictive commitment laws and for a return to treatment-premised commitments, and in the enactment of more restrictive "assisted outpatient treatment" legislation, such as New York's "Kendra's Law."[24] This has led to a troublesome "blurring" between civil and criminal mental disability law,[25] one that is ultimately anti-therapeutic.[26] I hope that the publication of this book clarifies many of the troubling issues in question and brings more coherence to this area of the law.

1.5   The structure of the book

The book begins with a short chapter on several jurisprudential filters[27] that must be understood if any of mental disability law is to make sense, followed by a chapter on the role of counsel.[28] I then consider substantive and procedural constitutional *civil* mental disability law,[29] followed by a "cusp" chapter that seeks to bridge the gap between civil and criminal mental disability law, looking at the role of mental health courts and the significance of international human rights law.[30] I conclude with four chapters on *criminal*

---

24 See Michael L. Perlin, *Therapeutic Jurisprudence and Outpatient Commitment: Kendra's Law as Case Study*, 9 PSYCHOL. PUB. POL'Y & L. 183 (2003).

25 See, e.g., Michael L. Perlin, Deborah A. Dorfman and Naomi M. Weinstein, *"On Desolation Row": The Blurring of the Borders between Civil and Criminal Mental Disability Law, and What It Means for All of Us*, 24 TEX. J. ON CIV. LIBS. & CIV. RTS. 59 (2018).

26 Id. at 117.

27 See *infra* Chapter 2. See, e.g., Michael L. Perlin, Talia Roitberg Harmon and Sarah Chatt, *"A World of Steel-Eyed Death": An Empirical Evaluation of the Failure of the Strickland Standard to Ensure Adequate Counsel to Defendants with Mental Disabilities Facing the Death Penalty*, 53 U. MICH. J. L. REF. 261 (2020) (discussing these filters).

28 See *infra* Chapter 3. On how, in many jurisdictions, the level of representation remains almost uniformly substandard, and, even within the same jurisdiction, the provision of counsel can be "wildly inconsistent," see Michael L. Perlin, *"You Have Discussed Lepers and Crooks": Sanism in Clinical Teaching*, 9 CLINICAL L. REV. 683, 690 (2003).

29 See *infra* Chapters 4 (civil commitment), 5 (institutional rights) and 6 (community rights).

30 See *infra* Chapter 7. See, e.g., Michael L. Perlin, *"Who Will Judge the Many When the Game is Through?": Considering the Profound Differences between Mental Health Courts and "Traditional" Involuntary Civil Commitment Courts*, 41 SEATTLE U. L. REV. 937 (2018); Michael L. Perlin, *Understanding the Intersection between International Human Rights and Mental Disability Law: The Role of Dignity*, in THE ROUTLEDGE HANDBOOK OF INTERNATIONAL CRIME AND JUSTICE STUDIES 191 (Bruce Arrigo and Heather Bersot eds., 2013).

mental disability law: incompetency,[31] insanity,[32] the criminal trial process, sentencing and correctional treatment rights,[33] and the death penalty.[34]

---

31 See *infra* Chapter 8.

32 See *infra* Chapter 9.

33 See *infra* Chapter 10.

34 See *infra* Chapter 11. Because of space limitations, this work omits chapters on sex offender law, tort law and on federal anti-discrimination statutes (although there is discussion of the case of *Olmstead v. L.C.*, 527 U.S. 581 (1999), *infra* 6.7). For more on these topics, see PERLIN AND CUCOLO, *supra* note 2, chs. 5, 11 and 12.

2   Some jurisprudential filters

It is impossible to understand developments in mental disability law without a full consideration of the malignant and corrosive impact of sanism, pretextuality, heuristic reasoning and (false) "ordinary common sense,"[1] or the potentially redemptive significance of the school of thought known as therapeutic jurisprudence.[2] "[These four] factors have 'poisoned and corrupted' all of mental disability law,"[3] have "malignantly distort[ed] both the legislative and judicial processes"[4] and have similarly "distort[ed] our abilities to rationally consider information."[5] The final filter—therapeutic jurisprudence—gives us hope that this area of law can be applied in a way that provides due process, and promotes wellness and an ethic of care.[6] It is impossible to understand developments in this area of the law without considering these factors, and their impact (both conscious and unconscious) on fact-finders.[7]

---

1 See Michael L. Perlin, Talia Roitberg Harmon and Sarah Chatt, *"A World of Steel-Eyed Death": An Empirical Evaluation of the Failure of the Strickland Standard to Ensure Adequate Counsel to Defendants with Mental Disabilities Facing the Death Penalty*, 53 U. Mich. J. L. Ref. 261, 278–82, 305–07 (2020). See generally Michael L. Perlin, The Hidden Prejudice: Mental Disability on Trial (2000).

2 See, e.g., Michael L. Perlin, *"Have You Seen Dignity?": The Story of the Development of Therapeutic Jurisprudence*, 27 U.N.Z. Law Rev. 1135 (2017); Michael L. Perlin, *"Changing of the Guards": David Wexler, Therapeutic Jurisprudence, and the Transformation of Legal Scholarship*, 63 Int'l J. L. & Psychiatry 3 (2019).

3 Michael L. Perlin and Meredith R. Schriver, *"You Might Have Drugs at Your Command": Reconsidering the Forced Drugging of Incompetent Pre-Trial Detainees from the Perspectives of International Human Rights and Income Inequality*, 8 Albany Gov't L. Rev. 381, 394 (2015).

4 Michael L. Perlin, *"Simplify You, Classify You": Stigma, Stereotypes and Civil Rights in Disability Classification Systems*, 25 Ga. St. U. L. Rev. 607, 607 (2009).

5 Id. at 622.

6 See Michael L. Perlin and Alison J. Lynch, *"All His Sexless Patients": Persons with Mental Disabilities and the Competence to Have Sex*, 89 Wash. L. Rev. 257, 278 (2014).

7 See generally Michael L. Perlin, *The Sanist Lives of Jurors in Death Penalty Cases: The Puzzling Role of Mitigating Mental Disability Evidence*, 8 Notre Dame J. L., Ethics & Pub. Pol. 239 (1994).

2.1   Sanism

Sanism dominates all mental disability law,[8] and reflects the "pathology of oppression."[9] It is a "largely invisible and largely socially acceptable" irrational prejudice of the same quality and character of other irrational prejudices that cause (and are reflected in) racism, sexism, homophobia, and ethnic bigotry.[10] Based predominantly upon stereotype, myth, superstition and deindividualization, it "infects both our jurisprudence and our lawyering practices . . . in unconscious response[s] to events both in everyday life and in the legal process."[11]

It reflects assumptions made by the legal system that mirror societal fears and apprehensions about mental disability and persons with mental disabilities; it ignores the most important question of all: why do we feel the way we do about "these people" (quotation marks understood)?[12]

2.2   Pretextuality

Sanist attitudes lead to pretextual decisions.[13] Pretextuality describes the ways that courts accept testimonial dishonesty—especially by expert witnesses—and engage similarly in dishonest (and frequently

---

8 Michael L. Perlin and Alison J. Lynch, *"Mr. Bad Example": Why Lawyers Need to Embrace Therapeutic Jurisprudence to Root out Sanism in the Representation of Persons with Mental Disabilities*, 16 WYO. L. REV. 299, 300 (2016).

9 Morton Birnbaum, *The Right to Treatment: Some Comments on its Development*, in MEDICAL, MORAL AND LEGAL ISSUES IN HEALTH CARE 97, 107 (Frank Ayd ed., 1974) (quoting civil rights lawyer Florynce Kennedy).

10 Michael L. Perlin, *"And My Best Friend, My Doctor/ Won't Even Say What It Is I've Got": The Role and Significance of Counsel in Right to Refuse Treatment Cases*, 42 SAN DIEGO L. REV. 735, 750 (2005).

11 Michael L. Perlin and Heather Ellis Cucolo, *"Tolling for the Aching Ones Whose Wounds Cannot Be Nursed": The Marginalization of Racial Minorities and Women in Institutional Mental Disability Law*, 20 J. GENDER, RACE & JUSTICE 431, 451–52 (2017). On how "sanist myths exert especially great power over lawyers who represent persons with mental disabilities," see Perlin, *supra* note 4, at 621.

12 See Michael L. Perlin and Mehgan Gallagher, *"Temptation's Page Flies out the Door": Navigating Complex Systems of Disability and the Law from a Therapeutic Jurisprudence Perspective*, 25 BUFFALO HUM. RTS. L. REV. 1, 27 (2018–19).

13 Heather Ellis Cucolo and Michael L. Perlin, *Promoting Dignity and Preventing Shame and Humiliation by Improving the Quality and Education of Attorneys in Sexually Violent Predator (SVP) Civil Commitment Cases*, 28 FLA. J. L. & PUB. POL'Y 291, 316 (2017).

meretricious) decisionmaking.[14] It "breeds cynicism and disrespect for the law, demeans participants, and reinforces shoddy lawyering, blasé judging, and, at times, perjurious and/or corrupt testifying."[15]

All aspects of mental disability law are pervaded by sanism and by pretextuality.[16] They exerted a stranglehold on mature mental disability law development,[17] and best explain the contamination of scholarly discourse and of lawyering practices alike.

2.3   Heuristics

Heuristics are a cognitive psychology construct that describes the implicit thinking devices that individuals use to simplify complex, information-processing tasks. Their use frequently leads to distorted and systematically erroneous decisions, and leads decision-makers to ignore or misuse items of rationally useful information.[18]

Through the "attribution" heuristic, we interpret a wide variety of additional information to reinforce pre-existing stereotypes.[19] Through the "typification" heuristic, we characterize a current experience via

---

14 See Michael L. Perlin and Naomi Weinstein, "*Said I, 'But You Have No Choice'": Why a Lawyer Must Ethically Honor a Client's Decision about Mental Health Treatment even if It Is Not What S/ he Would Have Chosen*, 15 Cardozo Pub. L. Pol'y & Ethics J. 73, 85 (2016):

> Pretextual devices such as condoning perjured testimony, distorting appellate readings of trial testimony, [and] subordinating statistically significant social science data . . . dominate the mental disability law landscape. Judges in mental disability law cases often take relevant literature out of context, misconstrue the data or evidence being offered, and/or read such data selectively, and/or inconsistently . . . In other circumstances, courts simply "rewrite" factual records so as to avoid having to deal with social science data that is cognitively dissonant with their view of how the world "ought to be" (citations omitted).

15 Perlin, *supra* note 10, at 750–51. On how courts "employ pretextuality as a 'cover' for sanist-driven decisionmaking," see Michael L. Perlin, *"Half-Wracked Prejudice Leaped Forth": Sanism, Pretextuality, and Why and How Mental Disability Law Developed as It Did*, 10 J. Contemp. Leg. Iss. 3, 30 (1999).

16 Michael L. Perlin, *"She Breaks Just Like a Little Girl": Neonaticide, the Insanity Defense, and the Irrelevance of "Ordinary Common Sense,"* 10 Wm. & Mary J. Women & L. 1, 25 (2003).

17 See Michael L. Perlin, *"Your Old Road Is/ Rapidly Agin'": International Human Rights Standards and Their Impact on Forensic Psychologists, the Practice of Forensic Psychology, and the Conditions of Institutionalization of Persons with Mental Disabilities*, 17 Wash. U. Global Studies L. Rev. 79, 101 (2018).

18 Heather Ellis Cucolo and Michael L. Perlin, *"They're Planting Stories in the Press": The Impact of Media Distortions on Sex Offender Law and Policy*, 3 U. Denv. Crim. L. Rev. 185, 212 (2013).

19 See, e.g., Michael L. Perlin, *"His Brain Has Been Mismanaged with Great Skill": How Will Jurors*

reference to past stereotypic behavior.[20] The "hindsight bias" causes people "to hold decisionmakers legally liable for outcomes that they could not have predicted."[21] Judges thus focus on information that confirms their preconceptions (i.e., confirmation bias), to recall vivid and emotionally charged aspects of cases (i.e., the availability heuristic), and to interpret information that reinforces the status quo as legitimate (i.e., system justification biases).[22]

Especially pernicious is the "vividness" heuristic, through which "one single vivid, memorable case overwhelms mountains of abstract, colorless data upon which rational choices should be made."[23] This heuristic—perhaps in the context of a TV "action news" story that a juror—or judge—saw about a defendant with a mental disability (a story that may or may not be true)—blocks the fact-finder's mind to actually *listening* to what the expert has to say.[24] The use of these heuristics blinds us "to . . . 'gray areas' of human behavior."[25]

2.4   "Ordinary common sense"

Ordinary common sense (OCS) is "a powerful unconscious animator of legal decision making"[26] that reflects "idiosyncratic, reactive

---

Respond to Neuroimaging Testimony in Insanity Defense Cases? 42 AKRON L. REV. 885, 892 (2009).

20 See, e.g., Michael L. Perlin, *Power Imbalances in Therapeutic and Forensic Relationships*, 9 BEHAV. SCI. & L. 111, 125 (1991).

21 Jeffrey J. Rachlinski, *A Positive Psychological Theory of Judging in Hindsight*, 65 U. CHI. L. REV. 571, 588 (1998).

22 Eden B. King, *Discrimination in the 21st Century: Are Science and the Law Aligned?* 17 PSYCHOL. PUB. POL'Y & L. 54, 58 (2011); see also Amos Tversky and Daniel Kahneman, *Availability: A Heuristic for Judging Frequency and Probability*, 5 COGNITIVE PSYCHOL. 207 (1973).

23 Michael L. Perlin, *"The Borderline Which Separated You from Me": The Insanity Defense, the Authoritarian Spirit, the Fear of Faking, and the Culture of Punishment*, 82 IOWA L. REV. 1375, 1417 (1997). Behavioral scientists are aware of the power of "distortions of vivid information." The "more vivid and concrete is better remembered, over recitals of fact and logic." Marilyn Ford, *The Role of Extralegal Factors in Jury Verdicts*, 11 JUST. SYS. J. 16, 23 (1986).

24 Michael L. Perlin, *"Deceived Me into Thinking/I Had Something to Protect": A Therapeutic Jurisprudence Analysis of When Multiple Experts Are Necessary in Cases in which Fact-Finders Rely on Heuristic Reasoning and "Ordinary Common Sense,"* 13 L.J. SOC'L JUST. 88, 105 (2020).

25 Perlin, *supra* note 16, at 6; see also Perlin and Cucolo, *supra* note 11, at 452.

26 Michael L. Perlin, *Psychodynamics and the Insanity Defense: "Ordinary Common Sense" and Heuristic Reasoning*, 69 NEB. L. REV. 3, 22–23, 29 (1990). See Richard K. Sherwin, *Dialects and Dominance: A Study of Rhetorical Fields in the Law of Confessions*, 136 U. PA. L. REV. 729, 737–38

decisionmaking,"[27] and "is a psychological construct that reflects the level of the disparity between perception and reality that . . . pervades the judiciary in deciding [mental disability law] cases."[28]

OCS is self-referential and non-reflective: "I see it that way, therefore everyone sees it that way; I see it that way, therefore that's the way it is."[29] It is supported by our reliance on heuristics-cognitive-simplifying devices that distort our abilities to rationally consider information.[30] It presupposes two "self-evident" truths: "First, everyone knows how to assess an individual's behavior. Second, everyone knows when to blame someone for doing wrong."[31]

2.5   Therapeutic jurisprudence

Therapeutic jurisprudence (TJ) recognizes that, as a therapeutic agent, the law can have therapeutic or anti-therapeutic consequences.[32] It asks whether legal rules, procedures and lawyer roles can or should be reshaped to enhance their therapeutic potential while not subordinating due process principles.[33] Importantly, "the law's use of mental health information to improve therapeutic functioning [cannot] impinge upon justice concerns."[34] "An inquiry into therapeutic outcomes does *not* mean that therapeutic concerns 'trump' civil rights and civil liberties."[35] Therapeutic jurisprudence "look[s] at law as it actually impacts people's lives,"[36] and TJ supports "an ethic of care,"[37]

(1988) (OCS is exemplified by the attitude of "[w]hat I know is 'self evident'; it is 'what everybody knows'").

27   Perlin, *supra* note 26, at 29.

28   Perlin and Weinstein, *supra* note 14, at 87–88.

29   Id. at 88.

30   See Perlin and Cucolo, *supra* note 11, at 453.

31   Michael L. Perlin, *Myths, Realities, and the Political World: The Anthropology of Insanity Defense Attitudes*, 24 BULL. AM. ACAD. PSYCHIATRY & L. 5, 17 (1996).

32   Perlin, *supra* note 19, at 912.

33   Perlin, *supra* note 10, at 751.

34   David B. Wexler, *Therapeutic Jurisprudence and Changing Concepts of Legal Scholarship*, 11 BEHAV. SCI. & L. 17, 21 (1993).

35   Michael L. Perlin, *A Law of Healing*, 68 U. CIN. L. REV. 407, 412 (2000).

36   Bruce J. Winick, *Foreword: Therapeutic Jurisprudence Perspectives on Dealing with Victims of Crime*, 33 NOVA L. REV. 535, 535 (2009).

37   Michael L. Perlin, *"I've Got My Mind Made Up": How Judicial Teleology in Cases Involving Biologically Based Evidence Violates Therapeutic Jurisprudence*, 24 CARD. J. EQUAL RTS. & SOC'L JUST. 81, 94 (2018) (quoting, in part, Bruce J. Winick and David B. Wexler, *The Use of Therapeutic*

seeking to bring about healing and wellness,[38] and valuing psychological health.[39]

One governing TJ principle is that the "law should . . . strive to avoid imposing anti-therapeutic consequences whenever possible. . . ."[40] TJ supports an ethic of care.[41]

The central principles of TJ include a commitment to dignity,[42] and what Professor Amy Ronner has described as the "three Vs":[43]

voice: litigants must have a sense of voice or a chance to tell their story to a decisionmaker;
validation: the decisionmaker needs to take seriously the litigant's story; and
voluntariness: in general, human beings prosper when they feel that they are making, or at least participating in, their own decisions.[44]

Virtually every aspect of mental disability law to be considered in this volume has been considered through a TJ filter.[45] These include, but are not limited to:

Jurisprudence in Law School Clinical Education: Transforming the Criminal Law Clinic, 13 CLINICAL L. REV. 605, 605–07 (2006)).

38 Perlin, *supra* note 37, at 94, citing Bruce Winick, *A Therapeutic Jurisprudence Model for Civil Commitment*, in INVOLUNTARY DETENTION AND THERAPEUTIC JURISPRUDENCE: INTERNATIONAL PERSPECTIVES ON CIVIL COMMITMENT 23, 26 (Kate Diesfeld and Ian Freckelton eds., 2003) (INVOLUNTARY DETENTION).

39 Id.

40 Bruce Winick, *A Therapeutic Jurisprudence Model for Civil Commitment*, in INVOLUNTARY DETENTION, *supra* note 38, at 26.

41 See e.g., Bruce J. Winick and David B. Wexler, *The Use of Therapeutic Jurisprudence in Law School Clinical Education: Transforming the Criminal Law Clinic*, 13 CLINICAL L. REV. 605, 605–07 (2006).

42 See BRUCE J. WINICK, CIVIL COMMITMENT: A THERAPEUTIC JURISPRUDENCE MODEL 161 (2005); Michael L. Perlin and Alison J. Lynch, *"She's Nobody's Child/The Law Can't Touch Her at All": Seeking to Bring Dignity to Legal Proceedings Involving Juveniles*, 56 FAM. CT. REV. 79 (2018).

43 See, e.g., Amy D. Ronner, *The Learned-Helpless Lawyer: Clinical Legal Education and Therapeutic Jurisprudence as Antidotes to Bartleby Syndrome*, 24 TOURO L. REV. 601, 627 (2008).

44 Amy D. Ronner, *Songs of Validation, Voice, and Voluntary Participation: Therapeutic Jurisprudence, Miranda and Juveniles*, 71 U. CIN. L. REV. 89, 94–95 (2002).

45 See MICHAEL L. PERLIN AND HEATHER ELLIS CUCOLO, MENTAL DISABILITY LAW: CIVIL AND CRIMINAL (3d ed. 2016) (2019 update), § 2-6, at 2-60 to 2-70.2.

- the provision of counsel,[46] and judicial attitudes,[47] especially in cases involving biologically based evidence,[48]
- the involuntary civil commitment process,[49] including assisted outpatient commitment[50] and the relationship between voluntary and involuntary commitment,[51]
- the right to treatment,[52]
- competency to consent to treatment,[53] the right to refuse medication[54] and the role of counsel at refusal-of-medication hearings,[55]
- institutional conditions in general,[56]

---

46 Perlin and Lynch, *supra* note 8; on the relationship between TJ and the provision of counsel to persons with mental disabilities in the community, see Alison J. Lynch and Michael L. Perlin, *"Life's Hurried Tangled Road": A Therapeutic Jurisprudence Analysis of Why Dedicated Counsel Must Be Assigned to Represent Persons with Mental Disabilities in Community Settings*, 35 BEHAV. SCI. & L. 353 (2017). See generally *infra* Chapter 3.

47 See Jessica Traguetto and Tomas Guimaraes, *Therapeutic Jurisprudence and Restorative Justice in the United States: The Process of Institutionalization and the Role of Judges*, 63 INT'L J. OFFENDER THER. & COMPAR. CRIMINOL. 1971 (2019). See generally *infra* Chapter 3.

48 See Perlin, *supra* note 37.

49 Michael L. Perlin, Keri Gould and Deborah A. Dorfman, *Therapeutic Jurisprudence and the Civil Rights of Institutionalized Mentally Disabled Persons: Hopeless Oxymoron or Path to Redemption?* 1 PSYCHOL. PUB. POL'Y & L. 80 (1995); Bruce Winick, *Therapeutic Jurisprudence and the Civil Commitment Hearing*, 10 J. CONTEMP. LEGAL ISSUES 37, 54 n.84 (1999). See generally *infra* Chapter 4.

50 Michael L. Perlin, Deborah A. Dorfman and Naomi M. Weinstein, *"On Desolation Row": The Blurring of the Borders between Civil and Criminal Mental Disability Law, and What It Means for All of Us*, 24 TEX. J. ON CIV. LIBS. & CIV. RTS. 59,76, 80 and 105–06 (2018). See generally *infra* Chapter 4.

51 Bruce J. Winick, *Competency to Consent to Voluntary Hospitalization: A Therapeutic Jurisprudence Analysis of* Zinermon v. Burch, 14 INT'L J.L.& PSYCHIATRY 169 (1991). See generally *infra* Chapter 4.

52 See Perlin, Gould and Dorfman, *supra* note 49. See generally *infra* Chapter 5.

53 Bruce Winick, *Competency to Consent to Treatment: The Distinction between Assent and Objection*, 28 HOUS. L. REV. 15 (1991); Julie Zito, Jozsef Vitrai and Thomas Craig, *Toward a Therapeutic Jurisprudence Analysis of Medication Refusal in the Court Review Model*, 11 BEHAV. SCI. & L. 151 (1993). See generally *infra* Chapter 5.

54 Deborah A. Dorfman, *Through a Therapeutic Jurisprudence Filter: Fear and Pretextuality in Mental Disability Law*, 10 N.Y.L. SCH. J. HUM. RTS. 805 (1993); Bruce J. Winick, *The Right to Refuse Mental Health Treatment: A Therapeutic Jurisprudence Analysis*, 17 INT'L J.L. & PSYCHIATRY 99 (1994). See generally *infra* Chapter 5.

55 Michael L. Perlin and Deborah A. Dorfman, *Is It More Than "Dodging Lions and Wastin' Time"? Adequacy of Counsel, Questions of Competence, and the Judicial Process in Individual Right to Refuse Treatment Cases*, 2 PSYCHOLOGY, PUB. POL'Y & L. 114 (1996). See generally *infra* Chapter 5.

56 See Michael L. Perlin and Alison J. Lynch, *"Toiling in the Danger and in the Morals of Despair": Risk, Security, Danger, the Constitution, and the Clinician's Dilemma*, 5 INDIANA J. L. & SOC'L EQUALITY 409 (2017). See generally *infra* Chapter 5.

- sexual autonomy, both in institutions and in the community,[57]
- the right to voluntarily receive mental health services in community settings,[58]
- the blurring of civil and criminal mental disability law,[59]
- problem-solving courts,[60] including a specific focus on mental health courts,[61]
- international human rights law,[62]
- competency to stand trial,[63] to plead guilty or to waive counsel,[64]
- all aspects of insanity defense law,[65]
- how jurors construe expert testimony,[66]
- all aspects of the sentencing process,[67]

---

57 See e.g., MICHAEL L. PERLIN AND ALISON J. LYNCH, SEXUALITY, DISABILITY AND THE LAW: BEYOND THE LAST FRONTIER? (2016); Perlin and Lynch, *supra* note 6. See generally *infra* Chapter 5.

58 Michael L. Perlin, *Law and the Delivery of Mental Health Services in the Community*, 64 AM. J. ORTHOPSYCHIATRY 194 (1994). See generally *infra* Chapter 6.

59 Perlin, Dorfman and Weinstein, *supra* note 50. See generally *infra* Chapter 7.

60 See, e.g., Bruce Winick, *Therapeutic Jurisprudence and Problem Solving Courts*, 30 FORDHAM URBAN L.J. 1055 (2003); John Petrila, *An Introduction to Special Jurisdiction Courts*, 26 INT'L J.L. & PSYCHIATRY 3 (2003). See generally *infra* Chapter 7.

61 Arthur J. Lurigio and Jessica Snowden, *Putting Therapeutic Jurisprudence into Practice: The Growth, Operations, and Effectiveness of Mental Health Court*, 30 JUST. SYS. J. 196 (2009); Ginger Lerner-Wren and Antoinette Appel, *A Court for a Nonviolent Defendant with a Mental Disability*, 31 PSYCHIATRIC ANNALS 453 (2001); Michael L. Perlin, *"Who Will Judge the Many When the Game is Through?": Considering the Profound Differences between Mental Health Courts and "Traditional" Involuntary Civil Commitment Courts*, 41 SEATTLE U. L. REV. 937 (2018). See generally *infra* Chapter 7.

62 Bruce J. Winick, *Therapeutic Jurisprudence and the Treatment of People with Mental Illness in Eastern Europe: Construing International Human Rights Law*, 21 N.Y.L. SCH. J. INT'L & COMP. L. 537 (2002); Michael L. Perlin, *"Abandoned Love": The Impact of* Wyatt v. Stickney *on the Intersection between International Human Rights and Domestic Mental Disability Law*, 35 LAW & PSYCHOL. REV. 121 (2011). See generally *infra* Chapter 7.

63 Michael L. Perlin and Alison J. Lynch, *"My Brain Is So Wired": Neuroimaging's Role in Competency Cases Involving Persons with Mental Disabilities*, 27 B.U. PUB. INT. L.J. 73 (2018). See generally *infra* Chapter 8.

64 Perlin and Gallagher, *supra* note 12; Bruce J. Winick, *Reforming Incompetency to Stand Trial and Plead Guilty*, in THERAPEUTIC JURISPRUDENCE APPLIED: ESSAYS ON MENTAL HEALTH LAW 233 (Bruce J. Winick ed., 1997). See generally *infra* Chapter 8.

65 See, e.g., MICHAEL L. PERLIN, THE JURISPRUDENCE OF THE INSANITY DEFENSE 417–45 (1994); Michael L. Perlin, *"God Said to Abraham/Kill Me a Son": Why the Insanity Defense and the Incompetency Status Are Compatible with and Required by the Convention on the Rights of Persons with Disabilities and Basic Principles of Therapeutic Jurisprudence*, 54 AM. CRIM. L. REV. 477 (2017); Perlin, Dorfman and Weinstein, *supra* note 50, at 87–90 and 109–11. See generally *infra* Chapter 9.

66 Perlin, *supra* note 24. See generally *infra* Chapter 10.

67 E.g., Keri Gould, *Turning Rat and Doing Time for Uncharged, Dismissed, or Acquitted Crimes:*

- the treatment of prisoners with severe mental disorders,[68] and
- all aspects of the death penalty.[69]

2.6   Conclusion

It is impossible to understand developments in mental disability law without considering these factors, and their impact (both conscious and unconscious) on fact-finders. These must be contextualized into all the discussions of the substance of mental disability law in each of the subsequent chapters.

Do the Federal Sentencing Guidelines Promote Respect for the Law? 10 N.Y.L. Sch. J. Hum. Rts. 835 (1993); Michael L. Perlin and Alison J. Lynch, *"In the Wasteland of Your Mind": Criminology, Scientific Discoveries, and the Criminal Process*, 4 Va. J. Crim. L. 304 (2016). See generally *infra* Chapter 10.

68 T. Howard Stone, *Therapeutic Implications of Incarceration for Persons with Severe Mental Disorders: Searching for Rational Health Policy*, 24 Am. J. Crim. L. 283 (1997). See generally *infra* Chapter 10.

69 Michael L. Perlin, *"Your Corrupt Ways Had Finally Made You Blind": Prosecutorial Misconduct and the Use of "Ethnic Adjustments" in Death Penalty Cases of Defendants with Intellectual Disabilities*, 65 Am. U. L. Rev. 1437 (2016); Michael L. Perlin, *"Merchants and Thieves, Hungry for Power": Prosecutorial Misconduct and Passive Judicial Complicity in Death Penalty Trials of Defendants with Mental Disabilities*, 73 Wash. & Lee L. Rev. 1501 (2016). See generally *infra* Chapter 11.

3 Counsel and judges

3.1 Introduction

The US Supreme Court has never ruled on the question of whether a person facing involuntary commitment to a psychiatric institution (or when seeking release from such an institution) has a right to counsel. However, *every* state and federal court that *has* considered the question has found that there is such a right. This reality should in no way minimize the significance of counsel issues (access, quality, means of assignment, and more) in all mental disability law.[1]

Closely related to these issues are those that reflect on the quality of judges in these cases (or whether there even are actual judicial officers hearing civil commitment cases). In all too many jurisdictions, judges are bored, disinterested or irritated at being assigned to do such cases. It is critical to consider these issues if we are to understand what happens in "real life" in civil commitment cases. This chapter will approach both these sets of issues.

3.2 Counsel[2]

3.2.1 Historical background

The record of the legal profession in providing meaningful advocacy services to persons with mental disabilities has historically been grossly inadequate.[3] Even where civil commitment hearings were

---

1 On the significance of counsel in one aspect of mental disability law (right to refuse treatment, see *infra* Chapter 5), see Michael L. Perlin, *"And My Best Friend, My Doctor/ Won't Even Say What It Is I've Got": The Role and Significance of Counsel in Right to Refuse Treatment Cases*, 42 SAN DIEGO L. REV. 735 (2005).

2 See generally MICHAEL L. PERLIN AND HEATHER ELLIS CUCOLO, MENTAL DISABILITY LAW: CIVIL AND CRIMINAL ch. 6 (3d ed. 2016) (2019 update).

3 Michael L. Perlin and Robert L. Sadoff, *Ethical Issues in the Representation of Individuals in the Commitment Process*, 45 LAW & CONTEMP. PROBS. 161 (Summer 1982).

required[4] and counsel mandated, counsel was not always provided;[5] "courts essentially defaulted in their responsibility to make judicial determinations for commitment."[6] All early surveys were in accord:

> [Historically,] traditional, sporadically-appointed counsel in mental health cases [were] unwilling to pursue necessary investigations, lack[ed] . . . expertise in dealing with mental health problems, and . . . suffered from "rolelessness," stemming from near total capitulation to experts, hazily defined concept[s] of success/failure, inability to generate professional or personal interest in [the] patient's dilemma, and lack of [a] clear definition of [the] proper advocacy function. [C]ounsel . . . functioned "as no more than a clerk ratifying the events that transpire[d], rather than influencing them."[7]

Commitment hearings were "an empty ritual,"[8] adding just a "falsely reassuring patina of respectability to the proceedings."[9] In those instances where counsel was actively involved, significantly fewer persons were committed.[10]

---

4 Prior to the early 1970s, court hearings were not required in many states as a prerequisite to civil commitment. See, e.g., Stanley C. Van Ness and Michael L. Perlin, *Mental Health Advocacy: The New Jersey Experience*, in MENTAL HEALTH ADVOCACY: AN EMERGING FORCE IN CONSUMERS' RIGHTS 62 (Louis E. Kopolow and Helene Bloom eds., 1977) (Kopolow and Bloom).

5 As of 1971, counsel was statutorily required in just 24 states. There were eight jurisdictions without any judicial hospitalization procedures; notice to the person facing hospitalization was required in only 26 of the other 42 states. THE MENTALLY DISABLED AND THE LAW 52, 54 (Samuel Jan Brakel and Ronald S. Rock eds., rev. ed. 1971).

6 Virginia Aldige Hiday, *The Attorney's Role in Involuntary Civil Commitment*, 60 N.C.L. REV. 1027, 1030 (1982).

7 Perlin and Sadoff, *supra* note 3, at 164, quoting Michael L. Perlin, *Representing Individuals in the Commitment and Guardianship Process*, in 1 LEGAL RIGHTS OF MENTALLY DISABLED PERSONS 497, 501 (Paul Friedman ed., 1979).

8 Hiday, *supra* note 6, at 1030, quoting Fred Cohen, *The Function of the Attorney and the Commitment of the Mentally Ill*, 44 TEX. L. REV. 424, 448 (1966).

9 Hiday, *supra* note 6, at 1030, quoting Elliot Andalman and David Chambers, *Effective Counsel for Persons Facing Civil Commitment: A Survey, a Polemic and a Proposal*, 45 MISS. L.J. 43, 72 (1974). A St. Louis survey found only two of 1,700 patients were released in so-called "contested cases," George Dix, *Acute Psychiatric Hospitalization of the Mentally Ill in the Metropolis: An Empirical Study*, [1968] WASH. U. L. REV. 485, 540.

10 *Developments in the Law: Civil Commitment of the Mentally Ill*, 87 HARV. L. REV. 1190, 1285 (1984).

3.2.2 Constitutional bases

3.2.2.1 *Competency of counsel*

3.2.2.1.1 Early cases Historically, the right to counsel was not applied to cases involving involuntary civil commitment.[11] This question was never taken seriously until the Supreme Court decided *In re Gault*,[12] extending basic procedural due process protections to juveniles facing delinquency proceedings that might result in incarceration in a state juvenile institution, applying such rights as notice,[13] confrontation of witnesses[14] and the privilege against self-incrimination.[15]

Less than a year later, the Tenth Circuit held that the constitutional right to counsel was equally applicable in civil commitment proceedings, specifically *rejecting* the state's argument that *Gault* was distinguishable:

> [L]ike *Gault*, and of utmost importance, we have a situation in which the liberty of an individual is at stake, and we think the reasoning in *Gault* emphatically applies. It matters not whether the proceedings be labeled "civil" or "criminal" or whether the subject matter be mental instability or juvenile delinquency. It is the likelihood of involuntary incarceration . . . which commands observance of the constitutional safeguards of due process.[16]

The failure to provide such counsel "may result in indefinite and oblivious confinement and work shameful injustice."[17] The Tenth Circuit's language was soon adopted in the lead case of *Lessard v. Schmidt*[18] and

---

11 See, e.g., David J. Rothman, The Discovery of the Asylum: Social Order and Disorder in the New Republic 143–44 (1971).

12 387 U.S. 1 (1967).

13 Id. at 33.

14 Id. at 57.

15 Id. at 50.

16 Heryford v. Parker, 396 F.2d 393, 396 (10th Cir. 1968).

17 Id. at 397.

18 349 F. Supp. 1078, 1097–98 (E.D. Wis. 1972), *vacated and remanded*, 414 U.S. 473, *on remand*, 379 F. Supp. 1376 (E.D. Wis. 1974), *vacated and remanded*, 421 U.S. 957 (1975), *reinstated*, 413 F. Supp. 1318 (E.D. Wis. 1976).

elsewhere,[19] some cases extending representation to "all significant stages" of the commitment process.[20]

Importantly, however, ~~case law is virtually silent on the question of what~~ *level* ~~of competency of counsel is~~ required to satisfy due process requirements in mental disability cases.[21] The US Supreme Court has paid attention to the question of *criminal defense* counsel's adequacy, but it has never touched on this question in the civil commitment context. It is necessary, then, to consider the case law that has developed since the Supreme Court's decision on effectiveness of counsel in criminal cases in the lead case of *Strickland v. Washington*[22] (and successor cases), and then assess decisions that have interpreted *Strickland* and its progeny in the civil commitment context.

3.2.2.1.2 The significance of Strickland v. Washington[23] In *Strickland*, the Supreme Court defined the Sixth Amendment constitutional right to counsel to include the right to the effective assistance of counsel. In its decision, the Court acknowledged that the role of counsel is critical to the ability of the adversarial system to best ensure that just results are produced. The Court did not elaborately define this constitutional requirement; subsequently, lower courts have set the bar shockingly low.

---

19 E.g., Sarzen v. Gaughan, 489 F.2d 1076, 1085 (1st Cir. 1973); Dorsey v. Solomon, 435 F. Supp. 725, 733 (D. Md. 1977); Bell v. Wayne County Gen. Hosp., 384 F. Supp. 1085, 1092–93 (E.D. Mich. 1974).

20 Lynch v. Baxley, 386 F. Supp. 378, 389 (M.D. Ala. 1974), superseded by statute as stated in Garrett v. State, 707 So. 2d 273 (Ala. Civ. App. 1997). The court defined "significant stages" as "all judicial proceedings and any other official proceedings at which a decision is, or can be, made which may result in a detrimental change in the conditions of the subject's liberty." Id. at n.5. Accord *In re* Beverly, 342 So. 2d 481, 489 (Fla. 1977). On the question of waiver of commitment counsel, courts have been split. Compare, e.g., U.S. v. Hall, 610 F.3d 727, 735 (D.C. Cir. 2010) (right to counsel may be knowingly and intelligently waived regardless of defendant's lawyering skills and experience), to *In re* Yoder, 682 N.E.2d 753 (Ill. App. 1997), *app'l denied*, 686 N.E.2d 1162 (Ill. 1997) (patient properly found unable to waive counsel or represent himself).

21 For one startling example in a criminal law context, a survey conducted by Harvard Medical School revealed that the "great majority" of defense counsel interviewed were unaware of the operative criteria for competency to stand trial. LABORATORY OF COMMUNITY PSYCHIATRY, HARVARD MEDICAL SCHOOL, FINAL REPORT, COMPETENCY TO STAND TRIAL AND MENTAL ILLNESS 1–6 (1973).

22 466 U.S. 668 (1984).

23 See generally MICHAEL L. PERLIN, MENTAL DISABILITY AND THE DEATH PENALTY: THE SHAME OF THE STATES 123–38 (2013).

The test for an ineffectiveness claim in *Strickland* is "whether counsel's conduct so undermined the proper function of the adversarial process that the trial court cannot be relied on as having produced a just result."[24] To determine whether counsel's assistance was "so defective as to require reversal,"[25] the Court established a two-part test:

> First, the defendant must show that counsel's performance was deficient. This requires showing that counsel made errors so serious that counsel was not functioning as the "counsel" guaranteed the defendant by the Sixth Amendment. Second, the defendant must show that the deficient performance prejudiced the defense. This requires showing that counsel's errors were so serious as to deprive the defendant of a fair trial, a trial whose result is reliable. Unless a defendant makes both showings, it cannot be said that the conviction or death sentence resulted from a breakdown in the adversary process that renders the result unreliable.[26]

The Court concluded that the new "objective," "reasonably effective assistance" standard need be measured by "simply reasonableness under prevailing professional norms."[27] Here, the Court would "indulge a strong presumption that counsel's conduct falls within the wide range of reasonable professional assistance."[28] It found that there was a duty for counsel to "make reasonable investigations or to make a reasonable decision that makes particular investigations unnecessary."[29] Even a "professionally unreasonable"[30] error will not result in reversal if such error "had no effect on the judgment."[31] A defendant must show prejudice, as measured by a showing of "a reasonable probability that, but for counsel's unprofessional errors, the result . . . would have been different."[32]

---

24 *Strickland*, 466 U.S. at 686. See generally Michael L. Perlin, Talia Roitberg Harmon and Sarah Chatt, *"A World of Steel-Eyed Death": An Empirical Evaluation of the Failure of the Strickland Standard to Ensure Adequate Counsel to Defendants with Mental Disabilities Facing the Death Penalty*, 53 U. Mich. J. L. Ref. 261 (2020).

25 *Strickland*, 466 U.S. at 687.

26 Id.

27 Id. at 687–88.

28 Id. at 689.

29 Id. at 691.

30 Id.

31 Id.

32 Id. at 694. The Court found that defendant's "[f]ailure to make the required showing of either deficient performance or sufficient prejudice defeats the ineffectiveness of the claim." Id. at 700.

Justice Marshall sharply dissented,[33] critiquing the majority's adoption of a performance standard "so malleable that, in practice, it will either have no grip at all or will yield excessive variation in the manner in which the Sixth Amendment is interpreted."[34] By this vagueness, he concluded, the Court has "not only abdicated its own responsibility to interpret the Constitution, but also impaired the ability of the lower courts to exercise theirs."[35]

3.2.2.1.3 Post-Strickland litigation Courts have been generally mixed in post-*Strickland* civil commitment cases.[36] However, in the most comprehensive and thoughtful post-*Strickland* case, the Montana Supreme Court had found the *Strickland* standards insufficient in an involuntary civil commitment case, and that *more* was required of assigned counsel.[37] The court stated:

> Although in numerous respects the procedural due process rights of an involuntary commitment patient-respondent are identical to those afforded an accused criminal defendant, the application of the *Strickland* standard is [not] appropriate in involuntary civil commitment proceedings. . . . *Strickland* simply does not go far enough to protect the liberty interests of individuals such as K.G.F., who may or may not have broken any law, but who, upon the expiration of a 90-day commitment, must indefinitely bear

---

33 Id. at 706.

34 Id. at 707.

35 Id. at 708. Justice Marshall characterized the standard as suffering from a "debilitating ambiguity," which will likely "stunt the development of Constitutional doctrine in this area." Id. at 708–09. Justice Brennan filed a separate opinion, concurring in part and dissenting in part. Id. at 701.

36 There has been little consistency between and among jurisdictions. Thus,

- An intermediate appellate court from Arizona ruled that an allegation of ineffective assistance of counsel at an involuntary commitment hearing required an evidentiary hearing. Matter of Pima Cty. Mental Health Serv., 757 P.2d 118 (Ariz. App. 1988);

- A Louisiana court found that the failure to appoint a lawyer from a specialized advocacy service was reversible error, as involuntary civil commitment law is "special and unfamiliar to most practitioners," thus making specialized representation necessary. *In re* C.P.K., 516 So. 2d 1323, 1324 (La. App. 1987); and

- An Illinois court reversed a commitment order where the trial court allowed the patient to discharge his attorney without any inquiry into the patient's ability to make a reasoned choice about the matter. Matter of Tiffin, 646 N.E.2d 285 (Ill. App. 1995).

On the other hand, in other Illinois cases, no prejudice was shown where counsel was not appointed until the day of the involuntary civil commitment hearing, Matter of McMahon, 581 N.E.2d 1208 (Ill. App. 1991), or where counsel failed to object to the admission of certain trial evidence, Matter of Robinson, 679 N.E.2d 818 (Ill. App. 1997).

37 Matter of Mental Health of K.G.F., 29 P.3d 485 (Mont. 2001), partially overruled in Matter of J.S., 401 P.3d 197 (Mont. 2017); In the Matter of J.S.W., 303 P.3d 741 (Mont. 2013) (same).

the badge of inferiority of a once "involuntarily committed" person with a proven mental disorder. . . .

Even a cursory review of legal commentary reveals the flawed reasoning of applying the . . . *Strickland* standard to involuntary civil commitment proceedings. . . . "[R]easonable professional assistance" cannot be presumed in a proceeding that routinely accepts—and even requires—an unreasonably low standard of legal assistance and generally disdains zealous, adversarial confrontation. *See generally* Michael L. Perlin, *Fatal Assumption: A Critical Evaluation of the Role of Counsel in Mental Disability Cases*, 16 Law & Hum. Behav. 39, 53–54 (1992) (identifying *Strickland* standard as "sterile and perfunctory" where "reasonably effective assistance" is objectively measured by the "prevailing professional norms").

[Also], the conduct of counsel during those few available hours prior to an involuntary commitment hearing or trial should be a key focal point of the inquiry as to whether the counsel's representation was effective.[38]

However, this "dramatic . . . launch[ing of] a rewriting of this area of the law"[39] was, in many ways, dissolved in 2017 when the Montana Supreme Court partially overruled *K.G.F.* and found that the standards and principles enunciated in *Strickland* also apply in civil commitment proceedings. *In the Matter of J.S.*[40] determined that the formalistic approach, designed in *K.G.F.*—to measure counsel's "effectiveness in the 'critical areas' of representation"—was an unnecessary requirement beyond the standards and principles enunciated in *Strickland* for measuring the effectiveness of counsel.[41]

Although the state Supreme Court recognized the significance of the court's opinion in *K.G.F.*, it ultimately concluded that "many of the circumstances which impelled this Court to reject *Strickland*, have proven unfounded," rejecting the notion that there is "an unreasonably low standard of legal assistance" offered in civil commitment

---

38 *K.G.F.*, 29 P.3d at 491–92. *K.G.F.* was disagreed with by the Washington Court of Appeals in *In re Detention of T.A.H.-L.*, 97 P.3d 767, 771–72 (Wash. App. 2004), that court noting:

> We do not share the Montana Supreme Court's dim view of the quality of civil commitment proceedings, or their adversarial nature, in the state of Washington. The *Strickland* standard appears to be sufficient to protect the right to the effective assistance of counsel for a civil commitment respondent in this state.

39 Perlin, *supra* note 1, at 738.

40 In the Matter of J.S., 401 P.3d 197 (Mont. 2017).

41 Id. at 209.

proceedings.[42] Significantly, however, in a subsequent case (holding that the Sixth Amendment's right to self-representation was not implicated by statute prohibiting a person from waiving right to counsel in civil commitment proceedings), the Montana Supreme Court made it clear that portions of the *K.G.F.* case still remained good law:

> Although we overruled ... *K.G.F.* on other grounds in ... *J.S.*, ... we reaffirmed the principle "that the right to effective assistance of counsel in civil commitment proceedings is premised upon the Fourteenth Amendment to the federal Constitution" and companion State constitutional provisions, not upon the Sixth Amendment. *In re J.S.*, ¶ 15.[43]

The *Strickland* standard offers almost no help in the resolution of constitutional questions dealing with adequacy of counsel for persons with mental disabilities. Although *K.G.F.* had offered a workable solution in such cases, the facts that (1) no other state has endorsed the *K.G.F.* methodology, and (2) the Montana Supreme Court gutted the *KG.F.* case of much of its strength and power leaves this area of the law highly problematic.[44]

3.2.3   Statutory provisions assigning counsel

There are statutory or regulatory provisions in each jurisdiction providing for the provision of counsel for a person facing involuntary civil commitment. These provisions range from terse (merely noting that the right exists) to expansive (setting out counsel's ethical duties). Neat pigeonholing is impossible; however, these statutes and rules can be roughly separated into these classifications:

(1)   those that merely set out the right;[45]
(2)   those that set out the right, providing for court appointment if the patient is indigent;[46]

---

42 Id. at 204–05.

43 Matter of S.M., 403 P.3d 324, 328 (Mont. 2017).

44 Assessing the performance of one federal circuit court of appeal in the context of death penalty cases involving defendants with mental disabilities, the author recently concluded that that circuit "regularly and consistently mocked the idea of adequate and effective counsel." Perlin, Harmon and Chatt, *supra* note 24, at 308.

45 See, e.g., GA. CODE ANN. § 37-3-141 (1997).

46 Statutes in this category provide for payment of appointed counsel in a variety of ways. See e.g., COLO. REV. STAT. § 27-10-127 (1997) (judicial department authorized to pay "sums directly to appointed counsel on a case-by-case basis or, on behalf of the state, to make lump sum grants

(3)   those that set out the right, providing for court appointment for indigent patients, and setting time limits for appointment;[47]

(4)   those that set out the right, providing for court appointment for indigent patients, and specifying counsel's roles;[48]

(5)   those that also extend the right to counsel to subsequent stages of the commitment proceeding;[49] and

(6)   those that also either establish some sort of organized system of providing such services or allow for the establishment of such a system.[50]

3.2.4   Other methods of assigning counsel

States have thus chosen to provide legal services in a variety of ways: through legislatively created, organized "mental health advocacy" programs; through other organized, legal services programs, usually on

---

and contract with individual attorneys, legal partnerships, legal professional corporations, public interest law firms, or nonprofit legal service corporations"); D.C. CODE ANN. § 21-543 (1997) (counsel to be compensated from patient's estate "or against any unobligated funds of the [Mental Health] Commission, as the court . . . directs . . .").

47 See, e.g., S.C. CODE ANN. § 44-17-530 (1997) (counsel to be appointed "within three days [exclusive of weekends and holidays] after the petition for judicial commitment"); S.D. CODIFIED LAWS ANN. § 27A-10-5 (1997) (patients have "the right to immediately contact or be represented by counsel").

48 See, e.g., ARIZ. REV. STAT. ANN. § 36-537 (1997):

The . . . attorney shall, for all hearings whether for evaluation or treatment, fulfill the following minimal duties:

1.   Within twenty-four hours of appointment, conduct an interview of the patient. The attorney shall explain to the patient his rights pending court-ordered treatment, the procedures leading to court-ordered treatment, the standards for court-ordered treatment and the alternative for becoming a voluntary patient. . . .

2.   At least twenty-four hours prior to the hearing, review the petition for evaluation, prepetition screening report, evaluation report, petition for treatment, the patient's medical records and the list of alternatives to court-ordered treatment.

3.   At least twenty-four hours prior to the hearing, interview the petitioner, if available, and his supporting witnesses, if known and available.

4.   At least twenty-four hours prior to the hearing, interview the physicians who will testify at the hearing, if available, and investigate the possibility of alternatives to court-ordered treatment.

Failure of the attorney to fulfill at least the duties prescribed by paragraphs 1 through 4 of this subsection may be punished as contempt of court.

49 Thus, North Carolina mandates that counsel "is also responsible for perfecting and conducting an appeal, if there is one." N.C. GEN. STAT. § 122C-270 (1997).

50 See, e.g., MICH. COMP. L. ANN. § 330.1454 (1997): ("If the state court administrator approves, a system of representation other than individual appointment may be created in any county or group of counties").

some sort of contractual basis; and on a variety of case-by-case bases, including "open list" appointments, "closed list" appointments, "rotating list" appointments and "special hire" appointments.

The quality of representation currently provided is uneven, varying from state to state, and, within a state, from county to county;[51] mostly, it remains "mediocre or worse."[52] In many jurisdictions, counsel is "woefully inadequate—disinterested, uninformed, roleless, and often hostile"[53] to the persons being represented.

3.2.5   Ethical issues/counsel's role[54]

What about ethical issues that surround counsel's role in civil commitment cases?

First, the attorney's initial interview with a person facing civil commitment is usually conducted on "alien territory," a factor that may "shape interview content."[55] When initial interviews are typically held randomly in corners of crowded wards—in a context dramatically unlike that of the prototypical attorney-client office interview—the interviewee often may become "suspicious, terrified, puzzled or simply distrustful of the attorney."[56]

Second, the attorney must have the ability to read and understand medical charts and the ability to communicate with mental disability professionals, essential aspects of investigation in the case of all persons facing civil commitment.[57]

Third, sensitivities must be heightened about events leading to hospitalization and the fact of hospitalization.[58]

---

51 See, e.g., Thomas Zander, *Civil Commitment in Wisconsin: The Impact of* Lessard v. Schmidt, 1976 WIS. L. REV. 503.

52 Michael L. Perlin, *"I Might Need a Good Lawyer, Could Be Your Funeral, My Trial": Global Clinical Legal Education and the Right to Counsel in Civil Commitment Cases,* 28 WASH. U. J. L. & POL'Y 241, 243 (2008).

53 Perlin, *supra* note 1, at 738.

54 See generally PERLIN AND CUCOLO, *supra* note 2, § 6-6.

55 Perlin and Sadoff, *supra* note 3, at 169.

56 Id. at 170.

57 *See Practice Manual: Preparation and Trial of a Civil Commitment Case,* 5 MENT. DIS. L. REP. 281, 285–87 (1981).

58 See generally ANDREW WATSON, PSYCHIATRY FOR LAWYERS 16–27 (2d ed. 1976).

Fourth, the attorney must be able to answer "classic social service" questions regarding alternatives to inpatient hospitalization of the client; such questions likely will play a significant factor in the court's disposition of the case:

- What halfway houses, community mental health centers, or patient-run alternatives are available?
- What economic benefits and entitlements might the patient receive outside the hospital?
- Is the alternative program one likely to survive economically . . . ?
- Is the program one specifically suited for persons with the client's condition?[59]

Fifth, civil commitment cases often involve multiple parties[60]—hospital staff, the community authority, a patient's family. Thus, an attorney often must conduct simultaneous multiple negotiations with parties and nonparties, often with "radically differing views as to [the] appropriate disposition."[61] This requires the development of unique negotiation skills.[62]

Sixth, the attorney's lawyering skills at the commitment hearing must be heightened in considering, for example, whether a certain witness should be called to the stand or whether the patient should testify.[63] More sophisticated counseling skills are also required.[64] Because the court will often be poorly informed as to both substantive and procedural commitment law,[65] the attorney will need to educate the court as to the law's nuances.[66]

59　Perlin and Sadoff, *supra* note 3, at 170.

60　See, e.g., N.C. GEN. STAT. § 122C-261 (1997). Compare Heller v. Doe, 509 U.S. 312 (1993) (Kentucky statute granting relatives party status at involuntary civil commitment hearings is not unconstitutional).

61　Perlin and Sadoff, *supra* note 3, at 171.

62　See generally ROGER FISHER, WILLIAM URY AND BRUCE PATTON, GETTING TO YES (3d ed. 2011).

63　See, e.g., Tyars v. Finner, 518 F. Supp. 502 (C.D. Cal. 1981), *rev'd*, 709 F.2d 1274 (9th Cir. 1983); Cramer v. Tyars, 151 Cal. Rptr. 653 (1979); State v. Mathews, 613 P.2d 88 (Or. App. 1980), *cert. denied*, 450 U.S. 1040 (1981).

64　See, e.g., DAVID BINDER AND SUSAN PRICE, LEGAL INTERVIEWING AND COUNSELING: A CLIENT-CENTERED APPROACH 192–210 (1977), updated in DAVID A. BINDER, PAUL BERGMAN AND SUSAN C. PRICE, LAWYERS AS COUNSELORS: A CLIENT CENTERED APPROACH (1991).

65　Hiday, *supra* note 6, at 1037.

66　ROBERT L. SADOFF, FORENSIC PSYCHIATRY: A PRACTICAL GUIDE FOR LAWYERS AND PSYCHIATRISTS 35, 47–48 (1985).

3.2.6   Rights are not self-executing

Legal rights are not necessarily self-executing.[67] A court's declaration of a right does not in itself provide that right.[68] Without counsel to guarantee enforcement, the rights "victories" that have been won in test case and law reform litigation in this area are unlikely to have any real impact on persons with mental disabilities.[69]

3.2.7   The myth of adequate counsel

The development of organized and regularized counsel programs has given rise to the supposition that such counsel is regularly available to persons with mental disabilities in individual matters involving their commitment to, retention in and release from psychiatric hospitals.[70] But, this is largely illusory.[71] Moreover, such representation is rarely available in a systemic way in law reform or test cases and is rarely provided in any systemic way in cases that involve counseling or negotiating short of actual litigation.

---

67 Bruce Winick, *Restructuring Competency to Stand Trial*, 32 UCLA L. REV. 921, 941 (1985). See also Grant Morris and J. Reid Meloy, *Out of Mind? Out of Sight: The Uncivil Commitment of Permanently Incompetent Criminal Defendants*, 27 U.C. DAVIS L. REV. 1, 8 (1993); Perlin, *supra* note 1, at 744.

68 See generally Donald Zeigler, *Rights Require Remedies: A New Approach to the Enforcement of Rights in the Federal Courts*, 38 HASTINGS L.J. 665 (1987).

69 An example: in 1972, the Supreme Court decided in *Jackson v. Indiana* that it violates due process to commit an individual awaiting criminal trial for more than the "reasonable period of time" needed to determine "whether there is a substantial chance of his attaining the capacity to stand trial in the foreseeable future." 406 U.S. 715, 733 (1972). Yet, this mandate is still ignored by about half of the states. See Winick, supra note 67, at 941; Morris and Meloy, *supra* note 67, at 8 (1993); Michael L. Perlin, *"For the Misdemeanor Outlaw?": The Impact of the ADA on the Institutionalization of Criminal Defendants with Mental Disabilities*, 52 ALABAMA L. REV. 193, 204 (2000); Andrew R. Kaufman, Bruce B. Way and Enrico Suardi, *Forty Years after* Jackson v. Indiana: *States' Compliance with "Reasonable Period of Time" Ruling*, 40 J. AM. ACAD. PSYCHIATRY & L. 261 (2012) (showing most states out of compliance with *Jackson*). See *infra* Chapter 8.

70 See, e.g., Alan Stone, *The Myth of Advocacy*, 30 HOSP. & COMMUN. PSYCHIATRY 819, 821–22 (1979) (charging that a "one-sided advocacy system" exists in which patients are regularly represented by zealous and conscientious lawyers); see also, e.g., French v. Blackburn, 428 F. Supp. 1351, 1357 (M.D.N.C. 1977), *aff'd*, 443 U.S. 901 (1979) (rejecting plaintiff's assumption that lawyer in involuntary civil commitment case will not act in client's best interest).

71 See M.C. Olley and James Ogloff, *Patients' Rights Advocacy: Implications for Program Design and Implementation*, 22 J. MENT. HEALTH ADMIN. 368, 369 (1995).

Empirical surveys consistently show that quality of counsel is the single most important factor in the disposition of cases in involuntary civil commitment systems and in the trial of mentally disabled criminal defendants.[72] Only when counsel is provided in an organized, specialized and regularized way is there more than a random chance of lasting, systemic change. Yet, few states appear willing to provide such counsel in such a manner.

3.2.8 Counsel's educative function

Structured counsel makes it more likely that all participants—including judges—are sensitized to the social, cultural and political issues involved in representation of such a marginalized class. We know that merely training lawyers about psychiatric techniques and psychological nomenclature makes little difference in ultimate case outcome; simply stated, education about the law and clinical details of mental illness is not enough.[73] For lawyers to provide truly adequate representation, they must also be "attitudinally and ethically" educated.[74]

The role of counsel in the representation of persons with mental disabilities is multi-textured, and it continually evolves. Systemic decision-makers need to acknowledge the complexity of this role, the historic shortcomings of sporadic counsel serving the population in question, and possible remedies for these problems. Yet, scant attention has been paid—neither by judges, nor by scholars, nor by practicing lawyers—to the questions posed here, ones that appear—inexplicably—"off the table" for purposes of legal discourse.[75]

---

72 See People v. Kerbs, 258 Cal. Rptr. 3d 67, 82 n.6 (Cal. App. 2020) (the quality of counsel is "the single most important factor in the disposition of involuntary civil commitment procedures," quoting MICHAEL L. PERLIN, MENTAL DISABILITY LAW: CIVIL AND CRIMINAL (2d ed. 1998) § 3B-11, pp. 362–63) (updated in PERLIN AND CUCOLO, *supra* note 2, §6-6.4, at 6-84).

73 Norman Poythress, *Psychiatric Expertise in Civil Commitment: Training Attorneys to Cope with Expert Testimony*, 2 LAW & HUM. BEHAV. 1 (1978). Poythress concluded that the "trained" lawyers' behavior in court was not materially different from that of "untrained" lawyers because the former group's *attitudes* toward their clients had not changed. Mere knowledge of cross-examination methods "did not deter them from taking [the] more traditional, passive, paternal stance towards the proposed patients." Id. at 15. As one trainee noted: "I really enjoyed your workshop, and I've been reading over your materials and its [sic] all very interesting, but this is the real world, and we've got to do something with these people. They're sick." Id.

74 See DAVID B. WEXLER, MENTAL HEALTH LAW 111 n.55 (1981).

75 On issues related to counsel at periodic review and on appeal, and the right to expert witnesses at trial, see PERLIN AND CUCOLO, *supra* note 2, §§ 6-8.1 to 6-8.2, and 6-9.

3.3   Judges[76]

Judges "generally have little judicial experience and little incentive to develop expertise in this area."[77] Their lack of interest "conveys the message that patients' rights ... are not important."[78] Simply put, judges subordinate mental disability law issues (a reflection and extension of their subordination of mentally disabled persons).[79]

This subordination translates into a failure to inform patients of their rights at such hearings. A study by Parry and Turkheimer revealed that, at the patient's initial hearing, fewer than one-third of judges told patients of their right to counsel, fewer than one-fourth told patients of their right to voluntary status and about two-fifths told patients of their right to appeal; by the second review hearing after 6 to 12 months in the hospital, less than 5 percent of judges mentioned the right to counsel and less than 8 percent mentioned voluntary admissions, while only 15 percent referred to the right to appeal.[80] There is no contesting Professor Sara Gordon's conclusion that "civil commitment proceedings tend to be short and perfunctory."[81]

Judges typically defer to the judgments of state experts[82] without any acknowledgement of the robust, valid and reliable evidence that tells us how imprecise clinical predictions of dangerousness often are.[83] They thus allow "psychiatrist experts [to] actually become the decision-makers in the civil commitment process," serving as "rubber stamps

---

76 See generally Michael L. Perlin, "Who Will Judge the Many When the Game is Through?": Considering the Profound Differences between Mental Health Courts and "Traditional" Involuntary Civil Commitment Courts, 41 SEATTLE U. L. REV. 937, 942–44 (2018).

77 Wenona Whitfield, Capacity, Competency, and Courts: The Illinois Experience, 14 WASH. U. J. L. & POL'Y 385, 404 (2004).

78 Michael L. Perlin, Keri K. Gould and Deborah A. Dorfman, Therapeutic Jurisprudence and the Civil Rights of Institutionalized Mentally Disabled Persons: Hopeless Oxymoron or Path to Redemption? 1 PSYCHOL. PUB. POL'Y & L. 80, 116 (1995).

79 Michael L. Perlin, Therapeutic Jurisprudence: Understanding the Sanist and Pretextual Bases of Mental Disability Law, 20 NEW ENG. J. ON CRIM. & CIV. CONFINEMENT 369, 377 (1994).

80 Charles D. Parry and Eric Turkheimer, Length of Hospitalization and Outcome of Commitment and Recommitment Hearings, 43 HOSP. & COMMUNITY PSYCHIATRY 65, 66 (1992).

81 Sara Gordon, The Danger Zone: How the Dangerousness Standard in Civil Commitment Proceedings Harms People with Serious Mental Illness, 66 CASE W. RES. L. REV. 657, 678 (2016).

82 Grant H. Morris, "Let's Do the Time Warp Again": Assessing the Competence of Counsel in Mental Health Conservatorship Proceedings, 46 SAN DIEGO L. REV. 283, 314 (2009).

83 See, e.g., Heller v. Doe, 509 U.S. 312, 323–24 (1993). There are "difficulties inherent in diagnosis of mental illness. It is thus no surprise that many psychiatric predictions of future violent behavior by the mentally ill are inaccurate." Id. See generally infra Chapter 4.

of psychiatrists' testimony."[84] As Professor Gordon points out, "civil commitment proceedings may not be given priority by judges with busy caseloads, who may therefore lack an incentive to carefully scrutinize psychiatrists' recommendations."[85]

---

84 William M. Brooks, *The Tail Still Wags the Dog: The Pervasive and Inappropriate Influence by the Psychiatric Profession on the Civil Commitment Process*, 86 N.D. L. Rev. 259, 285 (2010).

85 Gordon, *supra* note 81, at 678 (citing Paul S. Appelbaum, *Civil Commitment from a Systems Perspective*, 16 Law & Hum. Behav. 61, 66–67 (1992)).

4 Civil commitment law

4.1 Introduction[1]

Perhaps the most significant aspect of civil mental disability law is the law of involuntary civil commitment. Tens of thousands of individuals are subjected to these hearings yearly; to some extent, the substances and procedures of all of these hearings harken back to a grouping of cases decided by the US Supreme Court and certain state and federal courts in the 1970s. Those interested in this area of the law must familiarize themselves with the cases and their continuing significance.

4.2 Substantive civil commitment law

4.2.1 Brief history

Questions of legal responsibility for the care and maintenance of persons with mental disabilities date back over 2,500 years.[2] A millennium later, Roman law—as codified in the Codes and Institutes of Justinian[3]—"was troubled with problems that seem contemporary":[4]

> What was the legal status of a mentally disabled person during his lucid moments? Was he still under the protection of a guardian? If not, was it necessary to name a new guardian each time the illness returned?

---

1 See generally Michael L. Perlin and Heather Ellis Cucolo, Mental Disability Law: Civil and Criminal chs. 3 and 4 (3d ed. 2016) (2019 update).

2 See The Mentally Disabled and the Law 6 (Frank T. Lindman and Donald M. McIntyre eds., 1961) (Lindman and McIntyre) (quoting Carl Georg Bruns, Fontes Juris Romani Antiqui 23–24 (1871), citing the Twelve Tables of Rome, promulgated in 449 b.c.):

> If a person is a fool, let his person and his goods be under the protection of his family or his paternal relatives, if he is not under the care of anyone.

See also Judith S. Neaman, Suggestion of the Devil: The Origins of Madness 74–76 (1975).

3 See Lindman and McIntyre, *supra* note 2, at 6–7, nn.3–9.

4 Id.

And what was the status of the testament made by him during his lucid moments?[5]

In short, many contemporary questions also concerned the Romans.[6] In England, however, the first significant law was enacted about 700 years ago,[7] in which persons with mental disabilities were categorized as "lunatics" (grossly, mentally ill persons) or as "idiots" (grossly, intellectually disabled persons),[8] and in which the *parens patriae* responsibility of the sovereign toward the property and person of such individuals was noted.[9]

4.2.2 Early American developments

Early American developments reflected dual policy bases of commitment: (1) based on *police power* (the state's power to protect itself against breaches of the peace),[10] and (2) based on *parens patriae* (the state's power to act on behalf of persons with mental illness incapable of protecting their own welfare).[11] These sought to isolate the individual from the outside world sources of his or her illness.[12] Commitment matters were simply seen as administrative procedures.[13]

---

5 Id.

6 See also id. at 7 and id. n.10 (citing VISIGOTHIC CODE 2. 5. 10., in THE VISIGOTHIC CODE (FORUM JUDICUM) 67 (S. Scott ed., 1910) (insane persons, during lucid intervals, "shall not be prohibited from transacting business during those periods"). The Visigothic Code applied in France and Spain from the late fifth to the late seventh century. Lindman and McIntyre, *supra* note 2, at 7 n.9.

7 De Praerogativa Regis. See 17 Edw. 2, ch. 9–10 (1324) (enacted between 1255 and 1290).

8 See 1 BLACKSTONE, COMMENTARIES *302–04 (1783).

9 See *Developments in the Law: Civil Commitment of the Mentally Ill*, 87 HARV. L. REV. 1190, 1207–08 n.40 (1974) (*Developments*).

10 Hugh Alan Ross, *Commitment of the Mentally Ill: Problems of Law and Policy*, 57 MICH. L. REV. 945, 955 (1959). For general and classic statements, see District of Columbia v. Brooke, 214 U.S. 138, 149 (1909):

> [W]e are dealing with an exercise of the police power—one of the most essential of powers, at times the most insistent, and always one of the least limitable of the powers of government.

11 See generally *Developments, supra* note 9, at 1207–22; ALBERT DEUTSCH, THE MENTALLY ILL IN AMERICA: A HISTORY OF THEIR CARE AND TREATMENT FROM COLONIAL TIMES 59–71 (2d ed. 1949).

12 DAVID J. ROTHMAN, THE DISCOVERY OF THE ASYLUM: SOCIAL ORDER AND DISORDER IN THE NEW REPUBLIC 143 (1971).

13 NICHOLAS N. KITTRIE, THE RIGHT TO BE DIFFERENT: DEVIANCE AND ENFORCED THERAPY 64 (1973).

Medical superintendents wanted commitment laws to be "as simple and as uncomplicated as possible."[14] There were no legislative safeguards to protect the personal liberty of the allegedly mentally ill person.[15] Then, as a "cult of asylum swept the country,"[16] "therapeutic concerns were slowly being pushed into the background."[17] This growth cycle resulted in "larger and larger institutions."[18] And with this, "the serious consequences of the total lack of legislation defining commitment procedures became more manifest."[19]

4.2.3   Mental illness as a predicate to commitment

Some finding of "mental illness" must be a prerequisite to an involuntary civil commitment application. In holding in *Jackson v. Indiana*[20] that the due process clause applied to commitment procedures,[21] the US Supreme Court simply noted that the states "have traditionally exercised broad power to commit persons found to be mentally ill."[22] Similarly, some three years later, in declaring a "right to liberty" in *O'Connor v. Donaldson*,[23] the Court stressed that "it [cannot be seriously doubted that] a wholly sane and innocent person has a constitutional right not to be physically confined by the State when his freedom will pose a danger neither to himself nor to others."[24]

How is mental illness to be defined?[25] Involuntary civil commitment statutes present a "bewildering array" of broad, narrow and even circular definitions of mental illness for purposes of the involuntary civil

---

14 ROTHMAN, *supra* note 12, at 143.

15 DEUTSCH, *supra* note 11, at 420.

16 ROTHMAN, *supra* note 12, at 131.

17 GERALD N. GROB, MENTAL INSTITUTIONS IN AMERICA: SOCIAL POLICY TO 1875 205 (1973).

18 James Elkins, *Legal Representation of the Mentally Ill*, 82 W. VA. L. REV. 157, 169 (1979), quoting, in part, GROB, *supra* note 17, at 191.

19 DEUTSCH, *supra* note 11, at 422.

20 406 U.S. 715 (1972).

21 Id. at 738: "At the least, due process requires that the nature and duration of commitment must bear some reasonable relation to the purpose for which the individual is committed." See *infra* 4.2.5.

22 Id. at 736.

23 422 U.S. 563, 576 (1975).

24 Id. at 573 n.8.

25 Each state is free to define it as it wishes; there is no reason to expect that such definitions track the latest version of the American Psychiatric Association's DIAGNOSTIC AND STATISTICAL MANUAL (DSM).

commitment process,[26] some of which employ what could be characterized as (at least partially) *clinical* definitions[27] and others as *legal* standards.[28]

While the *meaning* of "mental illness" has not been extensively litigated, some courts have considered *substantive* standards. Thus, the North Carolina Court of Appeals rebuffed plaintiffs who had alleged that the state's involuntary civil commitment statute's definition of "mental illness" was "vague and arbitrary," as it did not require that "imminent danger" be shown or evidenced by some "overt act."[29] The court found that the operative definition of "mental illness"[30] was "certainly capable of being understood and objectively applied with the help of medical experts,"[31] and thus not constitutionally vague.[32]

4.2.4   On "dangerousness"

The most vexing question in the area of the involuntary civil commitment process has been the meaning of the word "dangerousness"—

---

26 See PERLIN AND CUCOLO, *supra* note 1, § 3-3.1, at 3-37.

27 See State v. Tanner, 2019 WL 1452924 (Ohio Ct. App. 2019), ¶ 19 (as defined in DIAGNOSTIC AND STATISTICAL MANUAL OF MENTAL DISORDERS (5th ed. 2013) (DSM-5), the patient was no longer mentally ill and therefore, recommended for release). But see *In re* Moll, 347 N.W.2d 67, 70 (Minn. App. 1984) (characterizing determination of mental illness as "a mixed question of legal and medical judgment").

28 See, e.g., OR. REV. STAT. § 426.005(1)(b) (1998) (recodified, OR. REV. STAT. § 426.005(1)(e)):

"Mentally ill person" means a person who, because of a mental disorder, is either:
(a) Dangerous to himself or others; or
(b) Unable to provide for his basic personal needs and is not receiving such care as is necessary for his health or safety.

That statutory definition was amended by the legislature and became effective on January 1, 2016. OR. LAWS 2015, ch. 433, § 1. The current version of the statute, ORS 426.005(1)(f)(B), defines a "person with mental illness" as "a person who, because of a mental disorder, is . . . [u]nable to provide for basic personal needs *that are necessary to avoid serious physical harm in the near future*, and is not receiving such care as is necessary *to avoid such harm.*"

29 Matter of Salem, 228 S.E.2d 649, 650 (N.C. App. 1976).

30 N.C. GEN. STAT. § 122-36(d)(i) (1974) reads:

The words "mental illness" shall mean an illness which so lessens the capacity of the person to use his customary self-control, judgment and discretion in the conduct of his affairs, and social relations as to make it necessary or advisable for him to be under treatment, care, supervision, guidance, or control. The words "mentally ill" shall mean a person with a mental illness.

31 *Salem*, 228 S.E.2d at 651.

32 Id. at 652.

is it a legal or a medical concept,[33] or a "socially defined condition"?[34] Few other concepts are as elusive or inspire the same "I-know-it-when-I-see-it" attitude.[35] Over 45 years ago, the American Psychiatric Association acknowledged that "'[D]angerousness' is neither a psychiatric nor a medical diagnosis, but involves issues of legal judgment and definition, as well as issues of social policy."[36] "Dangerousness" remains "amorphous"[37] and "vague,"[38] and is often misunderstood[39] and misapplied[40] in commitment decisionmaking.

How accurate are forensic mental health professionals in predicting dangerousness? Many of these predictions are "rooted in unsubstantiated fears and obscured by stereotypes."[41] At best, mental health professionals cannot predict long-term dangerousness accurately "at much better than a modest level of accuracy."[42] However, society has

---

33 See State v. Krol, 344 A.2d 289, 302 (N.J. 1975):

> [W]hile courts in determining dangerousness should take full advantage of expert testimony . . . , the decision is not one that can be left wholly to the technical expertise of the psychiatrists and psychologists. The determination . . . involves a delicate balancing of society's interest in protection from harmful conduct against the individual's interest in personal liberty and autonomy. This decision, while requiring the court to make use of the assistance which medical testimony may provide, is ultimately a legal one, not a medical one . . .

34 Donald Hermann, *Preventive Detention: A Scientific View of Man, and State Power*, [1973] U. ILL. L. FORUM 673, 685.

35 Compare Jacobellis v. Ohio, 378 U.S. 184, 197 (1964) (opinion of Stewart, J.) (defining "hard-core pornography"). See also Saleem Shah, *Dangerousness: A Paradigm for Exploring Some Issues in Law and Psychology*, 33 AM. PSYCHOLOGIST 224 (1978).

36 AMERICAN PSYCHIATRIC ASSOCIATION, CLINICAL ASPECTS OF THE VIOLENT INDIVIDUAL, Task Force Report 8, 33 (1974).

37 David T. Simpson, *Involuntary Civil Commitment: The Dangerousness Standard and Its Problems*, 63 N.C.L. REV. 241, 246 (1984).

38 Virginia Hiday, *Court Discretion: Application of the Dangerousness Standard in Civil Commitment*, 5 LAW & HUM. BEHAV. 275, 276 (1981).

39 E.g., Henry J. Steadman and Joseph Cocozza, *Psychiatry, Dangerousness and the Repetitively Violent Offender*, 69 J. CRIM. L. & CRIMINOL. 226 (1978).

40 E.g., Virginia Hiday and Lynn Smith, *Effects of the Dangerousness Standard in Civil Commitment*, 14 J. PSYCHIATRY & L. 433, 449–50 (1987).

41 Alexandra Douglas, *Caging the Incompetent: Why Jail-Based Competency Restoration Programs Violate the Americans with Disabilities Act under Olmstead v. L.C.*, 32 GEO. J. LEGAL ETHICS 525, 569 (2019).

42 Heather Ellis Cucolo and Michael L. Perlin, *"The Strings in the Books Ain't Pulled and Persuaded": How the Use of Improper Statistics and Unverified Data Corrupts the Judicial Process in Sex Offender Cases*, 69 CASE W. RES. L. REV. 637, 642 n.21 (2019) citing John Monahan, *Clinical and Actuarial Predictions of Violence*, in 1 MODERN SCIENTIFIC EVIDENCE: THE LAW AND SCIENCE OF EXPERT TESTIMONY § 7.2.2-1[2], 317 (David Faigman et al. eds., 1997). There is even sobering evidence that psychiatrists may be *less* accurate predictors than laypersons. See JOHN MONAHAN,

invested psychiatrists with "an aura of scientific infallibility,"[43] with "superior, almost superhuman powers . . . which are magical,"[44] and "continues to demand that psychiatrists predict violence."[45]

More recent research confirms that *some* predictions may be accurate as to the presence of certain social variables associated with danger-ousness: sex,[46] age, employment, prior history of violence, and drug or alcohol abuse.[47] Subsequent comprehensive research carried out by the MacArthur Foundation[48] has concluded that, while there appeared to be a "greater-than-chance relationship between mental disorder and violent behavior,"[49] mental health makes "at best a trivial contribution to the overall level of violence in society."[50]

THE CLINICAL PREDICTION OF VIOLENT BEHAVIOR 13, 22–25 (1981) (noting that psychiatrists might be less accurate predictors of future violence than laymen because of personal bias arising from fear of responsibility for erroneous release of a violent person).

43 See generally Paul Giannelli, *The Admissibility of Novel Scientific Evidence: Frye v. United States a Half-Century Later*, 80 COLUM. L. REV. 1197, 1237 (1980) ("The major danger of scientific evi-dence is its potential to mislead the jury; an aura of scientific infallibility may shroud the evidence and thus lead the jury to accept it without critical scrutiny").

44 John Gunn, *An English Psychiatrist Looks at Dangerousness*, 10 BULL. AM. ACAD. PSYCHIATRY & L. 143, 147 (1982). Gunn observed:

The psychiatrist is after all the medicine man who heals anxiety, the man we call upon to take away our fears. This is partly why we give him legal powers to protect us from insane violent people.

45 James C. Beck, *Psychiatric Assessment of Potential Violence: A Reanalysis of the Problem*, in THE POTENTIALLY VIOLENT PATIENT AND THE TARASOFF DECISION IN PSYCHIATRIC PRACTICE 84 (James C. Beck ed., 1985). Dr. Beck adds, however, that "none of us knows whether we can predict violence or not, although most of us [in clinical practice] believe we can." Id. at 90.

46 See, e.g., Jennifer Skeem, Carol Schubert, Stephanie Stowman, Stacy Beeson, Edward Mulvey, William Gardner and Charles Lidz, *Gender and Risk Assessment Accuracy: Underestimating Women's Violence Potential*, 29 LAW & HUM. BEHAV. 173 (2005).

47 E.g., Christopher Slobogin, *Dangerousness and Expertise Redux*, 56 EMORY L.J. 275 (2006); Joel Dvoskin and Kirk Heilbrun, *Risk Assessment and Release Decision-Making: Toward Resolving the Great Debate*, 29 J. AM. ACAD. PSYCHIATRY & L. 6 (2001); Jennifer Skeem, Joshua D. Miller, Edward Mulvey, Jenny Tiemann and John Monahan, *Using a Five-Factor Lens to Explore the Relation between Personality Traits and Violence in Psychiatric Patients*, 73 J. COUNSELING & CLIN. PSYCHOLOGY 454 (2005).

48 See McArthur Research Network on Mental Health and the Law, *The MacArthur Violence Risk Assessment Study*, 16 AM. PSYCHOL.-L. SOC. NEWSLETTER No. 3 (Fall 1996), at 1.

49 Monahan, *supra* note 42, § 7-2.2.1, at 314. Importantly, clinicians were found to be no better than chance when it came to predicting violence among female patients. *Mental Illness and Violent Crime*, NAT'L INST. OF JUSTICE RESEARCH PREVIEW (Oct. 1996), at 1 and 2.

50 Monahan, *supra* note 42, at 315. See also Jeffrey W. Swanson et al., *Psychotic Symptoms and Disorders and the Risk of Violent Behaviour in the Community*, 6 CRIM. BEHAV. & MENTAL HEALTH 209, 210 (1996) (mental disorder a "modest risk factor" for the occurrence of interper-

4.2.5   The significance of *Jackson v. Indiana*

Under the police power, the states have adopted a variety of commitment statutes premised on "the existence of a mental illness, defect, or disorder and a specified impact or consequence of the illness."[51] All flow from *Jackson v. Indiana*:[52] "the nature and duration of commitment [must] bear some reasonable relation to the purpose for which the individual is committed."[53] *Jackson* clarified that the due process clause applies to all institutional decisionmaking, and that all questions dealing with the "nature and duration" of commitment are constitutionally bound.[54] This "laid one of the key foundational points of all modern mental disability law,"[55] and "one of the lodestars of substantive civil commitment law."[56]

4.2.5.1   The constitutional contours

In addition, three other decisions—one from a federal district court, one from the US Supreme Court and one from a state Supreme Court—best sketched out the constitutional contours of the substance of civil commitment practice.

4.2.5.1.1   Lessard v. Schmidt   Lessard,[57] in its establishment of guidelines as to the meaning of "dangerousness," served as the model for the

---

sonal violent behavior); Kevin S. Douglas and Jennifer L. Skeem, *Violence Risk Assessment: Getting Specific about Being Dynamic*, 11 PSYCHOL. PUB. POL'Y & L. 347 (2005).

51 *Developments, supra* note 9, at 1201–02.

52 406 U.S. 715 (1972).

53 Id. at 738. *Jackson* challenged Indiana's system for pretrial commitment of persons awaiting trial for criminal offenses. The defendant, an intellectually disabled, deaf mute "with a mental level of a pre-school child," id. at 717, had been charged criminally with two counts of robbery (apparently purse snatching), id. After the court ordered a competency hearing, see IND. CODE ANN. § 9-1706(a) (Burns 1964), two psychiatrists reported that defendant was unable to comprehend the nature of the charges against him or participate in his defense, *Jackson*, 406 U.S. at 718, adding that his prognosis was "dim," and that it was doubtful that he had sufficient intelligence "ever to develop the necessary communication skills" so that he could stand trial, id. at 719. Further, Indiana had no facilities "that could help someone as badly off as [defendant] to learn minimal communication skills." Id.

54 Michael L. Perlin, *"Things Have Changed": Looking at Non-Institutional Mental Disability Law through the Sanism Filter*, 46 N.Y.L. SCH. L. REV. 535, 539 (2002–03).

55 Michael L. Perlin, Deborah A. Dorfman and Naomi M. Weinstein, *"On Desolation Row": The Blurring of the Borders between Civil and Criminal Mental Disability Law, and What It Means for All of Us*, 24 TEX. J. ON CIV. LIBS. & CIV. RTS. 59, 72 (2018).

56 PERLIN AND CUCOLO, *supra* note 1, COMMENT TO § 3-5.1.1, at 3-89.

57 349 F. Supp. 1078 (E.D. Wis. 1972), *vacated and remanded*, 414 U.S. 473, *on remand*, 379 F. Supp.

first generation of statutory challenges.[58] In a comprehensive opinion, it found state law to "require ... a finding of 'dangerousness' to self or others in order to deprive an individual of his or her freedom."[59] Dangerousness must be "based upon a finding of a recent overt act, attempt or threat to do substantial harm to oneself or another."[60] *Lessard* was the forerunner of a generation of involuntary civil commitment cases,[61] all making a finding that there must be a "real and present danger of doing significant harm"[62] to show dangerousness sufficient to support such a commitment.[63]

4.2.5.1.2   State v. Krol   The actual *legal* meaning of "dangerousness" was first given extended consideration in the New Jersey case of *State v. Krol*,[64] an appeal from an individual indefinite commitment order following a *criminal* finding of not guilty by reason of insanity (NGRI).[65] Declaring the commitment scheme unconstitutional,[66] the court noted the statutory lack of inquiry as to whether a particular defendant posed a "special risk of danger":[67]

> The fact that defendant is presently suffering from some degree of mental illness and that at some point in the past mental illness caused him to commit a criminal act, while certainly sufficient to give probable cause to inquire whether he is dangerous, does not in and of itself, warrant the infer-

---

1376 (E.D. Wis. 1974), *vacated and remanded*, 421 U.S. 957 (1975), *reinstated*, 413 F. Supp. 1318 (E.D. Wis. 1976).

58 Michael L. Perlin, Keri K. Gould and Deborah A. Dorfman, *Therapeutic Jurisprudence and the Civil Rights of Institutionalized Mentally Disabled Persons: Hopeless Oxymoron or Path to Redemption?* 1 Psychol. Pub. Pol'y & L. 80, 88 (1995).

59 *Lessard*, 349 F. Supp. at 1093.

60 Id.

61 See, e.g., Thomas Zander, *Civil Commitment in Wisconsin: The Impact of* Lessard v. Schmidt, [1976] Wis. L. Rev. 503, 559 ("*Lessard* ... will find its place in history ... as one of the first major judicial recognitions of civil commitment as more than a court authorized medical decision").

62 See, e.g., Doremus v. Farrell, 407 F. Supp. 509, 514–15 (D. Neb. 1975).

63 One district court described the standard as a "real and present threat of substantial harm to himself or to others." Lynch v. Baxley, 386 F. Supp. 378, 390 (M.D. Ala. 1974), superseded by statute as stated in Garrett v. State, 707 So. 2d 273 (Ala. Civ. App. 1997). Another court held that the basis for confinement must "lie in threatened or actual behavior stemming from the mental disorder, acts of a nature which the State may legitimately control; viz., that causing harm to self or others." Bell v. Wayne County Gen. Hosp., 384 F. Supp. 1085, 1096 (E.D. Mich. 1974).

64 344 A.2d 289 (N.J. 1975).

65 Id. at 293–94.

66 Id. at 305.

67 Id. at 295.

ence that he presently poses a significant threat of harm, either to himself or to others.[68]

Under this scheme, a mentally ill defendant who posed "no significant danger to society, may nevertheless be deprived of his liberty for an indefinite period of time because dangerousness is, in effect, presumed from continuing insanity."[69] The court found these defects of "constitutional dimension," relying on *Jackson* for the propositions that the commitment standard must bear a "reasonable relationship to the ostensible purpose for which the individual is committed" and that the state must make a "meaningful factual determination as to whether defendant actually meets the standard for commitment."[70] Thus, "the standard for commitment must be cast in terms of continuing mental illness and dangerousness to self or others, *not* in terms of continuing insanity alone."[71] The Court underscored: "The labels 'criminal commitment' and 'civil commitment' are of no constitutional significance."[72]

The court emphasized that "[d]angerous conduct [was] not identical with criminal conduct."[73] Dangerous conduct involved "not merely violations of social norms enforced by criminal sanctions, but significant physical or psychological injury to persons or substantial destruction of property."[74] The court warned:

> Persons are not to be indefinitely incarcerated because they present a risk of future conduct which is merely socially undesirable. Personal liberty and autonomy are of too great a value to be sacrificed to protect society against the possibility of future behavior which some may find odd, disagreeable, or offensive, or even against the possibility of future non-dangerous acts which

---

68 Id. (footnote omitted). The court noted that persons who are mentally ill are, "at most, only slightly more likely to commit harmful acts than the general population," and that even those who have committed prior criminal acts "have not been shown to be consistently substantially more dangerous than other persons suffering from mental illness." Id. at n.2.

69 Id. at 295.

70 Id. at 296.

71 Id. (emphasis added).

72 *Krol*, 344 A.2d at 297. But see Jones v. United States, 463 U.S. 354, 366 (1983) (under federal Constitution, NGRI finding sufficient foundation for commitment of insanity acquittee for "the purposes of treatment and the protection of society"), discussed *infra* Chapter 9.

73 *Krol*, 344 A.2d at 301.

74 Id. See also, e.g., State v. Woolridge, 794 P.2d 1258, 1258 (Or. App. 1990) ("mere threats of violence or verbal hostility may not be sufficient, standing alone, to show mental illness").

would be ground for criminal prosecution if actually committed. . . . [P]eople cannot be suppressed simply because they become public nuisances.[75]

Commitment requires "a substantial risk of dangerous conduct within the reasonably foreseeable future."[76] Evaluation of the *magnitude* of risk involves consideration of both the *likelihood* of dangerous conduct and the *seriousness* of the harm that may ensue if such conduct takes place.[77] Dangerousness is not a unitary concept;[78] a defendant might be dangerous "in only certain types of situations or in connection with relationships with certain individuals." Any evaluation of dangerousness in such situations must take into account "the likelihood that defendants will be exposed to such situations or come into contact with such individuals."[79]

4.2.5.1.3 O'Connor v. Donaldson Three years after *Jackson*, the Supreme Court examined the constitutional limitations on commitment in a *civil* case. Its decision in *O'Connor v. Donaldson*,[80] holding that a state "cannot constitutionally confine without more a nondangerous individual who is capable of surviving safely in freedom by himself or with the help of willing and responsible family members or friends,"[81] shaped "an important instrument [for a limited but numerically significant group of patients] in securing treatment or release from confinement."[82] It marked the first Supreme Court recognition of "the legitimacy of judicial involvement in activities previously considered to be the exclusive domain of psychiatrists."[83]

The Court established the constitutional boundaries of the "right to liberty":

> A finding of "mental illness" alone cannot justify a State's locking up a person against his will and keeping him indefinitely in simple custodial confinement. Assuming that that term can be given a reasonably precise content

---

75 *Krol*, 344 A.2d at 301–02 (citations omitted).

76 Id. at 302.

77 Id., citing Cross v. Harris, 418 F.2d 1095, 1100–01 (D.C. Cir. 1969).

78 See PERLIN AND CUCOLO, *supra* note 1, § 3-5.1.2, at 3-102.

79 *Krol*, 344 A.2d at 302.

80 422 U.S. 563 (1975).

81 Id. at 576.

82 *The Supreme Court: 1974 Term*, 89 HARV. L. REV. 70, 75 (1975).

83 Louis Kopolow, *A Review of Major Implications of the* O'Connor v. Donaldson *Decision*, 133 AM. J. PSYCHIATRY 379 (1976).

and that the "mentally ill" can be identified with reasonable accuracy, *there is still no constitutional basis for confining such persons involuntarily if they are dangerous to no one and can live in freedom.*

May the State confine the mentally ill merely to ensure them a living standard superior to that they enjoy in the private community? That the State has a proper interest in providing care and assistance to the unfortunate goes without saying. But the mere presence of mental illness does not disqualify a person from preferring his home to the comforts of an institution. . . .

May the State fence in the harmless mentally ill solely to save its citizens from exposure to those whose ways are different? One might as well ask if the State, to avoid public unease, could incarcerate all who are physically unattractive or socially eccentric. *Mere public intolerance or animosity cannot constitutionally justify the deprivation of a person's physical liberty.*[84]

4.2.5.1.4   Contextualizing the three cases   Lessard—still the highwater mark of involuntary civil commitment law[85]— assumed tremendous symbolic significance as the forerunner of an extensive body of case law requiring a finding of "dangerousness" precedent to a commitment finding. While its mandate of an "overt act" has been rejected more recently elsewhere, *Lessard*'s "dangerousness" requirement remains good law, and is still cited regularly.[86] *State v. Krol* remains the most articulate exposition of the *meaning of* "dangerousness," and few of the subsequent cyclical developments that have partially undercut some of *Lessard*'s underpinnings have eroded *Krol* as a national standard.

O'Connor stands beside *Jackson* as one of the Supreme Court's early "twin pillars" of civil commitment law.[87] Its reformative influence on state legislatures has been incalculable.[88]

---

84 Id. at 575–76 (citations omitted; emphasis added). Over 40 years later, courts continue to cite this paragraph. See, e.g., J.H. v. Prince George's Hosp. Ctr., 165 A.3d 664 (Md. App. 2017) (patients sought judicial review of orders for admission to hospital for involuntary psychiatric treatment).

85 See David F. Mrad and Erik Nabors, *The Role of the Psychologist in Civil Commitment*, in FORENSIC PSYCHOLOGY: EMERGING TOPICS AND EXPANDING ROLES 232, 235 (Alan Goldstein ed., 2006).

86 E.g., In the Matter of the Mental Commitment of D.J., 939 N.W.2d 890, 2020 WL 61062, *2 (Wis. Ct. App. 2020).

87 See Mrad and Nabors, *supra* note 85, at 235.

88 PERLIN AND CUCOLO, *supra* note 1, § 3-5.1.2, at 3-115.

4.2.6   Least restrictive alternative

Perhaps no other principle has permeated the full body of mental disability law and litigation as has the doctrine of the "least restrictive alternative" (LRA). The doctrine has its basis in the Supreme Court doctrine requiring the government "to pursue its ends by means narrowly tailored so as not to encroach unnecessarily on important competing interests."[89]

4.2.6.1   *Lake v. Cameron*

In *Lake v. Cameron*, the court interpreted local law to mandate the availability of "the entire spectrum of services . . . including outpatient treatment, foster care halfway houses, day hospitals, nursing homes, etc."[90] This was the first use of the LRA doctrine in mental disability law.[91]

4.2.6.2   *Lessard again*

This doctrine was first given *constitutional* life in the mental health context in *Lessard v. Schmidt*: "Even if the standards for an adjudication of mental illness and potential dangerousness are satisfied, a court should order full-time involuntary hospitalization only as a last resort."[92] The most "basic and fundamental right" was "the right to be free from unwanted restraint"; "persons suffering from the condition of being mentally ill, but who are not alleged to have committed any crime, cannot be totally deprived of their liberty if there are less drastic means for achieving the same basic goal."[93]

---

89 David Zlotnick, *First Do No Harm: Least Restrictive Alternative Analysis and the Right of Mental Patients to Refuse Treatment*, 83 W. VA. L. REV. 375, 381 (1981).

90 364 F.2d 657, 659–60 (D.C. Cir. 1966), quoting S. REP. No. 925, 88th Cong., 2d Sess. 31 (1964). Judge Bazelon added: "Deprivations of liberty solely because of the dangers to the ill persons themselves should not go beyond what is necessary for their protection." Id. at 660 (footnotes omitted).

91 See Nancy K. Rhoden, *The Limits of Liberty: Deinstitutionalization, Homelessness, and Libertarian Theory*, 31 EMORY L.J. 375, 422–23 (1982).

92 349 F. Supp. 1078, 1095 (E.D. Wis. 1972), *vacated and remanded*, 414 U.S. 473, *on remand*, 379 F. Supp. 1376 (E.D. Wis. 1974), *vacated and remanded*, 421 U.S. 957 (1975), *reinstated*, 413 F. Supp. 1318 (E.D. Wis. 1976).

93 Id.

The burden for exploring alternatives to institutionalization was placed on "the person recommending full-time involuntary hospitalization," who must prove:

> (1) what alternatives are available; (2) what alternatives were investigated; and (3) why the investigated alternatives were not deemed suitable. These alternatives include voluntary or court-ordered out-patient treatment, day treatment in a hospital, night treatment in a hospital, placement in the custody of a friend or relative, placement in a nursing home, referral to a community mental health clinic, and home health aide services.[94]

Lessard's reasoning was subsequently adopted elsewhere,[95] and was endorsed extensively in the literature. Its doctrinal importance as "one of the most important trends in mental health law" cannot be questioned.[96]

4.2.6.3   *Youngberg v. Romeo*

In expanding the LRA concept beyond the involuntary civil commitment process, the Third Circuit Court of Appeals had held in *Romeo v. Youngberg*[97] that involuntarily institutionalized persons with mental disabilities had a right to habilitation in the LRA.[98] The US Supreme Court, in vacating the Third Circuit's judgment,[99] declared a right to training and to "reasonably nonrestrictive confinement conditions,"[100] a phrase it neither elaborated upon nor further defined. This language, however, has had little impact on the application of the LRA doctrine to the commitment process; most subsequent cases have continued to demand relatively strict adherence to the appropriate statutory provisions.[101]

---

94 Id. at 1096.

95 See, e.g., Lynch v. Baxley, 386 F. Supp. 378, 392 (M.D. Ala. 1974), superseded by statute as stated in Garrett v. State, 707 So.2d 273 (Ala. Civ. App. 1997); Suzuki v. Quisenberry, 411 F. Supp. 1113, 1132–33 (D. Haw. 1976); Kesselbrenner v. Anonymous, 305 N.E.2d 903 (N.Y. 1973).

96 Bradley D. McGraw and Ingo Keilitz, *The Least Restrictive Alternative Doctrine in Los Angeles County Civil Commitment*, 6 WHITTIER L. REV. 35, 36 (1984).

97 644 F.2d 147 (3d Cir. 1980), *vacated* 457 U.S. 307 (1982).

98 Id. at 164–70.

99 *Youngberg*, 457 U.S. at 310–14.

100 Id. at 324.

101 Compare Goebel v. Colorado Dep't of Insts., 764 P.2d 785 (Colo. 1988), *suppl.*, 830 P.2d 995 (Colo.), *suppl.*, 830 P.2d 1036 (Colo. 1992) (construing state law, see COLO. REV. STAT. §§ 27-10-101; 27-10-116(1)(a) (1998), to provide treatment rights—including the LRA—for both involuntary and voluntary patients, but rejecting plaintiff's *Youngberg* claims, see 764 P.2d at 810 n.24).

4.2.7   Importance of an "overt act"

Courts have split dramatically over the question of constitutional necessity of an "overt act" as a prerequisite for a "dangerousness" finding,[102] following the requirement in *Lessard v. Schmidt* that such a finding must be premised on "a recent overt act, attempt or threat to do substantial harm to oneself or another,"[103] a phrase later adopted by other courts in similar statutory challenge cases.

This requirement, however, was specifically rejected by other courts in cases such as *United States ex rel. Mathew v. Nelson*,[104] which relied heavily on expert testimony that indicated "there are instances in which a psychiatrist can determine … that a mentally ill person is reasonably likely to injure himself or another even though the person's history does not include a recent overt act."[105]

4.2.8   Inability to care for oneself

Involuntary civil commitment has traditionally been premised on the bases of police power or *parens patriae*. Police power is generally the justification for commitments based on "dangerousness to self or others," the *parens patriae* doctrine for commitment has been premised on an individual's inability to protect his or her own welfare.

In *State ex rel. Hawks v. Lazaro*, the West Virginia Supreme Court of Appeals declared unconstitutional state law allowing for confinement on a showing of mental illness and being "in need of custody, care

---

102 For an analysis of the significance of risk assessment tools in making predictions about the need for commitment in this context, see Douglas Mossman, Allison H. Schwartz and Elise R. Elam, *Risky Business versus Overt Acts: What Relevance Do "Actuarial" Probabilistic Risk Assessments Have for Judicial Decisions on Involuntary Psychiatric Hospitalization?* 11 Hous. J. Health L. & Pol'y 365 (2012).

103 349 F. Supp. 1078, 1093 (E.D. Wis. 1972), *vacated and remanded*, 414 U.S. 473, *on remand*, 379 F. Supp. 1376 (E.D. Wis. 1974), *vacated and remanded*, 421 U.S. 957 (1975), *reinstated*, 413 F. Supp. 1318 (E.D. Wis. 1976).

104 461 F. Supp. 707 (N.D. Ill. 1978).

105 Id. at 711 (emphasis added). For the purposes of the case in question, "recent overt act" was defined, id. at 709–10 n.5, as:

(1) An act or an omission which physically injures the actor or another, or which constitutes a failure to care for one's self so as to guard against physical injury or provide for one's own physical needs,

(2) an attempt to commit such an act or omission, or

(3) a threat to commit such an act or omission.

or treatment in a hospital."[106] As the state could not demonstrate a compelling state interest "for hospitalizing a person in his own best interests," the need for hospitalization standing alone did not allow for state intervention.[107] The court underscored:

> It is possible for many nonviolent people, even those who suffer from a mental disease or retardation to such an extent that they are unable to earn a living, to live outside an institution, and when these people prefer to do so, regardless of the wisdom of their decision, or the strength of their reasoning powers, the constitution guarantees them the right to follow their own desires.[108]

On the other hand, the court would allow for commitment if an individual were a "passive" danger to self.[109] To meet this standard, the state must prove mental illness that "by sheer inactivity [on the part of the patient] will permit himself to die either of starvation or lack of care."[110]

4.2.9   Grave disability

In some jurisdictions, a person can be involuntarily civilly committed if he (or she) is found to be "gravely disabled," a "condition in which a person, as a result of a mental disorder, is unable to provide for his basic personal needs for food, clothing, and shelter."[111] However, in *Wetherhorn v. Alaska Psychiatric Institute*,[112] the Alaska Supreme Court concluded there would also need to be "reason to believe that the respondent's mental condition could be improved by the course of treatment sought."[113]

4.2.10   "Dangerousness to property"

While most substantive involuntary civil commitment litigation has focused on statutes dealing with behavior dangerous to self or to

---

106   202 S.E.2d 109, 116 (W. Va. 1974), quoting W. Va. Code § 27-5-4 (1965).

107   Id. at 123–24.

108   Id. at 123.

109   Id.

110   Id.

111   Cal. Welf. and Inst. Code § 5008(h)(1) (1997) (constitutionality upheld in Doe v. Gallinot, 486 F. Supp. 983 (C.D. Cal. 1979), aff'd, 657 F.2d 1017 (9th Cir. 1981)).

112   156 P.3d 371 (Alaska 2007).

113   Id. at 378, quoting Alaska Statute 47.30.730(a)(3).

others, several cases have considered the interplay between "danger-ousness" and damage to property.

In the lead case of *State v. Krol*, the New Jersey Supreme Court merely indicated that "dangerous conduct" involved, inter alia, "substantial destruction of property."[114] In striking down portions of Hawaii's involuntary civil commitment law in *Suzuki v. Yuen*,[115] however, the Ninth Circuit focused more closely on the questions raised by the danger occasioned by property damage.[116] Although the court did not decide "whether a state may *ever* commit one who is dangerous to property," it did find that the statute in question—allowing for com-mitment when one "threatens harm to *any* property"—was overbroad and thus unconstitutional,[117] as the protection of "just *any* property" was not sufficiently significant to support commitment.[118]

4.3 Procedural issues

Since 1972, there has been extensive litigation and legislation dealing with the constitutional appropriateness of procedures governing the involuntary civil commitment of individuals to psychiatric hospitals covering all phases of the commitment process, including the prehear-ing, hearing, dispositional phase and post-adjudication phases.

4.4 Contours of civil commitment hearings[119]

4.4.1 Right to final commitment hearing

The Constitution requires a judicial hearing prior to an order of invol-untary civil commitment.[120] Questions remain as to the extent of

---

114 State v. Krol, 344 A.2d 289, 301 (N.J. 1975). See *supra* 4.2.5.1.2.

115 617 F.2d 173 (9th Cir. 1980).

116 Id. at 176. The statute had provided for the commitment of one who is "mentally ill . . . and is dangerous to . . . property." HAWAII REV. STAT. § 334-60(b)(1)(B) (1976) (repealed 1984 Hawaii Sess. Laws ch. 188, § 2). See HAWAII REV. STAT. § 334-60.2 (Supp. 1984). See *Suzuki*, 617 F.2d at 175 n.2.

117 Id. (emphasis added).

118 Id. (emphasis added). See also, *In re* H.G., 632 N.W.2d 458, 462 (N.D. 2001) ("lack of prudence in business affairs is not the type of dangerousness to property envisioned by the statute as a basis for involuntary commitment").

119 On issues that arise prior to the actual hearing (e.g., how proceedings are initiated, the scope of screening procedures), see PERLIN AND CUCOLO, *supra* note 1, §§ 4-2.1 to 4-2.1.5.

120 E.g., Addington v. Texas, 441 U.S. 418, 425–27 (1979) (see *infra* 4.5.1).

procedural due process safeguards constitutionally required at such a hearing,[121] its timing, the patient's right to a continuance, the proper participants at such a hearing and the impact of a request for a jury trial.

4.4.1.1   *Time limitations*

The US Supreme Court summarily affirmed a district court decision upholding the constitutionality of a North Carolina statute providing for a final hearing within ten days of confinement.[122] Since this decision, state courts construing local statutes that stipulate specific time limitations for involuntary civil commitment hearings have interpreted these laws both narrowly and expansively.[123]

4.4.1.2   *Hearing waiver*

While certain state statutes expressly forbid waiver of commitment hearings,[124] others provide—in the case of initial waiver—for the right to a hearing "at any time during the period of commitment";[125] others allow for waiver if the court finds that it was "freely given."[126] Courts have generally approved of waivers in the involuntary civil commitment context where they are "knowing and intelligent," if made by counsel with "the approval of the [patient] and with the approval of the court."[127]

4.4.1.3   *Conduct and location of hearing*

Courts have split on the question of whether it is necessary for a judicial officer to conduct the involuntary civil commitment hearing.

---

121 See, e.g., Suzuki v. Quisenberry, 411 F. Supp. 1113, 1127 (D. Haw. 1976) (listing 12 mandatory procedural rights).

122 French v. Blackburn, 428 F. Supp. 1351, 1355 (M.D.N.C.), *aff'd*, 443 U.S. 901 (1977).

123 *Strict interpretations*: In several cases, appellate courts have held that, if a trial court has not scheduled a commitment hearing within the specified statutory time frame, the trial court loses jurisdiction over the patient, and has no choice but to dismiss the proceedings. E.g., State *ex rel.* Hashimi v. Kalil, 446 N.E.2d 1387 (Mass. 1983).

    Broad interpretations: A New Jersey appellate court has held that the addition of a 7-day observation period to the 20-day confinement period did not create an unconstitutionally "overlong time" between hospitalization and commitment hearing. Matter of Z.O., 484 A.2d 1287, 1291 (N.J. App. Div. 1984).

124 See, e.g., OHIO REV. CODE ANN. § 5122.15(H) (1998).

125 MASS. GEN. LAWS ANN. ch. 123, § 6(b) (1998). Initial waiver must be "in writing by the [patient] after consultation with his counsel." Id.

126 MINN. STAT. ANN. § 253B.08(5) (2012).

127 Lynch v. Baxley, 386 F. Supp. 378, 396 (M.D. Ala. 1974), superseded by statute as stated in Garrett v. State, 707 So.2d 273 (Ala. Civ. App. 1997).

There is some support for the position that a "neutral *judicial* officer" is required,[128] but it has more generally been held that it is not constitutionally objectionable for an administrative hearing tribunal to decide such matters.[129]

Commitment hearings have traditionally been discretionarily held at the hospital in which the subject is institutionalized[130] or at a location otherwise approved by the court.[131] Some modern statutes have given patients the right to object to "hospital hearings."[132] Importantly, commentators have expressed concern that "hospital hearings," "with the patient dressed in hospital garb, may introduce an element of unfairness," reinforcing the idea "that the individual should be in the hospital, and [reducing] his already shaken self-confidence."[133]

4.4.1.4   *Right to be informed of rights*

At least one state's courts have remanded commitment orders where patients were not advised of their statutory rights at the beginning of the commitment hearing or the proceeding for a continuation of the commitment.[134]

4.4.2   The substance of the hearing

4.4.2.1   *Right to be present*

Generally, state statutes provide for a patient's presence at an involuntary civil commitment hearing.[135] This right can be waived by the patient[136] if "freely given";[137] also, a patient can be excluded when "seriously disruptive,"[138] "totally incapable of comprehending and par-

---

128 See Suzuki v. Quisenberry, 411 F. Supp. 1113, 1128 (D. Haw. 1976).

129 See, e.g., Doremus v. Farrell, 407 F. Supp. 509, 516 (D. Neb. 1975). On the therapeutic jurisprudence implications of the use of non-judicial officers in general, see Michael L. Perlin, *"Man, I Ain't a Judge": The Therapeutic Jurisprudence Implications of the Use of Non-Judicial Officers in Criminal Justice Cases*, 64. AM. BEHAV. SCI. 1686 (2020).

130 See, e.g., VA. CODE § 37.2-820 (2012) (hearing "may be conducted by the district court judge or a special justice at the convenient facility or other place open to the public").

131 See, e.g., MICH. COMP. LAW ANN. § 330.1456(1) (1998).

132 See, e.g., WIS. STAT. ANN. § 51.20(5) (1997).

133 *Developments, supra* note 9, at 1281 n.107.

134 E.g., State v. Allison, 877 P.2d 660 (Or. App. 1994).

135 See, e.g., 405 ILL. COMP. STAT. ANN. 5/3-806 (1998); MINN. STAT. ANN. § 253B.08(5) (2012).

136 MINN. STAT. ANN. § 253B.08(5)(a) (2012).

137 Id.

138 Id.

ticipating in the proceedings"[139] or where the court "is satisfied by a clear showing that the respondent's attendance would subject him to substantial risk of serious physical or emotional harm."[140]

4.4.2.2   Right to in camera hearings

Most statutes provide that hearings be closed to the public on the theory that closure will "maximize candor from the respondent's family and other witnesses, and . . . minimize embarrassment to the respondent."[141] On the other hand, patients facing involuntary civil commitment usually have the right to request an open hearing.[142]

4.4.2.3   Right to recordation or transcript

Cases have generally found that a patient has a right to a complete record of the involuntary civil commitment hearing,[143] including "findings adequate for review."[144]

4.4.2.4   Right to notice

Many courts have held that mandatory notice is a required element of procedural due process.[145] Besides notice of "date, time, and place," such notice must inform the patient of "the basis of his detention,"[146]

> a clear statement of the purposes of the proceedings and of the possible consequences to the subject thereof, a statement of the legal standard upon which commitment is authorized, the names of the examining physicians and others who may testify in favor of their detention and the substance of their proposed testimony.[147]

---

139 Id.

140 405 ILL. COMP. STAT. ANN. 5/3-806 (1998).

141 See, e.g., Clifford D. Stromberg and Alan A. Stone, *A Model State Law on Civil Commitment of the Mentally Ill*, 20 HARV. J. LEGIS. 275, 344 n.232 (1983) (listing statutes).

142 Compare *In re* Elmore, 468 N.E.2d 97, 101 (Ohio Ct. App. 1983), affirming a commitment order in the face of a challenge to the court allowing a newspaper reporter into the hearing room, construing the controlling statute to vest discretion in the trial court "subject only to the right of the [patient] to require a public hearing."

143 E.g., Lynch v. Baxley, 386 F. Supp. 378, 396 (M.D. Ala. 1974), superseded by statute as stated in Garrett v. State, 707 So.2d 273 (Ala. Civ. App. 1997).

144 Id. at 396.

145 E.g., Suzuki v. Quisenberry, 411 F. Supp. 1113, 1127 (D. Haw. 1976).

146 *Lessard*, 349 F. Supp. at 1092.

147 *Suzuki*, 411 F. Supp. at 1127.

4.4.2.5   Right to present, confront and cross-examine witnesses

Most cases have found that due process requires that one subject to involuntary civil commitment be given the opportunity to offer evidence on his or her own behalf,[148] as such a right "is a fundamental element of due process of law."[149] One case—never cited in the 20 years since it was decided—has found that a patient has a due process right to testify in his or her own behalf at such a proceeding.[150]

4.4.2.6   Right to jury trial

The right to trial by jury is provided for in several state statutes;[151] however, courts are often reluctant to find a constitutional right to such a trial.[152] Commentators have concluded that, even if jury trials lead to the same results as judges' decisions, they will "be perceived as better protecting all citizens, which itself has value."[153]

4.4.2.7   Right to assert privilege against self-incrimination

Does the right to assert privilege against self-incrimination apply either in a pretrial psychiatric examination or at trial?[154] This issue was characterized by one commentator as "one of the most troublesome problems in judicial scrutiny of civil commitment procedures."[155]

---

148 E.g., Lynch v. Baxley, 386 F. Supp. 378, 394 (M.D. Ala. 1974), superseded by statute as stated in Garrett v. State, 707 So.2d 273 (Ala. Civ. App. 1997).

149 Id., citing Specht v. Patterson, 386 U.S. 605, 610 (1967), and quoting Washington v. Texas, 388 U.S. 14, 19 (1967).

150 Ibur v. State, 765 So.2d 275 (Fla. Dist. Ct. App. 2000).

151 Vicki G. Kaufman, *The Confinement of Mabel Jones: Is There a Right to Jury Trial in Civil Commitment Proceedings?* 6 FLA. ST. U. L. REV. 103, 113–14 n.60 (1978).

152 See, e.g., *In re* Jones, 339 So. 2d 1117 (Fla. 1976), *cert. denied*, 439 U.S. 972 (1977); County Attorney, Pima County v. Kaplan, 605 P.2d 912, 914 (Ariz. App. 1980).

153 Stromberg and Stone, *supra* note 141, at 381.

154 See, e.g., People v. Nayder, 435 N.E.2d 1317 (Ill. App. 1982) (not error—as violation of patient's constitutional right to *counsel*—to allow state to call respondent to testify as adverse party at involuntary civil commitment proceeding).

155 Daniel Shuman, *The Road to Bedlam: Evidentiary Guideposts in Civil Commitment Proceedings,* 55 NOTRE DAME L. REV. 53, 73 (1979). The lead case finding the privilege against self-incrimination applicable is Lessard v. Schmidt, 349 F. Supp. 1078 (E.D. Wis. 1972) (subsequent citations omitted), a case that "fortified" its conclusion by relying upon medical evidence indicating that patients "respond more favorably to treatment when they feel they are being treated fairly and are treated as intelligent, aware, human beings." 349 F. Supp. at 1101–02. Compare French v. Blackburn, 428 F. Supp. 1351, 1358–59 (M.D.N.C.), *aff'd*, 443 U.S. 901 (1977) ("To apply the

4.4.2.8 Right to a statement of reasons

Several courts have found that, along with a right to recordation of the proceedings in an involuntary civil commitment hearing, there is a right to a statement of the reasons relied upon by the fact-finder in support of commitment.[156]

4.5 Dispositional phase

4.5.1 Addington v. Texas

The Supreme Court addressed the burden of proof in *Addington v. Texas*,[157] from a jurisdiction where the preponderance standard had previously been applicable.[158] Noting that "civil commitment for any purpose constitutes a significant deprivation of liberty that requires due process protection,"[159] and that commitment "can engender adverse social consequences to the individual,"[160] the Court rejected the preponderance standard as "creat[ing] the risk of increasing the number of individuals erroneously committed" without furthering any legitimate state interests.[161] The Court explained: NO PoE

> Loss of liberty calls for a showing that the individual suffered from something more serious than is demonstrated by idiosyncratic behavior. Increasing the burden of proof is one way to impress the factfinder with the importance of the decision and thereby perhaps to reduce the chances that inappropriate commitments will be ordered.[162]

no BRD

The Court rejected the patient's argument that a "beyond a reasonable doubt" standard would be appropriate[163] as state power was not

---

privilege to the type of proceedings here challenged would be to destroy the valid purposes which they serve as it would make them unworkable and ineffective").

156 See, e.g., Lynch v. Baxley, 386 F. Supp. 378, 396 (M.D. Ala. 1974) (record must include "findings adequate for review"), superseded by statute as stated in Garrett v. State, 707 So.2d 273 (Ala. Civ. App. 1997); see also, Matter of S.J., 753 P.2d 319, 320–21 (Mont. 1988).

157 441 U.S. 418 (1979).

158 See State v. Turner, 556 S.W.2d 563 (Tex.), *cert. denied*, 435 U.S. 929 (1977).

159 *Addington*, 441 U.S. at 425, *citing*, inter alia, Jackson v. Indiana, 406 U.S. 715 (1972); Humphrey v. Cady, 405 U.S. 504 (1972).

160 Id. at 426.

161 Id.

162 Id. at 426–27.

163 Id. at 431.

being exercised "in a punitive sense,"[164] concluding that "layers of professional review and observation of the patient's condition, and the concern of family and friends generally will provide continuous opportunities for an erroneous commitment to be corrected."[165] It rejected the core principle of the criminal conviction analogy: "it is not true that the release of a genuinely mentally ill person is no worse for the individual than the failure to convict the guilty."[166]

The Court also looked at the "lack of certainty and the fallibility of psychiatric diagnosis," leading to a "serious question as to whether a state could *ever* prove beyond a reasonable doubt that an individual is both mentally ill and likely to be dangerous."[167] "The subtleties and nuances of psychiatric diagnosis [rendered] certainties virtually beyond reach in most situations."[168] It turned to a "middle level of proof that strikes a fair balance between the rights of the individual and the legitimate concerns of the state," and concluded that a burden "equal to or greater than . . . clear and convincing [proof]" was necessary to meet federal constitutional due process guarantees.[169]

4.5.2 Heller v. Doe

The Court subsequently considered this question in the context of commitment of persons with intellectual disabilities (then referred to as "mentally retarded"), from a different perspective: here, it considered the equal protection implications of a statutory scheme that established a heightened standard of review for involuntary civil commitment based on mental illness (beyond a reasonable doubt) but a lesser standard for commitments based on mental retardation (clear and convincing evidence). In *Heller v. Doe*, it found that these distinctions were constitutional and did not run afoul of the equal protection clause.[170]

---

164 *Addington*, 441 U.S. at 428.

165 Id. at 428–29.

166 And see id. at 429:

> One who is suffering from a debilitating mental illness and in need of treatment is neither wholly at liberty nor free of stigma. [Citations omitted.] It cannot be said, therefore, that it is much better for a mentally ill person to "go free" than for a mentally normal person to be committed.

167 Id.

168 Id.

169 Id. at 433.

170 509 U.S. 312, 320–28 (1993).

In *Heller,* the Supreme Court found that there was a rational basis for establishing a system with varying burdens of proof based upon the handicapping condition, finding "more than adequate justifications for the differences in treatment between the mentally retarded and the mentally ill."[171] It accepted Kentucky's arguments that mental retardation was easier to diagnose (since it becomes apparent during childhood and is generally supported by "evidence of the condition [that has] accumulated for years") than is mental illness (which may be sudden, may not manifest itself until after adulthood, and may be "difficult" to diagnose).[172]

Danger to self or others would be easier to establish in these cases as retardation was a "permanent, relatively static condition," so a determination of dangerousness may be made "with some accuracy" based on previous behavior of adults with mental retardation.[173] On the other hand, since "psychiatric predictions of future violent behavior by the mentally ill *are* inaccurate," it would have been "plausible" for the state to conclude that the dangerousness determination "was more accurate as to the mentally retarded than the mentally ill."[174]

In a scathing dissent, Justice Souter examined the differences between mental retardation and mental illness, rejecting the court's conclusion that persons with mental retardation are subject to "less invasive" treatment than are mentally ill persons, by examining the available social science evidence, which revealed that between 30 percent and 76 percent of all residents of facilities for persons with mental retardation received psychotropic medication.[175] These drugs are often misused,

---

171 Id. at 321.

172 Id. citing, in part, Addington v. Texas, 441 U.S. 418, 430 (1979).

173 *Heller,* 509 U.S. at 323.

174 Id. at 324 (emphasis added). The court also supported its decision by reference to the "much less invasive" means of treatment used following the institutionalization of persons with mental retardation. Mentally ill persons are subject to "intrusive inquiries" into their thoughts and the use of psychotropic drugs. On the other hand, persons with mental retardation, "in general, are not subjected to these medical treatments; rather they are provided 'habilitation,' which consists of education and training aimed at improving self-care and self-sufficiency skills." Id. This different treatment provides a rational basis for the statutory disparity. Id. at 325.

175 Id. at 342, citing James Intagliata and C. Rinck, *Psychoactive Drug Use in Public and Community Residential Facilities for Mentally Retarded Persons,* 21 PSYCHOPHARMACOLOGY BULL. 268, 272–73 (1985); Bradley K. Hill et al, *A National Study of Prescribed Drugs in Institutions and Community Residential Facilities for Mentally Retarded People,* 21 PSYCHOPHARMACOLOGY BULL. 279, 283 (1985); M.G. Aman and N.N. Singh, *Pharmacological Intervention,* in HANDBOOK OF MENTAL RETARDATION 347, 348 (Johnny L. Matson and James L. Mulick eds., 2d ed. 1991).

he concluded, and residents have been "seriously endangered and injured" by their misuse.[176] Nothing suggested that Kentucky institutions are "free from these practices."[177]

4.6 After the hearing

4.6.1 "Discharged pending placement" and "conditionally extended pending placement" statuses

One of the most difficult—seemingly virtually insoluble—problems of the involuntary civil commitment process is the dilemma of: what can be done in the case of a once-involuntarily committed patient who no longer meets the criteria for commitment or continued institutionalization but for whom there is no suitable and available alternative placement?

Notwithstanding application of rigorous procedural due process safeguards to the trials of commitment matters, it quickly became clear that, while "a significant number of patients no longer met the strict commitment criteria [of] mental illness and resulting dangerousness,"[178] many of these individuals could not be released because, as a result of years of hospitalization, such patients were often "left with no means of visible community support and could not survive on their own."[179]

The New Jersey Supreme Court offered an alternative in *In re S.L.*,[180] a consolidated appeal of cases involving patients, institutionalized for up to 52 years, who no longer met the commitment criteria, but "remained incapable of carrying on an independent and self-sufficient life."[181] In each case, the trial judge had classified the patients as "discharged pending placement" (DPP).[182] That is, orders were entered discharging

---

176 *Heller*, 509 U.S. at 343, citing Thomas S. by Brooks v. Flaherty, 699 F. Supp. 1178, 1186–87 (W.D.N.C. 1988), and Halderman v. Pennhurst State Sch. & Hosp., 446 F. Supp. 1295, 1307–08 (E.D. Pa. 1977).

177 *Heller*, 509 U.S. at 344.

178 Michael L. Perlin, *"Discharged Pending Placement": The Due Process Rights of the Nondangerous Mentally Handicapped with "Nowhere to Go,"* 5 DIRECTIONS IN PSYCHIATRY Lesson 21, at 2 (1985).

179 Id. See also O'Connor v. Donaldson, 422 U.S. 563, 576 (1975).

180 462 A.2d 1252 (N.J. 1983).

181 Id. at 1253.

182 Id. "DPP" matters are now referred to as "CEPP" cases ("conditionally extended pending placement"). See Matter of Commitment of Raymond S., 623 A.2d 249 (N.J. App. Div. 1993) (reversing commitment order).

the patients on paper, pending the discovery of an acceptable aftercare placement.[183]

The state Supreme Court concluded:

> Although the State does not have the authority to continue the legal commitment of the appellants, it is not required to cast them adrift into the community when the individuals are incapable of surviving on their own. In a proper exercise of its *parens patriae* authority, it may therefore of necessity continue the confinement of such persons on a provisional or conditional basis to protect their essential well-being, pending efforts to foster the placement of these individuals in proper supportive settings outside the institution.[184]

The court ordered that specific procedures be designed to "minimize restrictions on the person's liberty," with such restrictions "related to the underlying purpose of the confinement—ensuring a safe and orderly transition of the individual into an appropriate setting least restrictive of liberty."[185]

4.6.2   Right to periodic review

In *O'Connor v. Donaldson*, the US Supreme Court ruled that, even if the basis for an individual's original commitment was constitutionally adequate, confinement could not continue after the basis no longer existed.[186] Relying on this decision, the Connecticut Supreme Court, in *Fasulo v. Arafeh*, held that involuntarily confined civilly committed individuals be granted periodic judicial review of the propriety of their continued confinement.[187] The Court added:

> The burden should not be placed on the civilly committed patient to justify his right to liberty. Freedom from involuntary confinement for those who have committed no crime is the natural state of individuals in this country.[188]

---

183 *S.L.*, 462 A.2d at 1253.
184 Id. at 1258.
185 Id.
186 422 U.S. 563, 574–75 (1975).
187 378 A.2d 553, 556 (Conn. 1977).
188 Id. at 556–57.

The New Jersey Supreme Court endorsed and echoed *Fasulo*'s "eloquent . . . state[ment]" of the compelling reasons for so allocating the burden of proof at periodic review[189] in *State v. Fields*,[190] applying periodic review also to *insanity acquittees*.[191]

The New Jersey court concluded:

> Due process would seem to require a meaningful periodic review of the continued legitimacy of restraints on the liberty of all persons whose alleged dangerousness by reason of mental disability brought about these restrictions.[192]

Since *Fasulo* and *Fields*, nearly all jurisdictions provide a durational limitation on commitment.[193] The right to periodic review is now firmly entrenched in involuntary civil commitment law.[194]

4.7   Other forms of commitment[195]

4.7.1   Juvenile commitments

Traditionally, in almost all states, parents had been able to commit their children to mental institutions without any due process hearing or judicial scrutiny.[196] The child was denied access to "virtually all procedural protections—notice, hearing, appellate review, and habeas corpus—rights afforded all other patients institutionalized against their will."[197] This nearly unfettered discretion was subject to abuse, a problem especially heightened in families of low socioeconomic status.[198]

---

189 See generally Note, *Procedural Safeguards for Periodic Review: A New Commitment to Mental Patients' Rights*, 88 YALE L.J. 850, 861–65 (1979) (approving of *Fasulo*'s burden allocation).

190 390 A.2d 574, 583 (N.J. 1978).

191 See *infra* Chapter 9.

192 *Fields*, 390 A.2d at 580.

193 See, e.g., Wyatt v. King, 773 F. Supp. 1508 (M.D. Ala. 1991); Conner v. Branstad, 839 F. Supp. 1346, 1353 (S.D. Iowa 1993).

194 On the right to appeal, see PERLIN AND CUCOLO, *supra* note 1, §4-2.4.2.2.

195 Criminal commitments are discussed *infra* Chapters 8–10. On partial hospital commitments, see PERLIN AND CUCOLO, *supra* note 1, § 4-3.6.

196 James Ellis, *Volunteering Children: Parental Commitment of Minors to Mental Institutions*, 62 CALIF. L. REV. 840, 840 (1974).

197 Id. at 841.

198 Id. at 851–52.

In *Parham v. J.R.*[199] the US Supreme Court held that Georgia's juvenile commitment procedures were both reasonable and consistent with constitutional guarantees.[200] On the other hand, it ruled that:

- The risk of error was sufficiently great to mandate an independent inquiry by a "neutral factfinder" to determine whether statutory admission requirements were met;
- Although the hearing need not be formal nor conducted by a judicial officer, the inquiry must "carefully probe the child's background using all available services, including, but not limited to, parents, schools and other social agencies";
- The decision-maker had the authority to refuse to admit a child who does not meet the medical standards for admission; and
- The need for continued commitment must be periodically reviewed by a similarly independent procedure.[201]

The heart of the *Parham* opinion was its vision of the juvenile commitment process. There was a strong state interest "in not imposing procedural obstacles that may discourage the mentally ill or their families from seeking needed psychiatric assistance."[202] Such hearings might be, for parents, "too onerous, too embarrassing or too contentious," worried the Court, "speculat[ing] as to how many parents who believe they are acting in good faith would forego state-provided hospital care if such care is contingent on participation in an adversary proceeding designed to probe their motives and other private family matters in seeking the voluntary admission."[203]

Such hearings would also intrude into the parent-child relationship, the Court found. Without supporting citation, reference to the court

---

199 442 U.S. 584 (1979).

200 Id. at 620–21.

201 Id. at 606–07.

202 Id. at 605. This vision "simultaneously assumes (1) the persons at risk are genuinely mentally ill, (2) they are in need of psychiatric assistance and (3) such psychiatric assistance is available at the institutions to which the juveniles are being committed." See Michael L. Perlin, *An Invitation to the Dance: An Empirical Response to Chief Justice Warren Burger's "Time-Consuming Procedural Minuets" Theory in* Parham v. J.R., 9 BULL. AM. ACAD. PSYCHIATRY & L. 149, 151 (1981).

203 *Parham*, 442 U.S. at 605–06 (footnote omitted). He continued: "The state also has a genuine interest in allocating priority to the diagnosis and treatment of patients as soon as they are admitted to a hospital rather than to time-consuming procedural minuets before the admission." Id.

record or analysis of behavioral research, the Chief Justice set out his rationale:

> Another problem with requiring a formalized, factfinding hearing lies in the danger it poses for significant intrusion into the parent-child relationship. Pitting the parents and child as adversaries often will be at odds with the presumption that parents act in the best interests of their child . . .
>
> Surely, there is a risk [that such a hearing] would exacerbate whatever tensions already existed between the child and the parents. [T]here is a serious risk that an adversary confrontation will adversely affect the ability of the parents to assist the child while in the hospital . . . A confrontation over such intimate family relationships would distress the normal adult parents and the impact on a disturbed child almost certainly would be significantly greater.[204]

Justice Brennan, in a three-justice opinion, concurring in part and dissenting in part, charged that the majority "ignore[d] reality [when it] assume[d] blindly that parents act in their children's best interests when making commitment decisions,"[205] and recommended the institution of *post*-admission commitment hearings:

> [T]he interest in avoiding family discord would be less significant at this stage, since the family autonomy already will have been fractured by the institutionalization of the child. In any event, post-admission hearings are unlikely to disrupt family relationships.[206]

4.7.2   Voluntary commitments

There is statutory authority in virtually every state for the voluntary commitment of individuals to institutions for persons with mental disabilities. Typically, statutes provide that a person with mental illness can be admitted "if the superintendent deems such person clinically suitable for such admission";[207] in some jurisdictions, the patient must renew his or her voluntary status on a regular, periodic

---

204 Id. 442 U.S. at 610 (footnote omitted).

205 Id. at 632 (Brennan, J., concurring in part and dissenting in part).

206 Id. at 635 (Brennan, J., concurring in part and dissenting in part). In the companion Pennsylvania case, the court similarly reversed, and the *Parham* dissenters again dissented. Secretary of Public Welfare of Pennsylvania v. Institutionalized Juveniles, 442 U.S. 640, 646–50 (1979).

207 E.g., CONN. GEN. STAT. § 17A-506 (1998). See also, e.g., N.Y. MENTAL HYG. LAW §§ 9.15 and 9.17 (1998).

basis.[208] If a voluntary patient seeks release, local law generally provides for discharge within a relatively short period of time,[209] unless an involuntary commitment petition is filed during the discharge request's pendency.[210]

Many commentators have suggested that voluntary procedures are subject to abuse or involve substantial elements of coercion,[211] and that the distinction between "voluntary" and "involuntary" patients is often an "illusory" or "murky" one.[212] Also, after hospitalization, voluntary patients are often treated no differently than involuntary patients.[213]

4.7.2.1   *Zinermon v. Burch*

The US Supreme Court considered the question of voluntary commitment in *Zinermon v. Burch*,[214] holding that a voluntary patient could proceed with a civil rights damages action against state hospital officials where he charged that those officials should have known that he was incompetent to voluntarily commit himself to the hospital at the time he signed voluntary admission forms.[215]

This decision raises for the first time the concerns of a majority of the court as to the risks that some "voluntary" patients may not be competent to admit themselves to psychiatric facilities.[216] Justice Blackmun

---

208 See, e.g., 405 ILL. COMP. STAT. ANN. 5/3-404 (1998) (voluntary status must be reaffirmed after 30 days, and every 60 days thereafter); N.Y. MENTAL HYG. LAW § 9.25 (1998) (yearly review of voluntary status required).

209 See statutes collected in Stromberg and Stone, *supra* note 141, at 327–28 n.169 (mostly one to five days).

210 See, e.g., N.J. STAT. ANN. § 30:4-27.20 (1998).

211 Teresa Cannistraro, *A Call for Minds: The Unknown Extent of Societal Influence on the Legal Rights of Involuntarily and Voluntarily Committed Mental Health Patients*, 19 ANNALS HEALTH L. 425, 427 n.13 (2010); David Wexler, *Foreword: Mental Health Law and the Movement toward Voluntary Treatment*, 62 CALIF. L. REV. 671, 676 (1974).

212 Stanley Herr, *Civil Rights, Uncivil Asylums and the Retarded*, 43 U. CIN. L. REV. 679, 723 (1974); Wexler, *supra* note 211, at 676.

213 New York State Ass'n for Retarded Children, Inc. v. Rockefeller, 357 F. Supp. 752, 756 (E.D.N.Y. 1973). See also Cospito v. Califano, 89 F.R.D. 374, 380 (D.N.J. 1981): "[E]ven voluntary patients may be retained in the hospital against their will for observation periods and such persons are subject to formal, involuntary commitment procedures".

214 494 U.S. 113 (1990).

215 Id. at 130–39.

216 Id. at 132–35. Three years prior to the *Zinermon* decision, a New Jersey trial court had ruled that the right to judicial review extended to voluntary patients. See *In re* G.M., 526 A.2d 744, 745 (N.J. Ch. Div. 1987).

noted that "the very nature of mental illness" makes it "foreseeable" that such a person "*will* be unable to understand *any* proffered 'explanation and disclosure of the subject matter' of the forms that a person is asked to sign, and *will* be unable 'to make a knowing and willful decision' whether to consent to admission."[217]

In *Zinermon*, the Supreme Court was willing to "strip the facade"[218] from the category of "voluntary admission," and consider some of the realities of the voluntary process. By example, New Jersey responded to *Zinermon* by amending its court rules to provide that, in cases where patients wish to convert to voluntary status, "the court shall hold a hearing within twenty days to determine whether the patient had the capacity to make an informed decision to convert to voluntary status and whether the decision was made knowingly and voluntarily," providing that counsel "previously appointed" shall represent the patient at such a hearing.[219]

4.7.3 Outpatient commitments

Building on the concept of the LRA in involuntary civil commitment procedures,[220] most states permit some form of outpatient commitment (OPC). In enacting "Kendra's Law,"[221] responding to a brutal murder by an individual with serious mental disabilities,[222] the New York legislature made its intent clear:

> The legislature finds that there are mentally ill persons who are capable of living in the community with the help of family, friends and mental health professionals, but who, without routine care and treatment, may relapse and become violent or suicidal, or require hospitalization. The legislature further finds that there are mentally ill persons who can function well and safely in the community with supervision and treatment, but who without such assistance, will relapse and require long periods of hospitalization.[223]

---

217 *Zinermon*, 494 U.S. at 133 (emphasis added).

218 See Michael L. Perlin, *Are Courts Competent to Decide Questions of Competency? Stripping the Facade from* United States v. Charters, 38 U. KAN. L. REV. 957, 979–1001 (1990).

219 N.J. CT. R. 4:74-7(g)(1) (1998).

220 See *supra* 4.2.6.

221 See generally Michael L. Perlin, *Therapeutic Jurisprudence and Outpatient Commitment Law: Kendra's Law as a Case Study*, 9 PSYCHOL. PUB. POL'Y & L. 183 (2003).

222 Id. at 184.

223 1999 NY S.B. 5762, § 2.

Subject to this law were adult patients who "suffer[ed] from a mental illness"; and were "unlikely to survive safely in the community without supervision," with a history of noncompliance with treatments "that has resulted in one or more seriously violent acts, threats of violence or attempted violence, toward self or others within the last 48 months, or which has resulted in a hospitalization or receipt of mental health services at a correctional facility at least twice within the last 36 months," "were unlikely to voluntarily participate in treatment," and "will likely benefit from treatment . . . in order to prevent behavior likely to result in serious harm to the patient or others."[224]

Assisted outpatient treatment could be ordered for up to six months, if there was clear and convincing evidence establishing that the subject met these criteria, and that there was no appropriate or feasibly less restrictive alternative.[225]

In *Matter of K.L.*, the New York Court of Appeals found this a valid exercise of police power, holding that the due process and equal protection clauses did not require a judicial finding of incapacity prior to implementation of an assisted outpatient treatment plan, and that a provision allowing a noncompliant outpatient to be retained for up to 72 hours for psychiatric evaluation did not violate due process, equal protection or the Fourth Amendment right against unreasonable search and seizure.[226]

4.7.4 Emergency commitments

Virtually all states have traditionally provided for some sort of commitment process to provide for immediate apprehension and detention of persons in need of emergency commitment.[227] The process is typically begun by the issuance of a warrant, based on allegations by a police officer, certified mental health professional, family member or, in some cases, "any responsible person,"[228] that a person is reasonably believed to be imminently dangerous to himself or others.[229]

---

224 N.Y. Ment. Hyg. L. § 9.60 (C).

225 N.Y. Ment. Hyg. L. § 9.60 (J)(2).

226 774 N.Y.S.2d 472 (2004).

227 See, e.g., Michael Weissberg, *Chained in the Emergency Department: The New Asylum for the Poor*, 42 Hosp. & Commun. Psychiatry 317 (1991).

228 E.g., Utah Code Ann. § 62A-5-312 (1997).

229 See, e.g., Conn. Gen. Stat. § 17a-502 (1998); N.M. Stat. Ann. § 43-1-10 (1997). See Gross v.

Empirical studies tend to reveal that in many cases in which these laws are invoked no real emergency exists.[230] Because emergency procedures involve "a minimum of red tape and provide the quickest, easiest way to get a person to a hospital,"[231] they have often become a standard means of institutionalization, especially in areas without readily available (or cooperating) physicians.[232]

4.8   Transfer issues

4.8.1   Interinstitutional transfers

Significant case law has developed over the procedural due process limitations of transferring patients from public and private health care institutions and from prison and jail facilities to mental hospitals. Individuals who have not been subject to penal sanction must be entitled to at least as many rights in the process as those who have been either arrested and/or convicted of crime.[233]

4.8.2   Interhospital and intrahospital transfers

A federal district court in Pennsylvania has held that the due process clause entitles an involuntarily committed mental patient to a hearing prior to transfer from a minimum security facility to a maximum security institution.[234] In one of the few cases to explore the due process ramifications of the *closure* of a facility for persons with mental disabilities, the Illinois Supreme Court has held that, in conformity with *Youngberg v. Romeo*,[235] where closure resulted from "judgment exercised by a qualified professional," it would be erroneous to enjoin the planned implementation of a program through which residents of

---

Pomerleau, 465 F. Supp. 1167, 1173 (D. Md. 1979) (emergency confinement only permissible "where there has been some demonstration of overtly dangerous behavior").

230   See, e.g., Matter of Shennum, 684 P.2d 1073, 1076–78 (Mont.1984) (record failed to permit any finding of mental health emergency, and emergency statute thus inapplicable).

231   ALEXANDER D. BROOKS, LAW, PSYCHIATRY AND THE MENTAL HEALTH SYSTEM 751 (1974).

232   Robert D. Miller and Paul P. Fiddleman, *Involuntary Civil Commitment in North Carolina: The Result of the 1979 Statutory Changes*, 60 N.C. L. REV. 985, 1017 (1982). Such areas "tend to overutilize emergency commitment procedures in order to avoid the usual requirement for physician evaluations prior to admission, rather than use emergency procedures only for respondents presenting special risks." Id.

233   See Vitek v. Jones, 445 U.S. 480 (1980), discussed at length *infra* 4.8.3.

234   Eubanks v. Clarke, 434 F. Supp. 1022, 1029 (E.D. Pa. 1977).

235   457 U.S. 307 (1982). See generally Chapter 5.

a facility for persons with mental retardation could be transferred to eight other facilities throughout the state.[236]

4.8.3 Prison transfers

The US Supreme Court has held, in *Vitek v. Jones*, that virtually the entire panoply of procedural due process rights was applicable to prisoners who were subject to transfer to state mental hospitals.[237] In that case, where state law had allowed the transfer of a prisoner to a state mental hospital based on a finding by the designated mental health examiner that the prisoner "suffers from a mental disease or defect" that "cannot be given proper treatment" in a prison setting,[238] the Supreme Court concluded that the plaintiff had "a liberty interest that entitled him to the benefits of appropriate procedures in connection with determining the conditions that warranted his transfer to a mental hospital."[239]

The Court found that "[the plaintiff] retained a residuum of liberty that would be infringed by a transfer to a mental hospital without complying with minimum requirements of due process."[240] It emphasized that "the stigmatizing consequences of a transfer to a mental hospital for involuntary psychiatric treatment, coupled with the subjection of the prisoner to mandatory behavior modification as a treatment for mental illness constitute the kind of deprivations of liberty that require procedural protection."[241]

As to what procedural safeguards were due, the Court agreed with the district court that the following minima were required:

A. Written notice to the prisoner that a transfer to a mental hospital is being considered;

B. A hearing, sufficiently after the notice to permit the prisoner to prepare, at which disclosure to the prisoner is made of the evidence being relied upon for the transfer and at which an opportunity to be heard in person and to present documentary evidence is given;

---

236 Dixon Ass'n for Retarded Citizens v. Thompson, 440 N.E.2d 117, 123–25 (Ill. 1982).
237 445 U.S. 480, 494–96 (1980).
238 Id. at 484.
239 Id. at 490.
240 Id. at 491.
241 Id. at 494.

C. An opportunity at the hearing to present testimony of witnesses by the defense and to confront and cross-examine witnesses called by the state, except upon a finding, not arbitrarily made, of good cause for not permitting such presentation, confrontation, or cross-examination;

D. An independent decisionmaker;

E. A written statement by the factfinder as to the evidence relied on and the reasons for transferring the inmate;

* * *

G. Effective and timely notice of all the foregoing rights.[242]

The Supreme Court disagreed with the district court only as to the requirement of counsel. Whereas the trial court had also mandated the "[a]vailability of legal counsel, furnished by the state, if the inmate is financially unable to furnish his own," the Court found merely that "qualified and independent assistance" was required prior to transfer.[243]

---

242 Id. at 494–95.
243 Id. at 497, 500 (Powell, J., concurring in part).

5 Institutional rights[1]

5.1 The right to treatment[2]

The right to treatment is the centerpiece of all substantive rights of institutionalized persons with mental disabilities. It emerged from a seminal law journal article,[3] and was given its greatest impetus in the constitutional decision of *Wyatt v. Stickney*.[4] In 1982, the US Supreme Court dealt with some of the core issues raised in *Youngberg v. Romeo*,[5] and established a new methodology for the consideration of most adequacy-of-treatment claims. Both state constitutions and state-level "patients' bills of rights" are also relied upon as sources of this right.[6]

5.1.1 Historical background

Until 1960, the notion of a legal "right to treatment" was not a topic of great concern. At that time, Morton Birnbaum set the stage for 25 years of complex, "first impression" litigation that eventually reshaped the contours of mental disability law[7] Birnbaum, a lawyer and doctor, wrote to explicitly advocate for "the recognition and enforcement of the legal right of a mentally ill inmate of a public mental institution to adequate medical treatment for his mental illness."[8]

---

1 See Michael L. Perlin and Heather Ellis Cucolo, Mental Disability Law: Civil and Criminal chs. 7–9 (3d ed. 2016) (2019 update).

2 Cases and developments involving the right of *forensic* patients to refuse medication are discussed *infra* Chapters 8–11.

3 Morton Birnbaum, *The Right to Treatment*, 46 A.B.A. J. 499, 499 (1960).

4 325 F. Supp. 781 (M.D. Ala. 1971), 334 F. Supp. 1341 (M.D. Ala. 1972), 344 F. Supp. 373 (M.D. Ala. 1972), 344 F. Supp. 387 (M.D. Ala. 1972), *aff'd sub nom.* Wyatt v. Aderholt, 503 F.2d 1305 (5th Cir. 1974).

5 457 U.S. 307 (1982).

6 See generally Michael L. Perlin, *The Right to Treatment*, in The Sage Encyclopedia of Abnormal and Clinical Psychology 2897 (Amy Wenzel ed., 2017).

7 Michael L. Perlin, *The Rights of the Mentally Handicapped*, 4 Bull. Am. Acad. Psychiatry & L. 77, 78 (1976).

8 Birnbaum, *supra* note 3, at 499.

This was Birnbaum's central thesis: under "their traditional powers to protect the rights of our citizens," courts should consider whether a person institutionalized on account of mental illness "actually does receive adequate medical treatment" by "recognizing and enforcing the right to treatment."[9] If it were to be enforced, then "our substantive constitutional law would . . . include the concepts that . . . substantive due process of law does not allow a mentally ill person who has committed no crime to be deprived of his liberty by indefinitely institutionalizing him in a mental prison."[10] The declaration of this right would "force the legislatures to increase appropriations sufficiently to make it possible to provide adequate care and treatment so that the mentally ill will be treated in mental hospitals."[11]

5.1.2   Early case law

In 1966, a federal court of appeals declared a *statutory* right to treatment based on local law,[12] finding "the purpose of involuntary hospitalization is treatment, not punishment";[13] otherwise, "the hospital 'is transform[ed] . . . into a penitentiary where one could be held indefinitely for no convicted offense.'"[14] "Continuing failure to provide suitable and adequate treatment cannot be justified by lack of staff or facilities."[15]

5.1.3   *Wyatt v. Stickney*

The rationale of that decision was adopted in other cases,[16] but it was not until an obscure labor dispute in an Alabama state hospital led to one of the most influential mental disability law cases ever filed:

---

9 Id. at 503.

10 Id.

11 Id. This article led to the subsequent development of right-to-treatment litigation, see Michael Waterstone, *Disability Constitutional Law*, 63 EMORY L.J. 527, 534 n.28 (2014), earning Birnbaum the title of "father of the [right-to-treatment] doctrine," Michael L. Perlin, *Patients' Rights*, in PSYCHIATRY ch. 35, at 2 (Jesse O. Cavenar ed., 1985).

12 Rouse v. Cameron, 373 F.2d 451 (D.C. Cir. 1966).

13 Id. at 452.

14 Id. at 453, quoting, in part, Ragsdale v. Overholser, 281 F.2d 943, 950 (D.C. Cir. 1950) (Fahy, J., concurring).

15 Id. at 457.

16 See, e.g., United States *ex rel.* Schuster v. Herold, 410 F.2d 1071, 1088 (2d Cir. 1969); Nason v. Superintendent of Bridgewater State Hosp., 233 N.E.2d 908, 914 (Mass. 1968).

Wyatt v. Stickney.[17] A reduction in tax revenues[18] led to the firing of 99 employees at Bryce Hospital in Alabama; as a result, the only individuals who provided direct care mental health services were one Ph.D. clinical psychologist, three medical doctors with some psychiatric training (but no board-certified psychiatrist) and two M.S.W. social workers.[19]

There were other significant problems at Bryce:

> Dormitories are barnlike structures with no privacy for the patients. For most patients there is not even a space provided which he can think of as his own. The toilets in restrooms seldom have partitions between them. These are dehumanizing factors which degenerate the patients' self-esteem. Also contributing to the poor psychological environment are the shoddy wearing apparel furnished the patients, the non-therapeutic work assigned to patients (mostly compulsory, uncompensated household chores), and the degrading and humiliating admissions procedure which creates in the patient an impression of the hospital as a prison or as a "crazy house." Other conditions which render the physical environment at Bryce critically substandard are extreme ventilation problems, fire and other emergency hazards, and overcrowding caused to some degree by poor utilization of space.[20]

In light of this greatly uncontested evidence, District Court Judge Frank Johnson found that the programs in operation at the hospital "were scientifically and medically inadequate,"[21] failing "to conform to any known minimums established for providing treatment for the mentally ill."[22] Patients "unquestionably have a constitutional right to receive such individual treatment as will give each of them a realistic opportunity to be cured or to improve his or her mental condition."[23]

---

17 344 F. Supp. 373 (M.D. Ala. 1972), *aff'd in part, rev'd in part,* 344 F. Supp. 387 (M.D. Ala. 1972), *aff'd in part, rev'd in part sub nom.* Wyatt v. Aderholt, 503 F.2d 1305 (5th Cir. 1974). "This remarkable case has become the foundation of modern psychiatric jurisprudence and . . . must be studied by every serious scholar and practitioner." Milton Greenblatt, *Foreword,* in WYATT V. STICKNEY: RETROSPECT AND PROSPECT ix (L. Ralph Jones and Richard R. Parlour eds., 1981) (RETROSPECT).

18 The specific precipitant was a reduction in the sales tax on cigarettes, then the sole source of revenue available for hospital funding. Wyatt v. Aderholt, 503 F.2d 1305, 1307 (5th Cir. 1984).

19 *Wyatt,* 325 F. Supp. at 783.

20 *Wyatt,* 334 F. Supp. at 1343.

21 *Wyatt,* 325 F. Supp. at 784.

22 Id.

23 Id. On this point, the court cited, inter alia, Rouse v. Cameron, 373 F.2d 451 (D.C. Cir. 1966). See generally *supra* notes 12–15.

Adequate and effective treatment was "constitutionally required" because, "absent treatment, the hospital is transformed 'into a penitentiary where one could be held for no convicted offense'":[24]

> The purposes of involuntary hospitalization for treatment purposes is *treatment* and not mere custodial care or punishment. This is the only justification, from a constitutional standpoint, that allows civil commitments to mental institutions such as Bryce. According to the evidence in this case, the [hospital's] failure to supply adequate treatment is due to a lack of operating funds. The failure to provide suitable and adequate treatment to the mentally ill cannot be justified by a lack of staff or facilities.[25]

> * * *

> There can be no legal (or moral) justification for the State of Alabama failing to afford treatment—and adequate treatment from a medical standpoint—to the several thousand patients who have been civilly committed to Bryce for treatment purposes. To deprive any citizen of his or her liberty upon the altruistic theory that the confinement is for humane therapeutic reasons and then fail to provide adequate treatment violates the very fundamentals of due process.[26]

Subsequently, the court ruled that there were three "fundamental conditions for adequate and effective treatment programs in public mental institutions . . .":

> (1) a humane psychological and physical environment, (2) qualified staff in numbers sufficient to administer adequate treatment, and (3) individualized treatment plans.[27]

At a yet-later hearing, amici[28] and the parties "stipulated to a broad spectrum of conditions they feel are mandatory for a constitutionally

---

24 *Wyatt*, 325 F. Supp. at 784, quoting, in part, Ragsdale v. Overholser, 281 F.2d 943, 950 (D.C. Cir. 1960).

25 Id.

26 Id. at 784–85.

27 Id. at 1343.

28 Amici included the American Orthopsychiatric Association, the American Association on Mental Deficiency, the American Psychological Association, the American Civil Liberties Union, the National Association for Mental Health and the National Association for Retarded Children. The American Psychiatric Association declined to participate. See Robert L. Sadoff, *Changes in the Mental Health Law: Progress for Patients, Problems for Psychiatrists*, in 4 NEW DIRECTIONS IN MENTAL HEALTH SERVICES: COPING WITH THE LEGAL ONSLAUGHT 1, 2 (Seymour Halleck ed., 1979).

acceptable minimum treatment program."[29] These standards ranged in subject matter from the global (e.g., "Patients have a right to privacy and dignity") to the specific (e.g., "Thermostatically controlled hot water shall be maintained [at 180 °F] . . . for mechanical dishwashing"), and were established for persons with intellectual disabilities as well as those with mental illness. They covered the full range of hospital conditions—environmental standards, civil rights, medical treatment criteria, staff qualifications, nutritional requirements, and need for compliance with Life Safety Code provisions.[30] Importantly, the right "to the least restrictive conditions necessary to achieve the purposes of commitment" was specifically mandated.[31]

The Fifth Circuit substantially affirmed.[32] It noted that there was "no significant dispute" about conditions in the Alabama facilities in question: relying on its then-recent decision in *Donaldson v. O'Connor*:[33]

> [There, we] reasoned that the only permissible justifications for civil commitment, and for the massive abridgments of constitutionally protected liberties it entails, were the danger posed by the individual committed to himself or others, or the individual's need for treatment and care. We held that where the justification for commitment was treatment, it offended the fundamentals of due process if treatment were not in fact provided; and we held that where the justification was the danger to self or to others, then treatment had to be provided as the *quid pro quo* society had to pay as the price of the extra safety it derived from the denial of individuals' liberty.[34]

5.1.3.1 *Wyatt's impact on statutory and regulatory law*

Wyatt's massive influence on the development of state-level patients' bills of rights[35] and regulations[36] is beyond doubt. Its spirit permeates all federal statutes that provide rights to institutionalized persons with

---

29 *Wyatt*, 344 F. Supp. at 376.

30 Id. at 379–407.

31 Id. at 379, app. A, std. II (2).

32 *Wyatt*, 503 F.2d at 1310.

33 493 F.2d 507 (5th Cir. 1974), *remanded*, 422 U.S. 563 (1975). See *supra* Chapter 4.

34 *Wyatt*, 503 F.2d at 1312.

35 See generally *The Wyatt Standards: An Influential Force in State and Federal Rules*, 28 Hosp. & Commun. Psychiatry 374 (1977).

36 Harry Schnibbe, *Changes in State Mental Health Service Systems since* Wyatt, in Retrospect, *supra* note 17, at 173, 174.

mental disabilities. Section 504 of the Rehabilitation Act of 1973,[37] the Protection and Advocacy for Mentally Ill Individuals Act,[38] the Developmental Disabilities Assistance and Bill of Rights Act[39] and the Americans with Disabilities Act[40] have all drawn on *Wyatt* as their inspiration.

5.1.3.2   *Wyatt's impact on case law*

Wyatt dramatically influenced developments elsewhere.[41] Similar litigation was quickly filed in Ohio,[42] in Minnesota,[43] in Louisiana,[44] among other jurisdictions.[45] Although some of this impact abated after the *Youngberg* decision,[46] *Wyatt* continues to inform much of the important judicial decisionmaking in this area of the law.[47] The Supreme Court decision in *Olmstead v. L.C.*[48]—stressing Congress's aim (through the Americans with Disabilities Act) to eliminate isolation and segregation in large state psychiatric institutions—further supports this approach.[49]

5.1.4   *Youngberg v. Romeo*

In 1982, the Supreme Court directly confronted the question of the scope of substantive due process rights owed to persons institutionalized in facilities for persons with mental disabilities. Multiple courts had followed *Wyatt's* lead, locating a constitutional right to treatment

---

37   29 U.S.C. § 794 (1994).

38   42 U.S.C. § 10801 (1994).

39   42 U.S.C. § 6061 (1999).

40   42 U.S.C. § 12101 (1990) *et seq.*

41   See Michael L. Perlin, *"Abandoned Love": The Impact of* Wyatt v. Stickney *on the Intersection between International Human Rights and Domestic Mental Disability Law*, 35 LAW & PSYCHOL. REV. 121 (2011).

42   Davis v. Watkins, 384 F. Supp. 1196 (N.D. Ohio 1974).

43   Welsch v. Likins, 373 F. Supp. 487 (D. Minn. 1974).

44   Gary W. v. Louisiana, 437 F. Supp. 1209 (E.D. La. 1976).

45   Cases are collected in Philipp v. Carey, 517 F. Supp. 513, 517–19 (N.D.N.Y. 1981).

46   See *infra* 5.1.4.

47   See, e.g., Mahoney v. Lensink, 17 Conn. App. 130, 550 A.2d 1088, 1093 (1988), *aff'd in part, rev'd in part*, 213 Conn. 548, 569 A.2d 518 (1990) (citing *Wyatt* and *Youngberg*); Johnson v. Murphy, 2001 U.S. Dist. LEXIS 24013 (M.D. Fla. 2001) ("[After *Youngberg*], the Fifth Circuit's holdings in *Aderholt* and *Donaldson* are still binding precedent within the Eleventh Circuit").

48   527 U.S. 581 (1999); see *infra* 6.7.

49   See Michael L. Perlin, *"Their Promises of Paradise": Will* Olmstead v. L.C. *Resuscitate the Constitutional "Least Restrictive Alternative" Principle in Mental Disability Law?* 37 HOUS. L. REV. 999, 1013–14 (2000).

in the due process clause.[50] Many of these specified that the "right to treatment" included the right to the LRA setting.[51] When the Supreme Court granted defendants' petition for a writ of *certiorari* in *Youngberg v. Romeo*, it appeared that the Court had finally found what it perceived to be a suitable vehicle through which to shape the contours of the right.

5.1.4.1 *The majority opinion*

The plaintiff-respondent in *Youngberg* was a person with profound intellectual disabilities who was an involuntary resident of a Pennsylvania state institution who had suffered a series of 63 significant injuries, both self-inflicted and inflicted by other facility residents.[52] His mother filed a civil rights damages action, alleging that the defendants, facility administrators, knew or should have known that the plaintiff was suffering such injuries, and that their failure to protect him appropriately and prevent injuries violated the Eighth and Fourteenth Amendments.[53]

Initially, the Third Circuit found that the Fourteenth Amendment's due process clause was the proper source for determining the constitutional basis for the rights asserted by the plaintiff. The court found that "fundamental" liberty interests in freedom of movement and in personal security could be limited only by an "overriding, non-punitive" state interest, as well as a "liberty interest in habilitation designed to 'treat' their mental retardation."[54]

The Supreme Court vacated and remanded, holding that, in addition to the rights to "adequate food, shelter, clothing and medical care,"[55] plaintiff had a constitutionally protected Fourteenth Amendment liberty interest in "conditions of reasonable care and safety," "freedom from bodily restraint" and "such minimally adequate or reasonable training to ensure safety and freedom from undue restraint."[56]

---

50 See Philipp v. Carey, 517 F. Supp. 513, 517 (N.D.N.Y. 1981) (partial list).

51 See Richard Delgado, Michael N. Alexander, Peggy Bernardy and Fran Bremer, *"Concurrence" in Quotes: A Critical Assessment of Chief Justice Burger's Objections to a Right to Treatment for the Involuntarily Confined Mentally Ill*, 15 U.C. DAVIS L. REV. 527, 569–70 n.256 (1982).

52 457 U.S. at 310.

53 Id. at 311–12.

54 Id. at 313.

55 Id. at 315.

56 Id. at 319, 321 and 324.

In determining whether an individual plaintiff's constitutional rights were violated, the Court balanced these liberty interests against relevant state interests.[57] The standard: whether professional judgment was exercised.[58] A decision made by a professional is "presumably valid":[59] "liability may only be imposed when the decision by the professional is such a substantial departure from accepted professional judgment, practice or standards as to demonstrate that the person responsible actually did not base the decision on such a judgment."[60] The Court thus vacated and remanded.

Youngberg established a standard against which to assess treatment, training and habilitation claims. In declaring a right to "reasonably non-restrictive confinement conditions"[61] (a phrase that it neither defined nor elaborated upon), the Court acknowledged that it was essential to calibrate restrictivity of treatment: "such conditions of confinement would comport fully with the purposes of respondent's commitment," citing—in a "*cf.*" reference—*Jackson v. Indiana*.[62] The source of the phrase is left otherwise unexplained.

Nonetheless, the Court *has*, post-*Youngberg*, referred approvingly to the LRA concept in at least two mental disability law cases: in *Riggins v. Nevada* (on the question of the right of a competent insanity-pleading defendant to refuse antipsychotic medication during his trial),[63] and *Olmstead v. L.C.* (on the right of persons with mental disabilities to community-based treatment).[64]

---

57 Id. at 321.

58 Id. at 322.

59 Id. at 323. The term "professional" is defined in this manner, see, id. n.30:

> By professional decisionmaker, we mean a person competent, whether by education, training or experience, to make the particular decision at issue. Long-term treatment decisions normally should be made by persons with degrees in medicine or nursing, or with appropriate training in areas such as psychology, physical therapy, or the care and training of the retarded. Of course, day-to-day decisions regarding care—including decisions that must be made without delay—necessarily will be made in many instances by employees without formal training but who are subject to the supervision of qualified persons.

60 Id. In an action for damages against a professional in his or her individual capacity, there will be no liability if the professional "was unable to satisfy his normal professional standards because of budgetary constraints; in such a situation, good-faith immunity would bar liability." Id.

61 Id. at 324.

62 406 U.S. 715 (1972). See *supra* 4.2.5.

63 504 U.S. 127 (1992). See *infra* 9.5.4.

64 527 U.S. 581 (1999). See *infra* 6.7.

5.1.4.2 The concurrences

Concurring, Justice Blackmun—writing for himself and two others—stated he would grant the plaintiff an additional right beyond those articulated in the majority's opinion: the right to "such training as is reasonably necessary to prevent a person's pre-existing self-care skills from *deteriorating* because of his commitment."[65] An institutional resident's interest in not losing such skills "alleged a loss of liberty . . . quite distinct from—and as serious as—the loss of safety and freedom from unreasonable restraints."[66]

Chief Justice Burger wrote separately with one theme: "I would hold flatly that [plaintiff] has no constitutional right to training, or 'habilitation,' *per se.*"[67] It was also "clear" to the Chief Justice that the Constitution "does not otherwise place an affirmative duty on the State to provide any particular kind of training or habilitation—even such as might be encompassed under the essentially standardless rubric 'minimally adequate training' to which the Court refers."[68]

5.1.4.3 After Youngberg

Justice Blackmun's concurrence was a point of embarkation in a case that read the right to treatment more broadly than did *Youngberg.* In a case involving conditions at an inpatient facility for persons with intellectual disabilities, the Second Circuit found that such individuals had "a due process right to training sufficient to prevent basic self-care skills from deteriorating."[69] It ruled that institutional officials cannot "deprive the mentally retarded residents of their liberty interest in a humane and decent existence," and that such deprivation exists "when institution officials fail to exercise professional judgment in devising programs that seek to allow patients to live as humanely and decently as when they entered the school."[70] It also expanded on *Youngberg* by holding that the scope of the case reached *voluntary* as well as *involuntary* patients,[71] characterizing any distinction as "irrelevant."[72]

---

65 *Youngberg,* 457 U.S. at 327 (emphasis in original).
66 Id.
67 Id. at 329.
68 Id. at 330.
69 Society for Good Will to Retarded Children, Inc. v. Cuomo, 737 F.2d 1239, 1250 (2d Cir. 1984).
70 Id.
71 Id. at 1245–46.
72 Id. at 1247.

Other courts have construed *Youngberg* more narrowly. For example, one court relied in part on *Youngberg* to reject the plaintiffs' argument that confinement in a mental hospital is unconstitutional "unless the individual's mental illness is treatable."[73]

In the most important recent case, the Second Circuit relied in part on *Youngberg* in finding that plaintiffs—inmates of the Orange County (NY) Correctional Facility—had a right to discharge planning as part of their in-custody care while institutionalized,[74] allowing their claims that, because of their serious mental illnesses, their constitutional right to adequate medical care while incarcerated included such discharge planning.[75]

5.1.5 State patients' bills of rights

Other developments in the area of the right to treatment of this population followed the passage and subsequent implementation of state "patients' bills of rights."[76] These laws have not been a cure-all for the full range of treatment issues litigated in the five decades since *Wyatt v. Stickney* was filed, but they have provided important litigation tools for facility residents.[77]

Prior to the "due process revolution,"[78] few states regulated the substantive treatment of persons institutionalized because of mental disability. Only after *Wyatt*[79] did state legislatures take seriously these issues. The *Wyatt* standards[80] served as a role model for many of the states that either adopted new legislation or expanded existing statutes in the immediate aftermath of *Wyatt*.[81]

---

73 Project Release v. Prevost, 551 F. Supp. 1298, 1305–06 (E.D.N.Y. 1982), *aff'd*, 722 F.2d 960 (2d Cir. 1983). For the full range of other sorts of cases in which *Youngberg* has been applied, see PERLIN AND CUCOLO, *supra* note 1, § 7-5.3.

74 Charles v. Orange County, 925 F.3d 73 (2d Cir. 2019). See *infra* 10.4.2.

75 Id. at 80. See id. at 82, noting that *Youngberg* extended constitutional protections to civil detainees who were housed in institutions for persons with mental disabilities.

76 See *supra* 5.1.3.1.

77 See PERLIN AND CUCOLO, *supra* note 1, §§ 7-7 to 7-7.5.

78 See Michael L. Perlin, *Competency, Deinstitutionalization, and Homelessness: A Story of Marginalization*, 28 HOUS. L. REV. 63, 86 (1991).

79 See *supra* 5.1.3.

80 See id.

81 See, for a helpful earlier overview, Martha A. Lyon, Martin L. Levine and Jack Zusman, *Patients' Bills of Rights: A Survey of State Statutes*, 6 MENTAL DISABILITY L. REP. 178, 185–200 (1982).

These statutes generally tracked the *Wyatt* holdings, guaranteeing patients the right to "appropriate treatment and services," to an individualized treatment plan that is to be periodically reviewed, to an aftercare plan, to a humane treatment environment, and to privacy and safety. Other statutory provisions mandated a right to refuse treatment as well as other institutional rights flowing from the First Amendment. Although most of these statutes were neither all-encompassing nor uniform, their existence suggests that—to some extent, at least—state legislatures were beginning to respond to the moral imperative of cases such as *Wyatt*.[82]

5.2   The right to refuse treatment

5.2.1   Introduction

The US Supreme Court has never decided a civil right to refuse treatment case on the merits; yet, other courts are, generally, comfortable with the idea of at least a qualified right, both in civil and in forensic cases. These cases frequently look to state statutory law and state constitutional law as sources of this right.

5.2.2   History

The development in the early 1950s of a new type of psychiatric drug—one that appeared from the outset to be remarkably effective in limiting acute psychotic episodes[83]—revolutionized state mental hospital systems. Following disclosure by reformers such as Albert Deutsch of the "anguish and terror and sorrow and pain" experienced regularly by public psychiatric hospital patients,[84] the new drugs—mostly phenothiazines (the group that includes chlorpromazine (Thorazine))—were

---

For a subsequent survey, see Phil Brown and Christopher J. Smith, *Mental Patients' Rights: An Empirical Study of Variation across the United States*, 11 INT'L J.L. & PSYCHIATRY 157 (1988).

82 See Perlin, *supra* note 41, at 124; PERLIN AND CUCOLO, *supra* note 1, § 7-7.2, at 7-134.

83 For a comprehensive overview of the role of drug manufacturers in the creation and development of antipsychotic medications, see Douglas Mossman and Jill A. Steinberg, *Promoting, Prescribing, and Pushing Pills: Understanding the Lessons of Antipsychotic Drug Litigation*, 13 MICH. ST. U. J. MED. & J. 263 (2009).

84 Karl Menninger, *Introduction*, to ALBERT DEUTSCH, THE SHAME OF THE STATES 15, 17 (1948).

seen as a way to shorten hospital stays,[85] treat patients in community settings and ameliorate a major social ill.[86]

State hospital censuses dropped dramatically within a few years of the widespread use of these drugs, but both the physical and social costs associated with this widespread use became quickly apparent.[87] There were clearly significant positive effects of the use of these drugs—such as elimination or minimization of such psychotic symptomatology as hallucinations, lower recidivism rates, longer intervals between psychotic relapses, facilitation of deinstitutionalization, reduction of average hospital stay, and reduction in the level of fear and anxiety among patients' friends and families. However, significant problems emerged, including difficulties in prediction of individual responses to the drugs, in drug selection, and in dosage adjustments.[88]

Researchers began to ask whether the drugs actually helped all patients,[89] as evidence demonstrated that some patients deteriorated as a result of such drug administration.[90] Also, because of the traditionally significant high rate of misdiagnosis of psychiatric patients,[91] serious risks arose as to the misadministration of the drugs.[92] Finally, because of the milieu of the state facilities in which such a high percentage of patients received drugs, drugs became used for a variety of purposes unrelated to amelioration and/or cure of psychiatric ill-

---

85 JOHN A. TALBOTT, THE DEATH OF THE ASYLUM: A CRITICAL STUDY OF STATE HOSPITAL MANAGEMENT, SERVICES, AND CARE 26 (1978). This view is not a unanimous one. See, e.g., ANDREW T. SCULL, DECARCERATION: COMMUNITY TREATMENT AND THE DEVIANT 79–85 (2d ed. 1984), arguing that the changes in hospital stay patterns began *prior* to widespread use of psychiatric drugs and continued *independent* of such drug use.

86 See, e.g., TALBOTT, *supra* note 85, at 26–36.

87 See, e.g., Jonas Robitscher, *ECT and Invasive Therapies*, in CRITICAL ISSUES IN AMERICAN PSYCHIATRY AND LAW 303, 319–20 (Richard Rosner ed., 1982).

88 See, e.g., Nancy Rhoden, *The Right to Refuse Psychotropic Drugs*, 15 HARV. C.R.-C.L. L. REV. 363, 375–82 (1980).

89 See Mary Durham and John La Fond, *A Search for the Missing Premise of Involuntary Therapeutic Commitment: Effective Treatment of the Mentally Ill*, 40 RUTGERS L. REV. 303, 343–49 (1988).

90 John P. Davis, *Recent Developments in the Drug Treatment of Schizophrenia*, 133 AM. J. PSYCHIATRY 298 (1976).

91 See, e.g., H.J. Pope and J.F. Lipinski, *Diagnosis in Schizophrenia and Manic-Depressive Illness: A Reassessment of the Specificity of "Schizophrenic" Symptoms in the Light of Current Research*, 35 ARCH. GEN. PSYCHIATRY 811 (1976).

92 See Note, *Right to Refuse Antipsychotic Medication: A Proposal for Legislative Consideration*, 17 IND. L. REV. 1035, 1039 (1984).

nesses. They were often employed "for the convenience of staff and for punishment."[93]

In addition, toxic effects of the drugs in question became readily apparent:

> Temporary muscular side effects (disappearing on drug termination); dystonic reactions, such as muscle spasm in the eyes and face; irregular grimacing or writhing movements; tongue protrusion; akathisia (inability to stay still and agitation); and parkinsonisms (drooling, muscle stiffness, shuffling gait and tremors).[94]

Of all side effects, however, the most feared, and the one that appears to be the most irreversible, was found to be tardive dyskinesia:

> The tongue, mouth, and chin are common signs of tardive dyskinesia: the tongue sweeps from side to side, the mouth opens and closes, and the jaw moves in all directions. Fingers, arms and legs may display comparable movements; swallowing, speech or breathing can be affected as well. The movements are uncontrollable. . . . In severe cases, the involuntary movements impede walking and even digestion. Health can be endangered, and often the victim's appearance becomes grotesque. Tardive dyskinesia is common: estimates of the disorder's prevalence rates (the proportion of patients with tardive dyskinesia at any particular time) ranges as high as sixty-five percent; fifteen to twenty percent is a widely accepted estimate. It . . . usually persists throughout the patient's lifetime. There generally is no cure.[95]

Patients and counsel began to seek judicial relief to either terminate or alter unwanted medical treatment. Subsequent lawsuits established an agenda for the resolution of a "significant ethical conflict"[96] in which "patients' rights groups and their allies among the mental disability bar and bench stood alone pitted against the remainder of the mental health establishment."[97]

---

93 See Davis v. Hubbard, 506 F. Supp. 915, 926 (N.D. Ohio 1980).

94 BARRY FURROW, MALPRACTICE IN PSYCHOTHERAPY 61 (1980) (footnotes and citations omitted).

95 Sheldon Gelman, *Mental Hospital Drugs, Professionalism and the Constitution*, 72 GEO. L.J. 1725, 1742–43 (1984) (footnotes omitted), and sources cited id. at nn.85–90.

96 Robert L. Sadoff, *Patient Rights versus Patient Needs: Who Decides?* 44 J. CLINICAL PSYCHIATRY 27, 28 (1983).

97 Phil Brown, *The Right to Refuse Treatment and the Movement for Mental Health Reform*, 9 J. HEALTH POL., POL'Y & L. 291, 296 (1984).

5.2.3   Early constitutional approaches

The first constitutional cases involved persons in the criminal justice system, and were mostly litigated under Eighth Amendment "cruel and unusual punishment" theories.[98] At least one case—involving a patient who alleged that he was administered what he characterized as the "breath-stopping and paralyzing" drug succinylcholine as part of "aversive treatment"[99]—held that, if proven, such a practice would constitute "impermissible tinkering with the mental processes" in violation of the First Amendment.[100] Also, in *Scott v. Plante*,[101] "some form of notice and opportunity to be heard [was required] before [the patient] could be subjected to [involuntary drug] treatment."[102] In an analogous *prison* case, before a prisoner could be transferred into an experimental aversive behavior modification program, a hearing before a neutral fact-finder, with the right to present witnesses and cross-examination, was mandated.[103]

5.2.3.1   *Subsequent approaches*

The outlines of contemporary doctrine began to fill in with the litigation of the two cases "that are universally acknowledged to have set the stage for the legal debate on the extent of the right":[104] *Rennie v. Klein*[105] and *Rogers v. Okin*,[106] the source of most of the legal and social theories that have driven the debate in this area for 40+ years.

5.2.3.1.1   *Rennie, through the initial Third Circuit opinion*   In *Rennie*,[107] the court held squarely that the right to refuse medication—

---

98   See, e.g., Mackey v. Procunier, 477 F.2d 877, 877 (9th Cir. 1973) (state prisoner institutionalized at medical facility); Knecht v. Gillman, 488 F.2d 1136, 1136 (8th Cir. 1973) (inmates at state "Security Medical Facility").

99   *Mackey*, 477 F.2d at 877.

100   Id. at 878.

101   532 F.2d 939 (3d Cir. 1976).

102   Id. at 946.

103   Clonce v. Richardson, 379 F. Supp. 338, 348 (W.D. Mo. 1974).

104   Perlin, *supra* note 11, at 5.

105   462 F. Supp. 1131 (D.N.J. 1978), *supplemented*, 476 F. Supp. 1294 (D.N.J. 1979), *modified*, 653 F.2d 836 (3d Cir. 1981), *vacated and remanded*, 458 U.S. 1119 (1982), *on remand*, 720 F.2d 266 (3d Cir. 1983).

106   478 F. Supp. 1342 (D. Mass. 1979), *modified*, 634 F.2d 650 (1st Cir. 1980), *vacated and remanded*, 457 U.S. 291 (1982), *on remand*, 738 F.2d 1 (1st Cir. 1984).

107   The plaintiff was a highly intelligent, involuntary patient at a NJ state hospital. *Rennie*, 462 F. Supp. at 1134–35.

in the absence of an emergency[108]—is "founded on the emerging right to privacy," a right that includes the "right to protect one's mental processes from governmental interference" and "an individual's autonomy over his own body."[109] The right could only be qualified "where the government shows some strong countervailing interest."[110]

Several months later, the court expanded the suit into a class action on behalf of subclasses consisting of all adult patients at the five state mental health facilities,[111] and found that all involuntary patients had a "qualified right to refuse treatment" as well as a right to "due process . . . before drugs can be forcibly administered."[112] In order to implement these rights, specific and detailed procedures were mandated to assure conformity with the mandates of constitutional law.[113]

The trial court found that many patients who would normally be treated with psychotropics can improve without them, and smaller doses than are traditionally given can often be effective.[114] It reconfirmed the pervasive presence of drug side effects (including tardive dyskinesia), indicating that the drugs often inhibited a patient's ability to learn social skills that were needed to recover fully from psychosis, adding that "even acutely disturbed patients might have good reason to refuse these drugs."[115] All the New Jersey state hospitals were understaffed. Patients, who lived on "large, bleak and unpleasant wards," often had trouble seeing psychiatrists and were offered "little structured activity." The court quoted one expert witness's findings that drugs were the "be-all and end-all of hospitals" and further cited the startlingly candid observation of the medical director of a defendant institution that the hospital "uses medication as a form of control and as a substitute for treatment."[116] Widespread permanent neurological damage (often undiagnosed), including tardive dyskinesia and drug-induced parkinsonism, was found in 35 percent to 50 percent of all state hospital patients. Medication orders leaving discretion to staff

---

108 Id. at 1144.

109 Id. at 1142, 1144.

110 Id. at 1144, citing, inter alia, 1 PRESIDENT'S COMMISSION ON MENTAL HEALTH, REPORT 44 (1978).

111 Id. 476 F. Supp. at 1298.

112 Id. at 1307.

113 Id. at 1313–15.

114 Id. at 1298.

115 Id. at 1299.

116 Id.

for days and weeks were overused, despite specific hospital rules forbidding the practice. "Doctors also continue to use poor medication
practices," the court found, "including unjustified polypharmacy."[117]

"Forced drugging can be as intrusive as the involuntary confinement
resulting from commitment, and that drugging also has the potential
for permanent deprivation through long-term side effects." In determining the procedures necessary to afford the plaintiffs the right to
refuse treatment, the court added that it must consider "the degree of
vulnerability and helplessness of patients . . . as well as the history of
compelled medication through the use of forced injections which has
created a general belief that medication cannot be refused."[118]

On appeal, the Third Circuit Court of Appeals substantially affirmed
the trial court's ruling, premising its decision on the liberty clause of
the Fourteenth Amendment.[119] The court cited "dramatic" evidence
that "the risk of serious side effects stemming from the administration
of antipsychotic drugs is a critical factor in our determination that a
liberty interest is infringed by forced medication."[120] It was convinced
"there is a difference of constitutional significance between simple
involuntary commitment to a mental institution and commitment
combined with enforced administration of antipsychotic drugs."[121]

5.2.3.1.2   Rogers, through the First Circuit   In *Rogers v. Okin*, the trial
court ruled that the First Amendment's constitutional right of privacy encompassed refusal-of-medication decisions.[122] It enjoined the
defendants from "forcibly medicating committed patients with mental
disabilities, voluntary or involuntary, except in emergency circumstances, in which a failure to do so would bring about a substantial
likelihood of physical harm to the patient or others."[123]

---

117 Id. at 1300.

118 Id. at 1307.

119 *Rennie*, 653 F.2d at 844.

120 Id. at 843 and 843 n.8.

121 Id. at 844. On the other hand, the court sharply *limited* the extent of due process protections
available to patients who chose to exercise their right to refuse. The type of more stringent
protections previously ordered by the district court, including informal hearings to be held
before psychiatrists acting as fact-finders, was not required. Id. at 848–51.

122 478 F. Supp. at 1366–67.

123 Id. at 1371. The review of the evidence of the facilities in which *Rogers* plaintiffs were housed
tracked the *Rennie* findings. The Austin Unit of Boston State Hospital was a "drab, gloomy,
poorly lighted structure in a state of chronic disrepair"; the May Unit was similarly "in chronic
disrepair." Id. at 1356–57. Judge Tauro also made similar findings concerning drugs, finding

On appeal, the First Circuit Court of Appeals modified the trial court's ruling in *Rogers*, substantially affirming the finding that involuntarily committed mental patients had a qualified right to refuse the imposition of unwanted psychotropic medication, but significantly modifying both the remedy and the scope of the "emergency" exception to the general rule.[124]

5.2.4   The Supreme Court speaks

The Supreme Court's decision in *Mills v. Rogers* sidestepped the constitutional questions by remanding the case to the First Circuit Court of Appeals for consideration of the impact of an intervening decision by a Massachusetts *state court*.[125] In that case, *In re Richard Roe III*,[126] Massachusetts' highest court had held that a noninstitutionalized patient who was mentally incompetent (the plaintiff class in *Rogers* were institutionalized but mentally competent individuals) had a right to a judicial hearing to assert his or her desire to refuse treatment with antipsychotic drugs, a conclusion the state court had based "expressly . . . on the common law of Massachusetts"[127] as well as on the federal Constitution.[128]

In its *Mills* decision, the Court noted that all parties agreed that "the Constitution recognizes a liberty interest in avoiding the unwanted administration of antipsychotic drugs,"[129] but observed that the core dispute focused on the *definition* of this interest and an identification

---

multiple side-effects, including tardive dyskinesia, akathisia, akinesia, dystonia, and pseudo-Parkinsonian syndrome. Id. at 1360.

124 *Rogers*, 634 F.2d at 656–57:

In sum, we hold that the district court should not attempt to fashion a single "more-likely-than-not" standard as a substitute for an individualized balancing of the varying interests of particular patients in refusing antipsychotic medication against the equally varying interests of patients and the state—in preventing violence. . . . [T]he court should leave . . . difficult, necessarily ad hoc balancing to state physicians and limit its own role to designing procedures for ensuring that the patients' interests in refusing antipsychotics are taken into consideration and that psychotics are not forcibly administered absent a finding by a qualified physician that those interests are outweighed in a particular situation and less restrictive alternatives are unavailable.

125 *Mills*, 457 U.S. 291, 306 (1982).
126 421 N.E.2d 40 (Mass. 1981).
127 Id. at 51–52.
128 *Mills*, 457 U.S. at 301, and see id. at 301 n.17, quoting *Roe*, 421 N.E.2d at 42, and id. at n.1, and at 51 n.9.
129 Id. at 299.

of the conditions under which it might be outweighed by competing state interests.[130] The Court specifically "assume[d] that involuntarily committed mental patients do retain liberty interests protected by the Constitution and that these interests are implicated by the involuntary administration of antipsychotic drugs."[131]

The Court then restated a major principle of constitutional litigation: a state is always free, either under its own state constitution or under the common law, to create liberty or other due process interests broader than those minimally mandated by the federal Constitution.[132] Thus, it was "distinctly possible" that Massachusetts recognizes substantive liberty interests of incompetents "that are broader" than those recognized by the federal Constitution, as well as greater procedural protection of relevant liberty interests "than the minimum adequate to survive scrutiny under the Due Process Clause."[133] One week after the Court issued its decision in *Rogers*, it granted *certiorari* in *Rennie v. Klein*, and vacated and remanded to the Third Circuit for reconsideration, *not* in light of *Mills*, but in light of *Youngberg v. Romeo*.[134]

5.2.4.1   *The remand decisions*

5.2.4.1.1   *Rogers*   The First Circuit certified the case to the Massachusetts Supreme Judicial Court, which concluded (1) a committed mental patient is competent to make treatment decisions "until the patient is adjudicated incompetent by a judge";[135] (2) where there is such an incompetency adjudication, the judge, "using a substituted judgment standard, shall decide whether the patient would have consented to the administration of antipsychotic drugs";[136] and (3) that "no state interest" justified the use of such drugs "in a non-emergency situation without the patient's consent."[137] On the other hand, a patient *could* be treated against his or her will and without prior court

---

130   Id.

131   Id. at 299 n. 16.

132   Id. at 300.

133   Id. at 303–04.

134   Rennie v. Klein, 458 U.S. 1119 (1982). Youngberg v. Romeo, 457 U.S. 307 (1982), is discussed extensively *supra* 5.1.4.1.

135   Rogers v. Commissioner, Department of Mental Health, 458 N.E.2d 308, 310 (Mass. 1983).

136   Id.

137   Id. at 311.

approval to prevent the "immediate, substantial, and irreversible deterioration of a serious mental illness."[138]

Following this decision, the First Circuit ruled that these were "substantive rights created by legitimate, objective expectations derived from state law [and] entitled to the procedural protections of the Fourteenth Amendment,"[139] and that these rights "equal or exceed the rights provided in the federal Constitution."[140] It thus remanded the case to the district court to "issue a declaration stating that the Massachusetts Supreme Judicial Court ... has created for those patients a liberty interest under the Fourteenth Amendment of the Federal Constitution."[141]

5.2.4.1.2   Rennie   In *Rennie*, a sharply fractured Third Circuit reiterated the basic underlying substantive premise of its earlier decision—that involuntarily committed patients *do* have a constitutional right to refuse the administration of certain antipsychotic drugs.[142] The court also reaffirmed that the procedures specified in the state administrative bulletin satisfied due process requirements and remanded to the district court for further proceedings.[143]

The court also found that, after *Youngberg*, the concept of "least intrusive means" could no longer be employed.[144] Instead, the "accepted professional judgment" standard of *Youngberg*—that is, a decision to administer medication would be presumed to be valid unless it was shown to be a "substantial departure from accepted professional judgment, practice or standards"—was to be substituted.[145] On remand, the district court merely entered a brief order, consented to by all parties, permanently enjoining the defendants to comply with the most recent version of a state administrative bulletin, adding that the injunction

---

138 Id.
139 *Rogers*, 738 F.2d at 6.
140 Id. at 8–9.
141 Id. at 9.
142 See Rennie v. Klein, 720 F.2d 266 (3d Cir. 1983). There were five separate opinions released; no more than three judges joined in any opinion.
143 Id. at 270.
144 Id. at 269 (opinion by Garth, J.).
145 Id. The abandonment of the "least intrusive means" test was ordered over the pointed objections of four judges. See *Rennie*, 720 F.2d at 274, 276–77 (Weis, J., concurring, for himself and two others), and id. at 277 (Gibbons, J., dissenting).

"shall in no way affect the plaintiffs' rights or remedies under New Jersey state law."[146]

5.2.5   Other medication cases

Prior to the Supreme Court's remand decision in *Mills v. Rogers*, the highest state courts in other jurisdictions[147] and a federal district court in Ohio[148] had followed the lead of the *Rennie* and *Rogers* trial court decisions, finding that involuntarily committed patients had a qualified constitutional right to refuse treatment.

After the Supreme Court's decision in *Mills*, however, while many courts continued to endorse the earlier *Rogers/Rennie* model, others read these cases more restrictively in light of the Court's vacation and remand.[149] At least two cases, however, resurrected the least restrictive alternative (LRA) test abandoned by the Third Circuit on remand after the Supreme Court returned *Rennie* for reconsideration in light of *Youngberg v. Romeo*.[150]

Two basic due process models evolved in right-to-refuse cases: the "expanded due process model" and the "limited due process model."[151] The expanded due process approach resulted primarily from state court decisions based either on a state statute[152] or on state constitutional rights.[153] Under this model, patients are provided with procedural due process protections such as notice, counsel, the right to cross-examine witnesses, the right to present evidence (including expert testimony) and the right to appeal.[154] The limited due process model evolved from

---

146 Rennie v. Klein, No. 77-2624 (D.N.J., Aug. 16, 1984) (consent order).

147 *In re* Mental Health of K.K.B., 609 P.2d 747 (Okla. 1979); Goedecke v. Department of Institutions, 603 P.2d 123 (Colo. 1979); *In re* Boyd, 403 A.2d 744 (D.C. 1979).

148 Davis v. Hubbard, 506 F. Supp. 915 (N.D. Ohio 1980).

149 E.g., R.A.J. v. Miller, 590 F. Supp. 1319, 1322 (N.D. Tex. 1984).

150 Bee v. Greaves, 744 F.2d 1387 (10th Cir. 1984), *cert. denied*, 469 U.S. 1214 (1985); People v. Medina, 705 P.2d 961 (Colo. 1985).

151 See Michael L. Perlin and Deborah A. Dorfman, *"Is It More Than Dodging Lions and Wastin' Time?": Adequacy of Counsel, Questions of Competence, and the Judicial Process in Individual Right to Refuse Treatment Cases*, 2 PSYCHOLOGY, PUB. POL'Y & L. 114, 122–23 (1996).

152 See, e.g., Riese v. St. Mary's Hosp. & Medical Center, 243 Cal. Rptr. (Ct. App. 1987), *republished*, 271 Cal. Rptr. 199 (Ct. App. 1987), *superseded by* 751 P.2d 893 (Cal. 1988), *cause dismissed and order published*, 774 P.2d 698 (Cal. 1989).

153 See Rivers v. Katz, 504 N.Y.S.2d 74 (1986).

154 Michael L. Perlin, Keri K. Gould and Deborah A. Dorfman, *Therapeutic Jurisprudence and*

federal court decisions based on the US Constitution.[155] Under this model, mental health patients are provided with only minimal due process protections. Narrower administrative review is provided, and broad readings of the Fourteenth Amendment's due process clause are rejected.[156]

The most significant of the post *Rennie* and *Rogers* cases is probably *Rivers v. Katz*.[157] There, basing its decision solely on state constitutional and common-law grounds,[158] New York's highest court mandated a *judicial* determination "of whether the patient has the capacity to make a reasoned decision with respect to proposed treatment before the drugs may be administered pursuant to the State's *parens patriae* power."[159]

It rejected defendants' argument that involuntarily committed mental patients were "presumptively incompetent" to exercise this right because involuntary commitment included an implicit determination "that the patient's illness has so impaired his judgment as to render him incapable of making decisions regarding treatment and care."[160] The Court, rather, found that, without more, neither the fact of mental illness nor the fact of commitment "constitutes a sufficient basis to conclude that [such patients] lack the mental capacity to comprehend the consequences of their decision to refuse medication that poses a significant risk to their physical well-being."[161]

---

the Civil Rights of Institutionalized Mentally Disabled Persons: Hopeless Oxymoron or Path to Redemption? 1 PSYCHOL. PUB. POL'Y & L. 80, 112 (1995).

155 See, e.g., Project Release v. Prevost, 722 F.2d 960 (2d Cir. 1983).

156 Perlin, Gould and Dorfman, *supra* note 154, at 112. For other examples of this limited due process reading, see, e.g., Stensvad v. Reivitz, 601 F. Supp. 128 (W.D. Wis. 1985); *In re* L.R., 497 A.2d 753 (Vt. 1985).

157 After *Rivers*, many other state courts have turned to state law upon which to premise a finding of a right to refuse. See, e.g., Riese v. St. Mary's Hosp. & Medical Center, 243 Cal. Rptr. 241 (1987), *app'l dismissed as improvidently granted*, 259 Cal. Rptr. 669 (1988); Myers v. Alaska Psychiatric Institute, 138 P.3d 238 (Alaska 2006), expanded upon in Wetherhorn v. Alaska Psychiatric Institute, 156 P.3d 371 (Alaska 2007).

158 *Rivers*, 504 N.Y.S.2d at 78, 81–82.

159 Id. at 80–81.

160 Id. at 78.

161 Id. at 78–79. See id. at 79, quoting Alexander D. Brooks, *The Constitutional Right to Refuse Antipsychotic Medication*, 8 BULL. AM. ACAD. PSYCHIATRY & L. 179, 191 (1980):

  [T]here is ample evidence that many patients, despite their mental illness, are capable of making rational and knowledgeable decisions about medications. The fact that a mental

5.2.6   Considering other treatments

5.2.6.1   Introduction

It is also necessary to consider the implications of the right to refuse treatment doctrine for other treatment modalities.[162] Although the Supreme Court has never considered such a case, each modality raises important questions for the scholar and the practitioner.

5.2.6.2   Electroshock treatment

Electroshock (or electroconvulsive) therapy (ECT) is a controversial technique[163] by which a substantial current of electricity flows through a patient's brain, causing a convulsion characterized as the equivalent to an epileptic seizure.[164] It has been primarily used to relieve the symptoms of depression, but has also been employed in cases involving both acute and chronic schizophrenia.[165]

As a result of the treatment's evident physical intrusiveness,[166] reports of its use as punishment,[167] its apparent unpredictability[168] and a significant number of successful malpractice cases stemming from its negligent use,[169] multiple jurisdictions have enacted statutes regulating its use.[170]

---

patient may disagree with the psychiatrist's judgment about the benefit of medication outweighing the cost does not make the patient's decision incompetent.

162 Besides those discussed here, there are other modalities to consider. On psychotherapy, see PERLIN AND CUCOLO, *supra* note 1, § 8-9.2. On behavior modification, see id., § 8-9.5.

163 See, e.g., Caitlin Sandley, *Repairing the Therapist? Banning Reparative Therapy for LGB Minors*, 24 HEALTH MATRIX 247, 257 (2014).

164 New York City Health & Hosp. Corp. v. Stein, 335 N.Y.S.2d 461, 463–64 (Sup. Ct. 1972).

165 LOUIS LINN, A HANDBOOK OF HOSPITAL PSYCHIATRY: A PRACTICAL GUIDE TO THERAPY 41–42 (1969).

166 See, e.g., Note, *Conditioning and Other Technologies Used to "Treat?" "Rehabilitate?" "Demolish?" Prisoners and Mental Patients*, 45 S. CAL. L. REV. 616, 631–32 (1972).

167 See, e.g., Bonnie Burstow, *Electroshock as a Form of Violence against Women*, 12 VIOLENCE AGAINST WOMEN 372 (2006).

168 WALTER BROMBERG, FROM SHAMAN TO PSYCHOTHERAPIST: A HISTORY OF THE TREATMENT OF MENTAL ILLNESS 305–06 (1975).

169 E.g., Stone v. Proctor, 131 S.E.2d 297 (N.C. 1963).

170 See, e.g., People in the Interest of M.K.M., 765 P.2d 1075 (Colo. Ct. App. 1988); N.J. STAT. ANN. § 30:4-24(d).

In a damages case raising the question of whether an incompetent Veterans' Administration (VA) patient had a constitutional right to avoid its unwanted administration, the Seventh Circuit reversed a district court decision dismissing the plaintiff's complaint.[171] The court found that three constitutional interests implicated by compulsory medication—First Amendment interests in thinking and communicating freely; a liberty interest in personal security, dignity and bodily integrity; and a right to privacy in personal decisionmaking—were similarly implicated by compulsory ECT, characterized as a "highly intrusive and controversial form of treatment."[172] It reasoned that, if the plaintiff could prove that a defendant's decision to administer ECT "departed from accepted professional practice" under *Youngberg*, "a claim would be stated under even the most lenient reading of the Due Process Clause."[173]

5.2.6.3 *Psychosurgery*

The unpublished, yet carefully scrutinized opinion of *Kaimowitz v. Michigan Department of Mental Health*,[174] considered the constitutionality of a state-funded experimental psychosurgery program designed to test the efficacy of methods of reducing aggression among chronically violent state inmates by surgically destroying certain brain areas "which evidenced abnormal electrical discharge during periods of aggression."[175]

There, the court ruled:

(1) Patients involuntarily committed to state institutions were legally incapable of giving competent, voluntary, knowledgeable consent to experimental psychosurgery that would irreversibly destroy brain tissue.[176]

(2) The First Amendment rights to freedom of speech and freedom

---

171 Lojuk v. Quandt, 706 F.2d 1456, 1467 (7th Cir. 1983).

172 Id. at 1465, Among several "adverse effects" attributed to ECT were "memory loss and intellectual disorientation," along with the possibility of "permanent brain damage and a slowing of brain waves." Id.

173 Id. at 1467.

174 Civ. No. 73-19434-AW (Mich. Cir. Ct., Wayne Cty. July 10, 1973), reprinted in ALEXANDER D. BROOKS, LAW, PSYCHIATRY AND THE MENTAL HEALTH SYSTEM 902 (1974).

175 For a full description, see Note, Kaimowitz v. Department of Mental Health: *A Right to be Free from Experimental Psychosurgery*, 54 B.U.L. REV. 301 (1974).

176 *Kaimowitz, supra* note 175, at 911–16.

of expression presuppose a right to generate ideas and thoughts, which could be impaired or destroyed by such surgery.[177]

(3) The constitutional right to privacy would be thwarted by such an unwarranted intrusion into the patient's brain.[178]

Because "intrusive and irreversible" experimental psychosurgery often leads to "the blunting of emotions, the deadening of memory, [and] the reduction of affect, [thus] limit[ing] the ability to generate new ideas [and carrying with it a great] potential for injury to the [individual's] creativity," it can impinge on the individual's right "to be free from interference with his mental processes."[179] As there was no demonstration of a "compelling State interest in the use of experimental psychosurgery on involuntarily detained mental patients," the court found that the practice would be proscribed by the First Amendment.[180]

5.2.6.4   Seclusion and restraint

Seclusion-and-restraint cases are based on a wide range of legal theories. For instance:

- an Illinois intermediate appellate court has found that a plaintiff could seek recovery under the state mental health code for violations of seclusion-and-restraint policies,[181]
- the Eighth Circuit has found that an allegation that a prison medical director permitted a prisoner to be placed in restraints without medical approval stated a violation of constitutional rights,[182] and
- a Wisconsin intermediate appellate court reversed a grant of summary judgment to defendants where the trial court had failed to consider whether violations of seclusion-and-restraint policies were willful.[183]

---

177 Id. at 916–19.
178 Id. at 919–21.
179 Id.
180 Id. at 919.
181 Chadwick v. Al-Basha, 692 N.E.2d 390 (Ill. App. 1998).
182 Buckley v. Rogerson, 133 F.3d 1125 (8th Cir. 1998).
183 Schaidler v. Mercy Med. Center of Oshkosh, 563 N.W. 2d 554 (Wis. Ct. App. 1997).

5.3   Other institutional rights

5.3.1   Introduction

Early developments made it clear that systems-wide, right-to-treat-ment/institutional conditions suits were not always the appropriate means of vindicating the day-to-day civil rights of persons institution-alized because of mental disability. Litigation thus developed—based on the *Wyatt* standards[184] and on early jail and prison conditions cases[185]—in which plaintiffs sought judicial declarations that specific practices and policies violated the Constitution.

5.3.2   First Amendment rights

A series of cases explored the right of persons institutionalized because of mental disability to the free exercise of religion, and to visitation, free expression, the publication of newsletters, the free use of the mails and the use of a telephone.[186]

5.3.2.1   Free exercise of religion

The right to free exercise of religion gives competent patients a First Amendment right to refuse certain medical treatments absent a dem-onstration of a "grave and immediate danger to interests which the state may lawfully protect" that would justify overriding the patient's choice.[187]

5.3.2.2   Visitation

A federal district court struck down a state hospital policy that lim-ited the rights of patients to allocate available visiting hours among particular persons, on the grounds that it bore no rational relation-ship to legitimate security needs of the hospital or the provision of

---

184 See *supra* 5.1.3.

185 See, e.g., Jones v. North Carolina Prisoners' Labor Union, 433 U.S. 119, 129 (1977); Meachum v. Fano, 427 U.S. 215, 225 (1976); Pell v. Procunier, 417 U.S. 817, 822 (1974); Wolff v. McDonnell, 418 U.S. 539, 555–56 (1974).

186 See generally Michael L. Perlin and John Douard, *"Equality, I Spoke That Word as if a Wedding Vow": Mental Disability Law and How We Treat Marginalized Persons*, 53 N.Y.L. Sch. L. Rev. 9, 10 (2008–09), discussing Falter v. Veterans Admin., 502 F. Supp. 1178 (D.N.J. 1980) (raising these issues).

187 Winters v. Miller, 446 F.2d 65, 69 (2d Cir.), *cert. denied*, 404 U.S. 985 (1971).

an "adequate therapy program."[188] A second federal court ordered a facility for persons with intellectual disabilities to upgrade and increase "family visitation areas" as part of an omnibus conditions suit.[189]

5.3.2.3   Free expression

A federal district court has found that patients were subjected to excessive doses of forced medication as reprisals for expressing themselves freely about unpleasant drug side effects or for contacting counsel.[190] In the case of one patient-intervener, the court found that "the intervention of [counsel] caused reprisals [in the form of the withholding of a drug used to combat painful side effects] against the patient."[191]

5.3.2.4   Publication of newsletters

In an unreported consent decree, a district court approved a settlement by which defendant hospital administrators agreed to permit the distribution to patients of a newsletter published by a state legal services program.[192] Under the decree, patients were entitled to receive the newsletter in hospital common areas. In addition, defendants agreed to procedures that ensured that each hospitalized patient received a copy of the newsletter, and that forbade censorship over its contents.[193]

5.3.2.5   Free use of mails

The district court in *Wyatt v. Stickney* was the first court to hold that patients "have an unrestricted right to send sealed mail."[194] Other district courts have permanently enjoined hospital directors from censoring and interfering with patients' mail in any way—save for inspection within the patients' presence for contraband[195]—and have held that

---

188 Schmidt v. Schubert, 422 F. Supp. 57, 58 (E.D. Wis. 1976).

189 Society for Good Will to Retarded Children v. Cuomo, 572 F. Supp. 1300, 1360 (E.D.N.Y. 1983); compare Schmidt v. Schmidt, 459 A.2d 421 (Pa. Super. 1983) (noninstitutionalized, intellectually disabled adult woman with Down's syndrome could not be compelled by court order to visit her father following parents' separation).

190 See Rennie v. Klein, discussed *supra* 5.2.3.1.1.

191 *Rennie*, 476 F. Supp. at 1302.

192 B.P. v. Martin, Civ. No. H-78–104 (D. Conn. 1978), discussed in Michael L. Perlin, *Other Rights of Residents in Institutions*, in 2 LEGAL RIGHTS OF MENTALLY DISABLED PERSONS 1009, 1028 (Paul Friedman ed., 1979).

193 Id.

194 See generally *supra* 5.1.3.

195 Brown v. Schubert, 347 F. Supp. 1232, 1234 (E.D. Wis. 1972), *supplemented*, 389 F. Supp. 281,

the institution must give prior notice to the patient where there is to be any censorship, so that he or she can challenge its imposition.[196]

5.3.2.6   Use of telephones

Wyatt v. Stickney equated the right to visitation with the right to use of telephones while an inpatient:

> Patients shall have the same rights to visitation and telephone communication as patients at other public hospitals, except to the extent that [a] Qualified Mental Health Professional [imposes] special restrictions. . . .[197]

Subsequent courts have recognized that the telephone is a "valuable tool of communication," especially to patients who may live hundreds of miles from their site of hospitalization.[198] One district court has ruled that a cause of action would be stated in a case that alleged that a psychiatric hospital doctor and nurse monitored a patient's conversations with her attorney, as such conversations were "private and [might] be privileged."[199]

5.3.3   Sixth Amendment rights

There have been some modest developments surrounding the question of the right of counsel in matters challenging treatment conditions and the right of institutionalized persons to access to law libraries and the courts.

5.3.3.1   *Right to counsel in matters involving treatment while hospitalized and conditions of institutionalization*

Two circuits held that persons institutionalized by reason of mental disability are similarly entitled to meaningful access to counsel.[200] In

---

283–84 (E.D. Wis. 1975). See also Vallen v. Pierre, 2017 U.S. Dist. LEXIS 21213, at *5 (E.D.N.Y. Feb. 14, 2017) (patient has "right to the free flow of incoming and outgoing mail . . . protected by the First Amendment," citing, inter alia, Davis v. Goord, 320 F.3d 346, 351 (2d Cir. 2003)).

196   Davis v. Balson, 461 F. Supp. 842, 866–68 (N.D. Ohio 1978).

197   344 F. Supp. at 379, app. A, min. const. std. II (4).

198   Johnson by Johnson v. Brelje, 701 F.2d 1201, 1207–08 and 1208 n.7 (7th Cir. 1983), deemed "no longer viable," because of amendments to Illinois state statutes in Maust v. Headley, 959 F.2d 644, 648 (7th Cir. 1992).

199   Gerrard v. Blackman, 401 F. Supp. 1189, 1193 (N. D. Ill. 1975).

200   See, e.g., *Johnson by Johnson*, 701 F.2d at 1207–08 and 1208 n.8; see also Ward v. Kort, 762 F.2d

one, the Seventh Circuit struck down a hospital telephone policy that "severely restricted" patients' ability to communicate with their lawyers.[201] In the other case, the Tenth Circuit found that providing legal services to state hospital patients via a contractual relationship with a private law firm failed to pass constitutional muster.[202]

5.3.3.2   *Right of access to law libraries, counsel and the courts*

It has been established, in *Bounds v. Smith*, "that prisoners have a constitutional right of access to the courts," and that "remedial measures" may be necessary to ensure that access is "adequate, effective and meaningful."[203] To fulfill this right, prison authorities are required to assist inmates "by providing prisoners with adequate law libraries or adequate assistance from prisoners trained in the law."[204]

Thus, in an action brought by patients previously found incompetent to stand trial, the Seventh Circuit considered the institution's policies with regard to both the residents' use of telephones and access to a law library in light of the constitutional doctrine set down by the US Supreme Court in the *Bounds* case. It ruled that the plaintiffs "deserve no less constitutional protection" than was made available in *Bounds*. It thus struck down an institutional telephone policy that had limited patients to two ten-minute outgoing calls a week and allowed them no incoming calls, holding that such a policy "unreasonably restricts communications between [each plaintiff] and his attorney."[205]

On the question of the need for a law library, however, the Court disagreed with the plaintiffs. The right to meaningful access, it found, is satisfied if, "in lieu of a law library, adequate assistance of counsel is

---

856, 858 (10th Cir. 1985) ("there is no logic in holding that persons under mental commitment like plaintiffs are on a lower plane than convicted inmates").

201   *Johnson by Johnson*, 701 F.2d at 1207–08 n.7. The *Johnson* court also rejected plaintiffs' argument that they were similarly entitled to the establishment of a law library; because plaintiffs would be receiving adequate assistance of counsel (once the telephone policy was enjoined), a law library would not be required. Id. at 1208.

202   *Ward*, 762 F.2d at 858–60.

203   430 U.S. 817, 821–22 (1977).

204   Id. at 828.

205   *Johnson by Johnson*, 701 F. 2d.

provided."[206] Such adequate assistance would become available with the lifting of telephone restrictions.[207]

5.3.4 Other due process and treatment rights

5.3.4.1 Due process at disciplinary hearings

Following decisions that patients had a right to a procedural due process hearing prior to transfer from a minimum to a maximum security facility or from a prison to a psychiatric hospital, and a ruling that procedural due process safeguards are implicated when disciplinary action restricts liberty entitlements,[208] a federal district court held that such safeguards are similarly called into play in cases where a patient might be deprived of his or her right to treatment in the LRA setting because of similar disciplinary action.[209] In *Davis v. Balson*, the court divided disciplinary deprivations into two categories: (1) relatively minor deprivations, such as loss of yard or commissary privileges; and (2) relatively serious ones, such as seclusion, placement in restraints, transfer to a more secure ward or increase in medication. In matters involving minor deprivations, minimum procedural due process safeguards would include prehearing notice, a hearing before a fact-finder other than the complainant, and a written statement of the grounds for the removal of the privilege.[210] For more serious deprivations, minimum safeguards would include the right to written notice 24 hours prior to any hearing, the right to present testimony and call witnesses,[211] the right to a written statement of findings of fact and the evidence relied on, the right to an impartial fact-finder and the right to assistance at the hearing from another resident or staff member, "if the accused is illiterate or the issues complex."[212]

---

206 Id. 1208, citing *Bounds*, 430 U.S. at 828.

207 On the right to counsel at hospital staffings, see PERLIN AND CUCOLO, *supra* note 1, § 9-4.2.

208 See Eubanks v. Clarke, 434 F. Supp. 1022, 1028–29 (E.D. Pa. 1977); Evans v. Paderick, 443 F. Supp. 583, 585–86 (E.D. Va. 1977); Meachum v. Fano, 427 U.S. 215, 224 (1976).

209 See Davis v. Balson, 461 F. Supp. 842, 875–76 (N.D. Ohio 1978). See also Eckerhart v. Hensley, 475 F. Supp. 908, 926 (W.D. Mo. 1979).

210 461 F. Supp. at 877.

211 This right could be limited if "to do [otherwise] would unduly endanger institutional safety or rehabilitation goals." Id. at 878.

212 Id., adopting, *in toto*, the standards of Wolff v. McDonnell, 418 U.S. 539, 563–72 (1974).

5.3.4.2   *Due process rights in hospital fingerprinting practices*

The practice of fingerprinting and photographing state hospital patients—and subsequently transmitting the fingerprints and photographs to the Federal Bureau of Investigation and state law enforcement authorities—may, under certain circumstances, violate patients' rights under the equal protection clause.[213]

5.3.4.3   *Right to due process prior to imposition of restrictive security conditions*

Again, in *Davis*, patients charged that "security considerations have become paramount to treatment considerations" and that the "overwhelming and overriding presence of 'security' in the institution is both antitherapeutic and dehumanizing."[214] The court found that the facility was "operated primarily as a prison, and function[ed] only secondarily as a hospital for the mentally ill"; the maximum security environment "by its very nature . . . reduce[d] the normalization possible"; and, as a result of the security measures, "the atmosphere and interrelations were negative and nontherapeutic."[215] It found further that security measures were "so pervasive and oppressive as to infringe upon the plaintiffs' constitutional right to treatment,"[216] in ruling that defendants had not sufficiently accommodated the plaintiffs' right to treatment in the LRA.[217]

5.3.4.4   *Due process in seclusion-and-restraint decisionmaking*

Courts have applied procedural due process concepts to hospital decisionmaking in the imposition of restraints and seclusion practices.[218] In *Eckerhart v. Hensley*, the court found that, while advance notice and hearing were "not at all appropriate to the medical decision to use seclusion or restraints,"[219] due process mandated that "the *medical* decision to utilize physical restraints and seclusion be made in a con-

---

213   *Davis*, 461 F. Supp. at 868–72.

214   Id. at 855.

215   Id.

216   Id.

217   Id., quoting, in part, *Wolff*, 418 U.S. at 556.

218   See Eckerhart v. Hensley, 475 F. Supp. 908 (W.D. Mo. 1979); *Davis*, 461 F. Supp. 842, (N.D. Ohio 1978). On the interplay between right-to-refuse-treatment concepts and seclusion law, *see supra* 5.2.6.4.

219   475 F. Supp. at 926.

text designed to protect the patient from an arbitrary deprivation of personal liberty."[220] Hospital practices violated due process, "primarily [because of] the lack of documentation of patient behavior leading to the use of seclusion or restraints and of the reason to justify each incident. . . ."[221]

5.3.4.5   Right to exercise

The district court had held in *Wyatt v. Stickney* that patients "have a right to regular physical exercise several times a week," it being the hospital's duty to "provide facilities and equipment for such exercise."[222] Although patients' "freedom of movement may be restrained when and to the extent professional judgment deems it necessary to assure security or to provide needed treatment," even prison cases have held that the denial of outdoor exercise itself inflicts sufficient psychological harm on inmates so as to characterize the right to exercise as a "fundamental" one.[223]

5.3.4.6   Voting rights

Courts have outlawed discrimination against patients in matters involving voting rights. A New Jersey appellate court thus ruled that actions by a county elections board segregating patients' ballots was improper, and that a showing that a voter resides at a psychiatric hospital in itself was an insufficient basis on which to sustain a challenge to the patients' right to vote.[224] Subsequently, a federal court in Maine found that a state constitutional provision disenfranchising persons in psychiatric hospitals violated both the US Constitution and the Americans with Disabilities Act.[225]

5.3.4.7   Privacy rights/right-to-treatment records

Residents of a state forensic facility were allowed to proceed with their action alleging that state doctors and mental health officials disclosed confidential psychiatric and medical information in unsealed court

---

220 Id. at 926 (emphasis added).
221 Id. (footnote omitted).
222 344 F. Supp. at 380–81.
223 See, e.g., Laaman v. Helgemoe, 437 F. Supp. 269, 309 (D.N.H. 1977).
224 I/M/O Absentee Ballots Cast by Five Residents of Trenton Psychiatric Hosp., 750 A.2d 790 (N.J. App. Div. 2000).
225 Doe v. Rowe, 156 F. Supp. 2d 35 (D. Me. 2001).

documents, thus violating their constitutional right to privacy.[226] Elsewhere, a Wisconsin federal court has ruled that, under federal law, a state advocacy organization had a right to records of potential abuse and neglect at a private residential psychiatric facility.[227]

5.4   Penumbral rights

Among the most important penumbral rights is the right of persons institutionalized because of mental disability to voluntary sexual interaction.[228] Remarkably little attention has been paid to this, one of the most basic and fundamental of all civil and human rights. Only four of the states that adopted the *Wyatt* standards included that portion of those standards that guaranteed patients the right to reasonable interaction with members of the opposite sex.[229] Only a smattering of cases have been litigated elsewhere that have sought to vindicate this right.[230]

Consider *Foy v. Greenblott*.[231] There, an institutionalized patient and her infant child (conceived and born while the mother was a patient in a locked psychiatric ward) sued the mother's treating doctor for his failure to either maintain proper supervision over her so as to prevent her from having sex or to provide her with contraceptive devices and/or sexual counseling.[232] The court rejected the plaintiff's claims of improper supervision, finding that institutionalized patients had a

---

226 Hirschfeld v. Stone, 193 F.R.D. 175 (S.D.N.Y. 2000).

227 Wisconsin Coalition for Advocacy v. Czaplewski, 131 F. Supp. 2d 1039 (E.D. Wis. 2001). On challenges to hospital no-smoking policies, see PERLIN AND CUCOLO, *supra* note 1, § 9-6.6.

228 See generally MICHAEL L. PERLIN AND ALISON J. LYNCH, SEXUALITY, DISABILITY AND THE LAW: BEYOND THE LAST FRONTIER? (2016). See also, e.g., Michael L. Perlin, *Hospitalized Patients and the Right to Sexual Interaction: Beyond the Last Frontier?* 20 N.Y.U. REV. L. & SOC'L CHANGE 517 (1993–94); Michael L. Perlin and Alison J. Lynch, *"All His Sexless Patients": Persons with Mental Disabilities and the Competence to Have Sex*, 89 WASH. L. REV. 257 (2014).

229 Lyon, Levine and Zusman, *supra* note 81; see also Hannah Hicks, *To the Right to Intimacy and Beyond: A Constitutional Argument for the Right to Sex in Mental Health Facilities*, 40 N.Y.U. REV. L. & SOC. CHANGE 621, 649 (2016).

230 V.H. v. K.E.J. (*In re* Estate of K.E.J.), 887 N.E.2d 704 (Ill. App. 2008), *reh'g denied*, 2008 Ill. App. LEXIS 585 (May 29, 2008) (neither right to bear children nor right of personal inviolability is absolute in case of individual adjudicated as incompetent). See also, e.g., Conservatorship of Angela D., 83 Cal. Rptr. 2d 411 (App. 1999), *reh'g denied* (App. 1999) (finding that supervision of conservatee was not available as less invasive alternative form of contraception was supported by evidence).

231 190 Cal. Rptr. 84 (App. 1983). See Perlin, *supra* note 228, at 532–34.

232 *Foy*, 190 Cal. Rptr. at 87.

right to engage in voluntary sexual relations as an aspect of either the "least restrictive environment" or "reasonably non-restrictive confinement conditions," and that that right included "suitable opportunities for the patient's interactions with members of the opposite sex."[233]

On the other hand, it did characterize defendants' failure to provide plaintiff with contraceptive devices and counseling as a deprivation of her right to reproductive choice.[234] It also rejected a claim for "wrongful birth" by her infant child, concluding, "Our society has repudiated the proposition that mental patients will necessarily beget unhealthy, inferior or otherwise undesirable children if permitted to reproduce."[235]

The general lack of litigation in this area of the law may appear anomalous. Self-evidently, institutionalized persons do not lose their sexuality when they lose their liberty.[236] Yet, most states do not recognize their patients' right to personal, intimate relationships. Often, this right depends on the whim of line-level staff or on whether such interaction is seen as an aspect of an individual patient's treatment plan.[237] It has even been suggested that "sexual activities between psychiatric inpatients should be strictly prohibited, and when it occurs patients should be isolated . . . and tranquilized if necessary."[238] One hospital's guidelines stated, "If you develop a relationship with another patient, staff will get together with you to help decide whether this relationship is beneficial or detrimental to you."[239] Some, though certainly not all, of hospital staff are often hostile to the idea that patients are sexually active in any way,[240] and, especially, express an "abject fear" of patient pregnancies.[241] As a result of these attitudes, it is not a surprise that

---

233 Id. at 90 n.2.

234 Id. at 90.

235 Id. at 93.

236 See Susan Stefan, *Silencing the Different Voice: Competence, Feminist Theory, and Law*, 47 U. MIAMI L. REV. 763 (1993).

237 See Susan Stefan, *Whose Egg Is It Anyway? Reproductive Rights of Incarcerated, Institutionalized, and Incompetent Women*, 13 NOVA L. REV. 405 (1989).

238 As discussed in Renée Binder, *Sex between Psychiatric Inpatients*, 57 PSYCHIATRY Q. 121, 125 (1985).

239 Gabor Keitner and Paul Grof, *Sexual and Emotional Intimacy between Psychiatric Inpatients: Formulating a Policy*, 32 HOSP. & COMMUN. PSYCHIATRY 188, 193 (1981).

240 See, e.g., Michael L. Commons, Judi T. Bohn, Lisa T. Godon, Mark J. Hauser and Thomas G. Gutheil, *Professionals' Attitudes toward Sex between Institutionalized Patients*, 46 AM. J. PSYCHOTHERAPY 571 (1992).

241 Kalpana Elizabeth Dein, Paul Simon Williams, Irina Volkonskaia, Ava Kanyeredzi, Paula Reavey

there is a significant lack of literature and policy statements available to guide hospital practices.[242]

5.5   Economic rights[243]

5.5.1   Right of persons institutionalized because of mental disabilities to control their own assets

Persons institutionalized by reason of mental disability cannot be deprived of the right to control their own assets, absent a finding of incompetency, consistent with rudimentary due process safeguards.[244] A federal district court struck down as unconstitutional a Connecticut statute that authorized the state finance commissioner to serve as conservator of funds of any mentally ill person, with property or annual income of less than $5,000, committed or admitted to a state mental institution.[245]

and Gerard Leavey, *Examining Professionals' Perspectives on Sexuality for Service Users of a Forensic Psychiatry Unit*, 44 INT'L J.L. & PSYCHIATRY 15, 20–22 (2014).

242 See generally Michael L. Perlin and Alison J. Lynch, *"Love Is Just a Four-Letter Word": Sexuality, International Human Rights and Therapeutic Jurisprudence*, 1 CAN. J. COMPAR. & CONTEMP. L. 8 (2015).

243 Beyond the scope of this work are issues related to the right of patients to be compensated for institutional work, see PERLIN AND CUCOLO, *supra* note 1, §§ 9-7.1 to 9-7.1.13, and the right of the state to bill institutionalized patients for their care and maintenance, see id. §§ 9-7.3 to 9-7.3.3.

244 See, e.g., Vecchione v. Wohlgemuth, 377 F. Supp. 1361 (E.D. Pa. 1974), *further proceedings*, 426 F. Supp. 1297 (E.D. Pa.), *aff'd*, 558 F.2d 150 (3d Cir.), *cert. denied*, 434 U.S. 943 (1977); McAuliffe v. Carlson, 377 F. Supp. 896 (D. Conn. 1974), *rev'd on other grounds*, 520 F.2d 1305 (2d Cir. 1975), *cert. denied*, 427 U.S. 911 (1976).

245 *McAuliffe*, 377 F. Supp. at 904. And see id. at 905: such hospital admission "does not support even a presumption that a mental patient is incompetent," the state's irrefutable presumption of incompetency violated due process.

6   Rights of persons with mental disabilities in community settings

6.1   Introduction[1]

The theoretical underpinnings of a right to aftercare are found in early cases that established both a right to treatment and a right to the least restrictive alternative (LRA) in commitment decisionmaking. These cases established the basic principles that served as the initial underpinning in the attempted structuring of a constitutional right to deinstitutionalization:[2]

> [T]here is a constitutional right to liberty (the "natural state of individuals"); before one can be deprived of that right, the process of deprivation must comport with strict due process procedures to minimize the risk of error (and to place such risk on the committing agency, not the person at risk) so that institutionalization is seen as the last resort; if a person is to be institutionalized, that institutionalization cannot meet constitutional muster if it does not offer a person a reasonable opportunity to receive such care and treatment in a humane environment as to enhance that person's likelihood of being released ... it is impermissible to presume a person incompetent to manage his affairs because of his status as a patient.[3]

---

1 See MICHAEL L. PERLIN AND HEATHER ELLIS CUCOLO, MENTAL DISABILITY LAW: CIVIL AND CRIMINAL ch. 10 (3d ed. 2016) (2019 update).

2 See especially O'Connor v. Donaldson, 422 U.S. 563 (1975); Lessard v. Schmidt, 349 F. Supp. 1078 (E.D. Wis. 1972), *vacated and remanded*; and Wyatt v. Stickney, 325 F. Supp. 781 (M.D. Ala. 1971), 334 F. Supp. 1341 (M.D. Ala. 1972), 344 F. Supp. 373 (M.D. Ala.), 344 F. Supp. 387 (M.D. Ala.), *aff'd sub nom.* Wyatt v. Aderholt, 503 F.2d 1305 (5th Cir. 1974).

3 Michael L. Perlin, *Rights of Ex-Patients in the Community: The Next Frontier?* 8 BULL. AM. ACAD. PSYCHIATRY & L. 33, 33–34 (1980) (footnotes omitted).

6.2   Statutory right-to-deinstitutionalization cases—
Dixon v. Weinberger

The first case to focus specifically on a right to community treatment or aftercare was brought on behalf of patients at a Washington, D.C. hospital, where "hundreds of patients ... were being improvidently held at the facility because, in the pat phrase of both the institutional and the community social service providers: 'There's nowhere else for them to go.'"[4] In *Dixon v. Weinberger*, the court found that, under local statutes, the plaintiffs had a statutory right to aftercare, and that this right had been violated by the local government's failure to provide suitable alternative facilities for those St. Elizabeth's patients who no longer met the statutory criteria for hospitalization.[5] There was a specific affirmative obligation on the part of local officials to place those patients "determined suitable for placement in alternative facilities in proper facilities that are less restrictive alternatives to the hospital ... such alternatives including but not being limited to nursing homes, foster homes, personal care homes, and halfway houses."[6]

Subsequently,[7] a monitoring committee reported that the local government was "out of compliance with the *Dixon* Consent Order in virtually every regard."[8] The blue-ribbon panel concluded:

> The members of the *Dixon* class should not be asked to wait any longer. They cannot afford to pay—with their freedom and their dignity—for the District defendants' chronic inability to provide adequate mental health services.[9]

Finally, in 1997, a federal court ruled that appointment of a receiver to oversee the D.C. Commission on Mental Health Services was necessary to implement the court orders as an "appropriate remedy" after 22 years of unsuccessful attempts at compliance.[10]

---

4 Id. at 35.

5 405 F. Supp. 974, 977–78 (D.D.C. 1975).

6 Id. at 979.

7 Dixon v. Harris, Civ. No. 74–285 (D.D.C. April 30, 1980), reported in 14 CLEARINGHOUSE REV. 784 (1980).

8 REPORT TO THE COURT, RECOMMENDATIONS OF THE DIXON IMPLEMENTATION MONITORING COMMITTEE TO ACHIEVE THE DISTRICT DEFENDANTS' COMPLIANCE WITH THE DIXON CONSENT ORDER 21 (Sept. 30, 1982).

9 Id. at 22.

10 Dixon v. Barry, 967 F. Supp. 535 (D.D.C. 1997).

6.2.1   Other early deinstitutionalization litigation

Subsequent cases were settled on terms close to those ordered initially by the *Dixon* court. By way of example, Massachusetts state officials agreed to undertake specific programs that would provide a comprehensive system of community mental health and retardation services by offering less restrictive residential facilities and nonresidential treatment and support programs for former residents of Northampton State Hospital.[11] Defendants promised to "use their best efforts to insure . . . full and timely financing" of the programs in question.[12]

6.3   Right to deinstitutionalization—a procedural approach

After the limitations of cases such as *Dixon v. Weinberger* became apparent, this question continued to be asked:

> [W]hat can be done in the case of a once-involuntarily committed patient who no longer meets the criteria for commitment or continued institutionalization but for whom there is no suitable and available alternative placement?[13]

Thus, because of the "universality of the problem, the apparent lack of acceptable practical solutions, and the courts' general reluctance to grant relief to litigants seeking the declaration of a constitutional right to aftercare services in the community," the New Jersey Supreme Court attempted a different approach in *In re S.L.*,[14] ruling that special placement hearings would be scheduled in cases involving individuals who were "not able to survive in the community independently or with the help of family or friends."[15] At such hearings:

> the court shall inquire into the needs of the individual for custodial and supportive care, the desires of the individual regarding placement, the type of facility that would provide the needed level of care in the least restrictive

11 Brewster v. Dukakis, 675 F.2d 1, 2 (1982).

12 Id.

13 Michael L. Perlin, *"Discharged Pending Placement": The Due Process Rights of the Nondangerous Institutionalized Mentally Handicapped with "Nowhere to Go,"* 5 DIRECTIONS IN PSYCHIATRY Lesson 21, at 2 (1985).

14 462 A.2d 1252 (N.J. 1983), discussed extensively *supra* 4.6.1.

15 Id. at 1258.

manner, the availability of such placement, the efforts of the State to locate such placement and any other matters it deems pertinent.[16]

6.4   Is there a constitutional right to aftercare?

In *Halderman v. Pennhurst State School*,[17] plaintiffs' lawyers sought to merge arguments in support of a constitutional right to habilitation and a right to the LRA in "a direct assault on institutionalization of retarded persons."[18] There, the district court found that institutional conditions violated residents' rights to minimally adequate habilitation, to freedom from harm and to "non-discriminatory habilitation." In addition, it held that conditions violated the state statutory right to minimally adequate habilitation and federal statutory right—under § 504 of the Rehabilitation Act—to nondiscriminatory habilitation.[19] The trial judge found that "the confinement and isolation of the retarded in . . . Pennhurst is segregation in a facility that clearly is separate and *not* equal,"[20] and that the equal protection clause prohibited such segregation "in an isolated institution . . . where habilitation does not measure up to minimally adequate standards."[21]

On appeal, the Third Circuit substantially affirmed, with one major modification, but on a nearly totally different legal basis.[22] The court found that there was a private cause of action under the Developmentally Disabled Assistance and Bill of Rights Act (DD Act).[23] That law, the court found, provided persons with mental retardation an enforceable federal statutory right to treatment.[24] The court also read applicable state law to find a statutory right to treatment on which relief could be sought in federal court under a pendent jurisdiction

---

16 Id.

17 446 F. Supp. 1295 (E.D. Pa. 1978), *modified*, 612 F.2d 84 (3d Cir. 1979), *rev'd*, 451 U.S. 1 (1981), *reinstated*, 673 F.2d 647 (3d Cir. 1982), *rev'd*, 465 U.S. 89 (1984).

18 David Ferleger and Penelope Boyd, *Anti-Institutionalization: The Promise of the* Pennhurst *Case*, 31 STAN. L. REV. 717, 739 (1979).

19 *Pennhurst*, 446 F. Supp. at 1314–24.

20 Id. at 1321–22 (emphasis in original).

21 Id. at 1322.

22 See *Pennhurst*, 612 F.2d at 95–100.

23 42 U.S.C. §§ 6001–6081 (1976). The Act has since been recodified, and several pertinent sections renumbered. See 42 U.S.C. §§ 15901 *et seq.* The section numbers used in the court's opinion will be employed in this work.

24 See *Pennhurst*, 612 F.2d at 95.

theory,[25] and further found that this right was guaranteed in the LRA setting.[26]

However, these expansive readings were summarily rejected by the Supreme Court in its first *Pennhurst* decision (*Pennhurst I*).[27] The Court construed the DD Act as merely a "federal-state grant program whereby the Federal Government provided financial assistance to participating States to aid them in creating programs to care for and treat the developmentally disabled."[28] It noted that the Act was "voluntary," that the states were given the choice of complying with the conditions set forth in the Act or "forgoing the benefits of federal funding,"[29] and that there was no language in the "Bill of Rights" provision of the Act requiring compliance for the receipt of federal funding.[30]

Following this sharply-criticized decision,[31] the Third Circuit reinstated in its entirety its initial ruling, premising its holding solely on the basis of Pennsylvania *state* law, ruling that the Pennsylvania Supreme Court "had spoken definitively" in holding that the state mental retardation act required the state to provide care to persons with mental retardation in the least restrictive environment.[32] However, the Supreme Court again reversed and remanded.[33]

In its most intensely split institutional decision of the twentieth century,[34] the Court held that the decision below, in which a *federal*

---

25 Id. at 100–03.

26 Id. at 103–07.

27 Pennhurst State School & Hosp. v. Halderman, 451 U.S. 1 (1981) (*Pennhurst I*).

28 Id. at 11.

29 Id.

30 Id. at 13. Justice White, writing for himself and Justices Brennan and Marshall, dissented in part, arguing that the majority's opinion "misconceives the important purposes Congress intended § 6010 to serve[: the] establish[ment of] requirements which participating States had to meet in providing care to the developmentally disabled," id. at 34–35, adding that Congress was "deadly serious in stating that the developmentally disabled had entitlements which a State must respect if it were to participate in a [grant] program, id. at 37. Justice Blackmun also concurred in part. Id. at 27.

31 See, e.g., David Ferleger and Patrice M. Scott, *Rights and Dignity: Congress, the Supreme Court, and People with Disabilities after* Pennhurst, 5 W. NEW ENG. L. REV. 327, 345 (1983) (Court "distorted the major issue," and engaged in a "contorted framing" of the issues, creating an opinion that "eschews . . . logic").

32 *Pennhurst*, 673 F.2d at 651, citing *In re* Schmidt, 429 A.2d 631 (Pa. 1981).

33 465 U.S. 89 (1984) (*Pennhurst II*)

34 See, e.g., David Rudenstine, Pennhurst *and the Scope of Federal Judicial Power to Reform Social Institutions*, 6 CARDOZO L. REV. 71, 72 (1984).

court ordered *state* officials to conform their conduct to *state* law, violated the Eleventh Amendment,[35] which bars such action when the state is the real party in interest, even if only prospective injunctive relief was being sought.[36]

The Court again remanded to the Third Circuit to consider whether the *other* grounds originally relied on by the district court (the Eighth and Fourteenth Amendments and § 504 of the Rehabilitation Act) or *other* independent bases (other sections of the DD Act and the Court's intervening decision in *Youngberg v. Romeo*) were sufficient grounds on which the court of appeals' decision could be sustained.[37]

Following this remand, the parties reached a settlement, ending the litigation. Under this settlement, the state agreed that it would close Pennhurst and never again use the institution as a residential facility for persons with mental retardation.[38] Both state and county defendants agreed to provide community living arrangements to those members of the plaintiff class "for whom such placement is deemed appropriate," along with such community services "as are necessary to provide each person with minimally adequate habilitation" until the individual is no longer in need of such services.[39]

Defendants also agreed to develop, review and monitor individual, written habilitation plans for each member of the plaintiff class, and to afford each plaintiff:

(1) protection from harm; (2) safe conditions; (3) adequate shelter and clothing; (4) medical, health-related, and dental care; (5) protection from physical and psychological abuse, neglect, or mistreatment; (6) protection

---

35 See *Pennhurst II*, 465 U.S. at 120.

36 Id. at 105–06.

37 Id at 125. In a brief dissent, Justice Brennan wrote to reiterate his position that the Eleventh Amendment bars only federal suits against states by citizens of other states. Id. at 125–26. In a lengthy and angry dissent, Justice Stevens characterized the majority as having reached a "perverse result," referring to the state's position as being "utterly without support." Id. at 127, 130. In the years following *Pennhurst*, the Supreme Court split bitterly time after time on questions of the scope of the Eleventh Amendment and sovereign immunity. See, e.g., Virginia Office for Protection & Advocacy v. Stewart, 563 U.S. 247 (2011); Kimel v. Florida Bd. of Regents, 528 U.S. 62 (2000).

38 Halderman v. Pennhurst State Sch. & Hosp., 610 F. Supp. 1221, 1226–27 (E.D. Pa. 1985).

39 Id. at 1227.

from unreasonable restraint and the use of seclusion; and (7) protection from the administration of excessive or unnecessary medication.[40]

State defendants agreed to make available sufficient funds to create sufficient community placement and services for Pennhurst residents, to allow for the facility's closing by the target date, and to provide for community residents with mental retardation not residing there.[41] The court stressed:

> [S]uch transfers can be accomplished with a minimum of disruption by employing a program of preplacement visits in order to afford an opportunity for them to become familiar with their new living arrangements. The Court is well aware that many of the Pennhurst residents will encounter an emotional reaction to a new life outside the institution. However, the Court finds that with care and sensitivity, such transfers can be accomplished without harm to the individual.[42]

It concluded:

> This settlement is more than just a termination of litigation; it is the beginning of a new era for retarded persons. [All] parties . . . are now in complete agreement that the retarded citizens of this Commonwealth have a right to care, education and training in the community. It is a recognition by [all defendants] that retarded persons are not subjects to be warehoused in institutions, but that they are individuals, the great majority of whom have a potential to be productive members of society.[43]

This order provided plaintiffs with most—virtually all—of the relief they sought from Pennhurst when the case was originally filed. However, it did fall short of what the plaintiffs' counsel had articulated as one of the primary goals of the case: "the end of more than a century of incarceration of the retarded in the United States."[44] Nevertheless, it is the broadest and most comprehensive attempt to force mental disability policymakers and governmental officials to alter the way they

---

40 Id.
41 Id.
42 Id. at 1231.
43 Id. at 1233–34.
44 David Ferleger, *The Future of Institutions for Retarded Citizens: The Promise of the* Pennhurst *Case*, MENTAL RETARDATION & L. 29, 31 (1978).

think about—and operationally deal with—institutionalization of persons with mental disabilities.[45]

6.5   A right to services in the community?

On the other hand, attempts by plaintiffs' lawyers to have the constitutional right to treatment extended to community facilities was struck a blow in *Youngberg v. Romeo*,[46] finding that there was no general right to services in the community.[47] In the broadest reading of *Youngberg* prior to the Supreme Court's decision in *DeShaney v. Winnebago County Department of Social Services*,[48] a federal district court in North Carolina had extended *Youngberg*'s holding to apply to *noninstitutionalized* patients with mental retardation as well.[49] There, where the plaintiff, a nineteen-year old who had been "shuffled" through 40 foster homes and institutions since being given up for adoption at birth, was housed in a community placement "because there is no place else for him to go," the court found the *Youngberg* standards appropriate.[50] Even though not institutionalized as a ward of the state at the time of the trial, "he may be required to return to" his former institutionalized status; like the plaintiff in *Youngberg*, and thus the state "has control over [his] liberty and care."[51]

On appeal, the Fourth Circuit substantially affirmed. Although the plaintiff resided in a community setting, "he remains a legally incompetent adult who is a ward of a [state] guardian," and the principles of *Youngberg* continue to control.[52] While *Youngberg* counseled deference to professional judgment, the Supreme Court "did not allow the professionals free rein."[53]

---

45 See generally Martha Minow, *When Difference Has Its Home: Group Homes for the Mentally Retarded, Equal Protection and Legal Treatment of Difference*, 22 HARV. C.R.-C.L. L. REV. 111, 113 and 161–68 (1987).

46 457 U.S. 307 (1982). See generally *supra* 5.1.4.

47 Id. at 319.

48 489 U.S. 189 (1989), discussed below.

49 Thomas S. by Brooks v. Morrow, 601 F. Supp. 1055 (W.D.N.C. 1984), *aff'd and modified*, 781 F.2d 367 (4th Cir.), *cert. denied sub nom.* Kirk v. Thomas S., 476 U.S. 1124, *cert. denied sub nom.* Childress v. Thomas S., 479 U.S. 869 (1986).

50 *Thomas S. by Brooks*, 601 F. Supp. at 1057.

51 Id.

52 *Thomas S. by Brooks*, 781 F.2d at 374.

53 Id.

But then, in *DeShaney*, where plaintiff's mother and son alleged that, once the state took the son into custody to protect him from his abusive father, it owed an affirmative duty to protect him in a reasonably competent manner, the Supreme Court held that the due process clause did not obligate the state to protect its citizens from one another; the state's affirmative act of restraining an individual's freedom to act on his or her own behalf—through institutionalization or other similar restraint on personal liberty—was a prerequisite to any state obligation to provide care.[54]

On the other hand, courts have cited *DeShaney* for the proposition that, once a state accepts an individual into its care and custody, it "has assumed responsibility for the safety and well-being of the resident,"[55] and have emphasized that *Youngberg* remains good law after *DeShaney*.[56]

6.6   Civil rights in the community—introduction

Persons with mental disabilities have a right to be free from discrimination in community housing and zoning matters, and in a wide range of civil rights in community settings. The most important case is *City of Cleburne v. Cleburne Living Center*.[57]

---

54 489 U.S. 189, 197–99 (1989). Dissenting in *DeShaney*, Justice Blackmun's begins the last paragraph of his dissent with: "Poor Joshua! Victim of repeated attacks by an irresponsible, bullying, cowardly, and intemperate father, and abandoned by respondents who placed him in a dangerous predicament and who knew or learned what was going on, and yet did essentially nothing. . . ." Id. at 214. As of the writing of this book, this dissent has been cited in 198 law review articles accessible on the Westlaw data base. See also K.L. v. Edgar, 941 F. Supp. 706, 716–19 (N.D. Ill. 1996), finding no right to services once a patient has been discharged, analogizing the case to "the sad case of Joshua DeShaney."

55 People First of Tenn. v. Arlington Developmental Center, 878 F. Supp. 97, 101 n.8 (W.D. Tenn. 1992).

56 Shaw by Strain v. Strackhouse, 920 F.2d 1135, 1146 (3d Cir. 1990). Beyond the scope of this work are issues related to the relationship between deinstitutionalization and homelessness. See PERLIN AND CUCOLO, *supra* note 1, §§ 10-4 to 10-4.5, and Michael L. Perlin, *Competency, Deinstitutionalization, and Homelessness: A Story of Marginalization*, 28 HOUS. L. REV. 63 (1991).

57 473 U.S. 432 (1985). Although the holding of the case is limited to facilities for persons with intellectual disabilities (referred to in the litigation as "mental retardation"), id. at 445–46, subsequent litigation has made it clear that *Cleburne* has not been without impact on cases involving mental illness as well. See, e.g., Township of West Orange v. Whitman, 8 F. Supp. 2d 408 (D.N.J. 1998); Pacific Shores Properties, LLC v. City of Newport Beach, 730 F.3d 1142 (9th Cir. 2013).

The facts in *Cleburne* were virtually uncontested. A private individual purchased a building in the city with the intention of leasing it to Cleburne Living Center (CLC) for a group home for 13 individuals with mental retardation, as it was then characterized. After both the Planning and Zoning Commission and the city council held hearings and voted to deny the special use permit, CLC filed suit in federal court, alleging that the ordinance was facially invalid because it discriminated against persons with mental retardation in violation of the equal protection clause.[58]

On first appeal, the Fifth Circuit had held that mental retardation was a quasi-suspect classification, and that the validity of the ordinance should thus be assessed under the standard of intermediate level scrutiny.[59] Such additional scrutiny was particularly appropriate in a housing discrimination case because of the importance of the benefit withheld by the ordinance: without group homes, persons with mental retardation could never hope to integrate themselves into the community.[60] The court thus held the ordinance facially invalid and invalid as applied.[61]

Subsequently, the Supreme Court noted that the rule that legislation is presumptively valid "gives way . . . when a statute classifies by race, alienage or national origin."[62] Thus, it concluded, the Fifth Circuit had erred in characterizing mental retardation as a quasi-suspect classification calling for "a more exacting standard of judicial review than is normally accorded economic and social legislation."[63] On the other hand, the Court stressed, this refusal to adopt quasi-suspect classification "does not leave [persons with mental retardation] entirely unprotected from invidious discrimination."[64] Use of the rational relationship standard "affords governments the latitude necessary,

---

58 *Cleburne*, 473 U.S. at 437.

59 *Cleburne*, 726 F.2d 191, 197 (5th Cir. 1984). While the Court of Appeals found strict scrutiny inappropriate (because mental retardation was, in fact, relevant to many legislative actions), it further found that the history of "unfair and often grotesque mistreatment" of persons with mental retardation made it likely that discrimination reflected "deep-seated prejudice." Id. In addition, it found that persons with mental retardation lacked political power, id., and that their condition was "immutable." Id. at 198.

60 Id. at 199–200.

61 Id. at 200.

62 *Cleburne*, 473 U.S. at 440.

63 Id. at 442.

64 Id. at 446.

both to pursue policies designed to assist the retarded in reaching their full potential, and to freely and efficiently engage in activities that burden the retarded in what is essentially an incidental manner."[65]

In the case before it, the Court found that the record reflected no rational basis for suggesting that CLC's home would "pose any special threat to the city's legitimate interests."[66] The Court thus affirmed the Fifth Circuit's judgment "insofar as it holds the ordinance invalid as applied."[67]

The Court scrutinized—and rejected—the factors on which the city based its insistence on a special use permit. Most importantly, although the city was concerned with "negative attitudes" of adjacent property owners and fears of nearby elderly neighborhood residents, such "unsubstantiated" negative attitudes or fear were not permissible bases for discriminatory treatment:[68] "Private biases may be outside the reach of the law, but the law cannot, directly or indirectly, give them effect."[69]

The opinion concluded:

> The short of it is that requiring the permit in this case appears to us to rest on an irrational prejudice against the mentally retarded, including those who would occupy the [CLC] facility and who would live under the closely supervised and highly regulated conditions expressly provided for by state and federal law.[70]

---

65 Id. Thus, the state cannot rely on a classification whose relationship to an alleged goal is "so attenuated as to render the distinction arbitrary or irrational," id., citing Zobel v. Williams, 457 U.S. 55, 61–63 (1982); United States Dep't of Agriculture v. Moreno, 413 U.S. 528, 535 (1973), or one which includes objectives such as a "bare . . . desire to harm a politically unpopular group," id. at 447, citing *Moreno*, 413 U.S. at 534.

66 Id. at 448.

67 Id.

68 Id.

69 Id. (quoting Palmore v. Sidoti, 466 U.S. 429, 432–34 (1984)). Also, the Court dismissed objections to the facility being located both across the street from a junior high school (whose students might "harass" CLC residents) and on a "five hundred year flood plain." Since 30 students with mental retardation attended the nearby school, the Court found the city's fears concerning the school to be "vague [and] undifferentiated." The Court also found that concern as to a possible bi-millennial flood could not justify a meaningful distinction in treatment between a group home and, for instance, a permitted nursing home. Id. at 436–37 n.3 and 449.

70 Id. at 450.

Justice Stevens concurred, arguing that cases involving categorizations based on conditions such as mental retardation "do not fit well into sharply defined classifications."[71] Given the history of "unfair and often grotesque mistreatment" to which persons with mental retardation have been subjected, he was "convince[d]" that the city required a permit "because of the irrational fears of neighboring property owners, rather than for the protection of the mentally retarded persons who will reside in [CLC's] home."[72] Justice Marshall—for himself, Justice Brennan and Justice Blackmun—concurred in part and dissented in part, agreeing only with the majority's holding that persons with mental retardation cannot be "deemed presumptively unfit to live in a community" and that retardation "cannot be a proxy" for the deprivation of "rights and interests without regards to variations in individual ability." He stressed that persons with mental retardation had been subject to a "'lengthy and tragic' history of segregation and discrimination that can only be called grotesque."[73] Given the importance of the interest at stake and the history of discrimination, the equal protection clause, according to Justice Marshall, "requires us to do more than review the [ordinance's] distinctions . . . as if they appeared in a taxing statute or in economic or commercial legislation."[74]

6.6.1   Civil rights of ex-patients in the community—state-level decisions

A significant amount of litigation has arisen in contexts *corollary* to the subject's status as ex-patient, in attempts to "vindicat[e] the civil rights and basic rights of citizenship of individual mentally handicapped persons."[75] Courts have thus outlawed status discrimination against former patients and community mental health center residents in such areas as voting,[76] family law matters,[77] employment,[78] jury service,[79]

---

71 Id. at 452.

72 Id. at 455.

73 Id.

74 Id. at 464.

75 Perlin, *supra* note 3, at 38.

76 E.g., Doe v. Rowe, 156 F. Supp. 2d 35 (D. Me. 2001) (overturning Maine constitutional provision disenfranchising individuals under guardianship by reason of mental illness).

77 E.g., Baer v. Baer, 738 A.2d 923 (Md. App. 1999) (alimony); Matter of Johnson, 658 N.Y.S.2d 780 (Sup. 1997) (annulment); Saldarriaga v. Saldarriaga, 121 S.W.3d 493 (Tex. App. 2003) (divorce).

78 E.g., Donovan v. New Floridian Hotel, Inc., 676 F.2d 468 (11th Cir. 1982).

79 On a criminal defendant's right to object to the state's exclusion of jurors who had contact with individuals suffering from mental disorders, see State v. Strauss, 779 S.W.2d 591 (Mo. App.), *application for transfer denied* (1989) (no such right).

courtroom access,[80] sexual autonomy,[81] and access to welfare[82] and (SSI) Supplemental Security Income benefits.[83]

In the broadest related decision, the Arizona Supreme Court ruled that both the state and county were statutorily compelled to provide mental health care to chronically mentally ill community patients.[84] And a New Jersey appellate court ruled that state statutes that prohibited the placement in community residences of insanity acquittees violated federal housing law.[85]

6.7   *Olmstead v. L.C.*

In *Olmstead v. L.C.*,[86] the Supreme Court qualifiedly affirmed a decision by the Eleventh Circuit that had provided the first coherent answer to the question of the right of institutionalized persons with mental disabilities to community services under the Americans with Disabilities Act (ADA), and found that the ADA entitled plaintiffs—residents of Georgia State Hospital—to treatment in an "integrated community setting" as opposed to an "unnecessarily segregated" state hospital.[87]

Plaintiffs challenged their hospital placement on the grounds that the ADA entitled them to "the most integrated setting appropriate to [their] needs."[88] The district court granted summary judgment to plaintiffs, finding that the state's failure to place them in an "appropriate community-based program" so violated the ADA, and the state

---

80 E.g., Green v. North Arundel Hospital Association, Inc., 785 A.2d 361 (Md. Ct. App. 2001), *cert. denied*, 535 U.S. 1055 (2002).

81 E.g., Doe v. Bell, 754 N.Y.S.2d 846 (2003).

82 E.g., Duc Van Le v. Ibarra, 843 P.2d 15 (1992), *cert. denied*, 510 U.S. 1085 (1994).

83 E.g., *In re* Minus, No. 142-24-5334 (H.E.W. Soc. Sec. Admin., Bureau of Hearings and Appeals 1979), cited in Perlin, *supra* note 3, at 42 n.66.

84 Arnold v. Department of Health Servs., 775 P.2d 521 (Ariz. 1989), discussed in Jose M. Santiago, *The Evolution of Systems of Mental Health Care: The Arizona Experience*, 147 AM. J. PSYCHIATRY 148 (1990). On later aspects of the *Arnold* litigation, see Shijie Feng, *Madness and Mayhem: Reforming the Mental Health Care System in Arizona*, 54 ARIZ. L. REV. 541, 544 (2012), concluding that the "courtroom victory . . . did not translate into sustainable improvements in the mental health arena."

85 Matter of Commitment of J.W., 672 A.2d 199 (N.J. App. Div. 1996).

86 527 U.S. 581 (1999). See PERLIN AND CUCOLO, *supra* note 1, § 11-3.2.

87 138 F.3d 893, 897 (11th Cir. 1998), *aff'd in part, rev'd in part and vacated in part*, 527 U.S. 581 (1999).

88 Id. at 895.

appealed.[89] On appeal, the Eleventh Circuit affirmed the judgment that the state had discriminated against the plaintiffs, but also remanded for further findings related to the state's defense that the relief sought by plaintiffs would "fundamentally alter the nature of the service, program, or activity."[90]

On appeal, the Supreme Court qualifiedly affirmed. After setting out the provisions of the ADA that focused on the institutional segregation and isolation of persons with disabilities, and the discrimination faced by persons with disabilities (including "exclusion . . . and segregation"),[91] the Court reviewed the key Department of Justice regulations, including the "integration mandate" regulation, pointing out that the case, as presented, did *not* challenge their legitimacy.[92] It then set out its holding:

> Unjustified isolation, we hold, is properly regarded as discrimination based on disability. But we recognize, as well, the States' need to maintain a range of facilities for the care and treatment of persons with diverse mental disabilities, and the States' obligation to administer services with an even hand. Accordingly, we further hold that the Court of Appeals' remand instruction was unduly restrictive. In evaluating a State's fundamental-alteration defense, the District Court must consider, in view of the resources available to the State, not only the cost of providing community-based care to the litigants, but also the range of services the State provides others with mental disabilities, and the State's obligation to mete out those services equitably.[93]

The Court endorsed the Department of Justice's position that "undue institutionalization qualifies as discrimination 'by reason of . . . disability,'" and characterized the ADA as having "stepped up earlier measures to secure opportunities for people with developmental disabilities to enjoy the benefits of community living," stressing the law's comprehensiveness.[94] It focused on what it saw as Congressional judgment supporting the finding that "unjustified institutional isolation of persons with disabilities is a form of discrimination":

---

89 Id.

90 Id., citing 28 C.F.R. § 35.130(b)(7).

91 See 42 U.S.C. §§ 12101(a)(2), (3), (5).

92 *Olmstead*, 527 U.S. at 582.

93 Id. at 597.

94 Id. at 599, discussing 42 U.S.C. § 6010(2), as construed in Pennhurst State Sch. & Hosp. v. Halderman, 451 U.S. 1, 24 (1984). Other aspects of *Pennhurst* are discussed *supra* 6.4.

First, institutional placement of persons who can handle and benefit from community settings perpetuates unwarranted assumptions that persons so isolated are incapable or unworthy of participating in community life. Cf. Allen v. Wright, 468 U.S. 737, 755 . . . (1984) ("There can be no doubt that [stigmatizing injury often caused by racial discrimination] is one of the most serious consequences of discriminatory government action."); Los Angeles Dept. of Water and Power v. Manhart, 435 U.S. 702, 707, n.13 . . . (1978) ("'In forbidding employers to discriminate against individuals because of their sex, Congress intended to strike at the entire spectrum of disparate treatment of men and women resulting from sex stereotypes.'") . . . Second, confinement in an institution severely diminishes the everyday life activities of individuals, including family relations, social contacts, work options, economic independence, educational advancement, and cultural enrichment. . . . Dissimilar treatment correspondingly exists in this key respect: In order to receive needed medical services, persons with mental disabilities must, because of those disabilities, relinquish participation in community life they could enjoy given reasonable accommodations, while persons without mental disabilities can receive the medical services they need without similar sacrifice. . . .[95]

The ADA did *not* "condone[] termination of institutional settings for persons unable to handle or benefit from community settings"; states "generally may rely on the reasonable assessments of its own professionals" in determining whether an individual is eligible for community-based programs, and that there was no requirement that "community-based treatment be imposed on patients who do not desire it."[96]

The Court then turned to the questions of remedy and enforcement, concluding:

Sensibly construed, the fundamental-alteration component of the reasonable-modifications regulation would allow the State to show that, in the allocation of available resources, immediate relief for the plaintiffs would be inequitable, given the responsibility the State has undertaken for the care and treatment of a large and diverse population of persons with mental disabilities.[97]

---

95 *Olmstead*, 527 U.S. at 600.

96 Id. at 602. None of these issues, however, were present in the case before it: Georgia's professionals determined that community-based treatment would be appropriate for the plaintiffs, both of whom desired such treatment. Id. at 587.

97 Id. at 604.

In summary:

> Under Title II of the ADA, States are required to provide community-based treatment for persons with mental disabilities when the State's treatment professionals determine that such placement is appropriate, the affected persons do not oppose such treatment, and the placement can be reasonably accommodated, taking into account the resources available to the State and the needs of others with mental disabilities.[98]

Justice Kennedy concurred, urging "caution and circumspection" in the enforcement of the *Olmstead* case.[99] After stressing that persons with mental disabilities "have been subject to historic mistreatment, indifference, and hostility,"[100] he traced what he saw as the history of deinstitutionalization: that, while it has permitted "a substantial number of mentally disabled persons to receive needed treatment with greater freedom and dignity," it has "had its dark side" as well.[101] Here he quoted extensively from the writings of E. Fuller Torrey:

> For a substantial minority . . . deinstitutionalization has been a psychiatric Titanic. Their lives are virtually devoid of "dignity" or "integrity of body, mind, and spirit." "Self-determination" often means merely that the person has a choice of soup kitchens. The "least restrictive setting" frequently turns out to be a cardboard box, a jail cell, or a terror-filled existence plagued by both real and imaginary enemies.[102]

He feared that "[s]tates may be pressured into attempting compliance on the cheap, placing marginal patients into integrated settings devoid of the services and attention necessary for their condition and urged "caution and circumspection" and "great deference to the medical decisions of . . . responsible, treating physicians."[103] Justice Thomas dissented.[104]

---

98 Id. at 607. Justice Stevens concurred, stating that he would have preferred simply affirming the Eleventh Circuit's opinion, but joined in all of Justice Ginsburg's opinion, except for the remedy-enforcement portion. Id. at 607–08.

99 Id. at 610.

100 Id. at 608.

101 Id. at 609–10.

102 Id. (quoting E. FULLER TORREY, OUT OF THE SHADOWS 11 (1997)).

103 Id.

104 Id. at 625.

Olmstead was the first time that the Supreme Court had ruled on the applicability of the ADA to community-based treatment programs. It breathed important life into the Congressional findings on questions of institutional segregation, discrimination and exclusion, focusing on the way that "unjustified isolation . . . is properly regarded as discrimination based on disability."[105] It comprehended how the ADA had "stepped up" prior Congressional efforts in this area.[106] Finally, it underscored how institutional isolation "perpetuates unwarranted assumptions that persons so isolated are incapable or unworthy of participating in community life," and "severely diminishes the everyday life activities of institutionalized individuals."[107]

6.8   Other economic rights of persons with mental disabilities

The issue of whether ex-patients and workers in community facilities for persons with intellectual disabilities have a right to fair compensation under federal wage statutes for labor performed has been infrequently addressed. Two cases have held that such laws *are* applicable, both as to minimum wage[108] and as to overtime[109] provisions.

In one, the Eleventh Circuit affirmed a district court decision enjoining certain hotel owners from violating these provisions and awarding over 200 employees—all ex-mental patients, who were paid as little as $.17 per hour in such capacities as kitchen help, maids and waitresses— nearly $200,000 in back wages.[110] In the other case, the Sixth Circuit ruled that the Tenth Amendment did not insulate a private corporation that provided services to individuals with mental retardation in a community setting from similar minimum wage provisions.[111]

---

105 Id. at 582.

106 Id. at 583.

107 Id. The argument has been advanced that for people deprived of liberty in institutions, *Olmstead* has a constitutional dimension; unnecessary institutionalization violates the equal protection clause because it fails to meet contemporary strict scrutiny level of review, defined as "mature strict scrutiny," arguing that the rationale of *City of Cleburne*, see *supra* 6.6, no longer applies. See David Ferleger, *People with Disabilities, the Constitution and "Mature Strict Scrutiny,"* CIVIL RTS. INSIDER (March 2020); David Ferleger, *The Constitutional Right to Community Services: Olmstead and Equal Protection*, 40 J. & MED. 101 (2020).

108 See 29 U.S.C. § 206(a) and 29 U.S.C. § 215(a)(2).

109 See 29 U.S.C. § 207 and 29 U.S.C. § 215(a)(5).

110 Donovan v. New Floridian Hotel, Inc., 676 F.2d 468, 469–70, 476 (11th Cir. 1982).

111 Skills Development Servs. v. Donovan, 728 F.2d 294, 299 (6th Cir. 1984).

7 Between civil and criminal mental disability law

7.1 Introduction

The first six chapters of this book have dealt, primarily, with civil mental disability law. The following four will deal with criminal mental disability law. This chapter bridges the gap between those two major sub-areas[1] by discussing (1) the proliferation of mental health courts, and (2) the significance of international human rights law principles.

7.2 Mental health courts[2]

As discussed in Chapter 3, if there has been *any* constant in modern mental disability law, "it is the near-universal reality that counsel assigned to represent individuals at involuntary civil commitment cases is likely to be ineffective,"[3] a reality known since the modern era of mental disability law began.[4] Early empirical research showed that most lawyers prepared much less for civil commitment cases than for

---

1 On the complexity of multiple systems of disability law, see Michael L. Perlin and Mehgan Gallagher, *"Temptation's Page Flies out the Door": Navigating Complex Systems of Disability and the Law from a Therapeutic Jurisprudence Perspective*, 25 Buffalo Hum. Rts. L. Rev. 1 (2018–19) (discussing differences between social and medical models of disability).

2 Much of this section is adapted from Michael L. Perlin, *"Who Will Judge the Many When the Game is Through?": Considering the Profound Differences between Mental Health Courts and "Traditional" Involuntary Civil Commitment Courts*, 41 Seattle U. L. Rev. 937 (2018).

3 See, e.g., Michael L. Perlin, *"I Might Need a Good Lawyer, Could Be Your Funeral, My Trial": Global Perspective on the Right to Counsel in Civil Commitment Cases*, 28 Wash. U. J. L. & Pol'y 241, 241 (2008).

4 See, e.g., George E. Dix, *Acute Psychiatric Hospitalization of the Mentally Ill in the Metropolis: An Empirical Study*, [1968] Wash. U. L. Rev 485, 540 (discussed *supra* 3.2.1, n.9); *In re* Judicial Commitment of C.P.K., 516 So. 2d 1323, 1325 (La. Ct. App. 1987) (reversing commitment order where trial court failed to comply with statute expressing explicit preference for representation by state Mental Health Advocacy Service, rejecting as "untenable" argument that trial court should be excused "since it did not know . . . whether the Service really existed").

other cases, many did not speak to clients before the hearing, and they "rarely took an adversary role to obtain release of their clients whom psychiatrists had recommended for commitment."[5] It was clear that only in those jurisdictions that had dedicated counsel programs was there any coherent body of reported civil commitment case law.[6] Such offices represent a small percentage of those subject to commitment.[7] Involuntary civil commitment trials remain the "disfavored stepchild in the large family of concerns that must be addressed by the justice system."[8]

But consider the parallel universe of mental health courts (MHCs).[9] One of the most important contemporaneous developments in the way that *criminal defendants* with mental disabilities are treated in the criminal process has been the creation and expansion of MHCs, a "problem-solving court."[10] The creation of these courts is particularly critical as we—tardily—begin to come to grips with the ways that persons with mental disabilities are disproportionately arrested for

---

5 Virginia Aldigé Hiday, *Are Lawyers Enemies of Psychiatrists? A Survey of Civil Commitment Counsel and Judges*, 140 Am. J. Psychiatry 323, 326 (1983).

6 See, e.g., Michael L. Perlin, *"You Have Discussed Lepers and Crooks": Sanism in Clinical Teaching*, 9 Clinical L. Rev. 683, 708–09 (2003), discussed *supra* 1.2, n.14.

7 See Michael L. Perlin and Heather Ellis Cucolo, Mental Disability Law: Civil and Criminal (3d ed. 2016) (2019 update), §§ 6-4.2 to 6-4.3. See also, Henry A. Dlugacz and Christopher Wimmer, *The Ethics of Representing Clients with Limited Competency in Guardianship Proceedings*, 4 St. Louis U. J. Health L. & Pol'y 331, 353–54 (2011):

> There are also institutional pressures: The attorney who depends on the goodwill of others in the system (e.g., judges, state attorneys, or prosecutors) may pull his punches, even unwittingly, in order to retain credibility for future interactions (which he would put to use for his future clients). Judges want cases resolved.

8 Paul S. Appelbaum, *Civil Commitment from a Systems Perspective*, 16 Law & Hum. Behav. 61, 66 (1992), as quoted in Sara Gordon, *The Danger Zone: How the Dangerousness Standard in Civil Commitment Proceedings Harms People with Serious Mental Illness*, 66 Case W. Res. L. Rev. 657, 678 (2016).

9 See generally Michael L. Perlin, *"The Judge, He Cast His Robe Aside": Mental Health Courts, Dignity and Due Process*, 3 Mental Health L. & Pol'y J. 1 (2013) (Perlin, *Cast His Robe*); Michael L. Perlin, *"There Are No Trials inside the Gates of Eden": Mental Health Courts, the Convention on the Rights of Persons with Disabilities, Dignity, and the Promise of Therapeutic Jurisprudence*, in Coercive Care: Law and Policy 193 (Bernadette McSherry and Ian Freckelton eds., 2013) (Perlin, *Gates of Eden*).

10 See, e.g., Greg Berman and John Feinblatt, *Problem-Solving Courts: A Brief Primer*, 23 Law & Pol'y, 125, 127 (2001); Greg Berman and Aubrey Fox, *The Future of Problem-Solving Justice: An International Perspective*, 10 U. Md. L.J. Race Relig. Gender & Class 1, 3 (2010); see also Ursula Castellano, *The Politics of Benchcraft: The Role of Judges in Mental Health Courts*, 42 Law & Soc. Inquiry 398, 398 (2017).

"nuisance crimes."[11] There is a wide range of dispositional alternatives available to judges in these cases[12] and an even wider range of judicial attitudes.[13] And the entire concept of MHCs is certainly not without controversy.[14]

There is no question, however, that MHCs offer a radically new approach to the problems at hand. They become even more significant because of their articulated focus on dignity,[15] as well as their embrace of TJ, their focus on procedural justice, and their use of the principles of restorative justice.[16]

---

11 See, e.g., Michael L. Perlin and Alison J. Lynch, *"Had to Be Held Down by Big Police": A Therapeutic Jurisprudence Perspective on Interactions between Police and Persons with Mental Disabilities*, 43 FORDHAM URB. L.J. 685, 687–89 (2016); Alison J. Lynch and Michael L. Perlin, *"Life's Hurried Tangled Road": A Therapeutic Jurisprudence Analysis of Why Dedicated Counsel Must Be Assigned to Represent Persons with Mental Disabilities in Community Settings*, 35 BEHAV. SCI. & L. 353 (2017). Michael L. Perlin and Alison J. Lynch, *"To Wander off in Shame": Deconstructing the Shaming and Shameful Arrest Policies of Urban Police Departments in Their Treatment of Persons with Mental Disabilities*, in SYSTEMIC HUMILIATION IN AMERICA: FINDING DIGNITY WITHIN SYSTEMS OF DEGRADATION 175 (Prof. Daniel Rothbart ed., 2018) (Perlin and Lynch, *To Wander Off in Shame*). On the lack of continuity of care in such cases, see Naomi Weinstein and Michael L. Perlin, *"Who's Pretending to Care for Him?": How the Endless Jail-to-Hospital-to-Street-Repeat Cycle Deprives Persons with Mental Disabilities the Right to Continuity of Care*, 8 WAKE FOREST J.L. & POL'Y 455 (2018).

12 See, e.g., Henry J. Steadman, Allison D. Redlich, Patricia Griffin, John Petrila and John Monahan, *From Referral to Disposition: Case Processing in Seven Mental Health Courts*, 23 BEHAV. SCI. LAW 215, 220–21 (2005).

13 See, e.g., Michael S. King, *Should Problem-Solving Courts Be Solution-Focused Courts?* 80 REV. JUR. U.P.R. 1005, 1008 (2011).

14 See, e.g., Tammy Seltzer, *A Misguided Attempt to Address the Criminal Justice System's Unfair Treatment of People with Mental Illness*, 11 PSYCHOL. PUB. POL'Y & L. 570, 576 (2005). For a sobering empirical critique of such courts in one jurisdiction, see E. Lea Johnston and Conor Flynn, *Mental Health Courts and Sentencing Disparities*, 62 VILL. L. REV. 685 (2017).

15 See Ginger Lerner-Wren, *Mental Health Courts: Serving Justice and Promoting Recovery*, 19 ANNALS HEALTH L. 577, 593 (2010) (explaining dignity in the context of MHCs).

16 See MICHAEL L. PERLIN, A PRESCRIPTION FOR DIGNITY: RETHINKING CRIMINAL JUSTICE AND MENTAL DISABILITY LAW 88–96 (2013) (A PRESCRIPTION FOR DIGNITY) (discussing restorative justice); Jessica Burns, *A Restorative Justice Model for Mental Health Courts*, 23 S. CAL. REV. L. & SOC. JUST. 427, 447–54 (2014); Thomas L. Hafemeister, Sharon G. Garner and Veronica E. Bath, *Forging Links and Renewing Ties: Applying the Principles of Restorative and Procedural Justice to Better Respond to Criminal Offenders with a Mental Disorder*, 60 BUFF. L. REV. 147, 201–02 (2012) (on procedural justice); Henry J. Steadman, Susan Davidson and Collie Brown, *Law and Psychiatry: Mental Health Courts: Their Promise and Unanswered Questions*, 52 PSYCHIATRIC SERVICES 457, 457–58 (2001) (discussing TJ in this context). On the relationship between these three approaches, see A PRESCRIPTION FOR DIGNITY, *supra* at 96–98.

MHCs are set up differently in different jurisdictions. There are now over 375 such courts in operation in the United States,[17] some dealing solely with misdemeanors,[18] some dealing solely with nonviolent offenders[19] and some dealing with no such restrictions.[20]

7.2.1 Structure of MHCs

Although there is no single prototype, virtually all MHCs include a special docket handled by a particular judge, with the primary goal of diverting defendants from the criminal justice system and into treatment.[21] MHCs are premised on team approaches;[22] representatives from justice and treatment agencies assist the judge in screening offenders to determine whether they would present a risk of violence if released to the community, devising appropriate treatment plans, and supervising and monitoring the individual's performance in treatment.[23]

---

17 Nat'l Drug Ct. Resource Ctr., *Drug Treatment Courts by State*, accessed October 6, 2020 at https://perma.cc/FP6Z-RBMK, cited in Donald M. Linhorst and P. Ann Dirks-Linhorst, *Mental Health Courts: Development, Outcomes, and Future Challenges*, 54 JUDGES' J. 22, 22 (2015).

18 See, e.g., Ursula Castellano, *Courting Compliance: Case Managers as "Double Agents" in the Mental Health Court*, 36 LAW & SOC. INQUIRY 484, 490 (2011).

19 See, e.g., Julie Grachek, *The Insanity Defense in the Twenty-First Century: How Recent United States Supreme Court Case Law Can Improve the System*, 81 IND. L.J. 1479, 1495 (2006).

20 See, e.g., E. Leah Johnston, *Theorizing Mental Health Courts*, 89 WASH. U. L. REV. 519, 521 (2012). See generally Carol Fisler, *Building Trust and Managing Risk: A Look at a Felony Mental Health Court*, 11 PSYCHOL. PUB. POL'Y & L. 587 (2005) (on expansion of these courts to include felony prosecutions).

21 Roger A. Boothroyd, Norman G. Poythress, Annette McGaha and John Petrila, *The Broward Mental Health Court: Process, Outcomes, and Service Utilization*, 26 INT'L J.L. & PSYCHIATRY 55, 55 (2003). At least one evaluation has concluded "most . . . defendants have been 'nuisance' offenders who have a high incidence of drug co-morbidity, treatment plan noncompliance, and recidivism. . . . Their high recidivism rate and the problem of severe jail overcrowding made the mental health court experiment especially attractive to some county policy makers." Gerald Nora, *Prosecutor as "Nurse Ratched"? Misusing Criminal Justice as Alternative Medicine*, 22 CRIM. JUST. 18, 22 (2007).

22 See, e.g., Arthur J. Lurigio and Jessica Snowden, *Putting Therapeutic Jurisprudence into Practice: The Growth, Operations, and Effectiveness of Mental Health Court*, 30 JUST. SYS. J. 196, 210–11 (2009).

23 Bruce J. Winick, *Outpatient Commitment: A Therapeutic Jurisprudence Analysis*, 9 PSYCHOL. PUB. POL'Y & L. 107, 125–26 (2003). On the role of jail as a potential sanction in cases of noncompliant defendants, see Allison Redlich, Henry J. Steadman, John Monahan, Pamela Clark Robbins and John Petrila, *Patterns and Practice in Mental Health Courts: A National Survey*, 30 LAW & HUM. BEHAV. 347, 355–56 (2006).

The MHC judge functions as part of a mental health team that assesses the individual's treatment needs,[24] deciding whether there can be safe release to the community.[25] The team formulates a treatment plan; a court-employed case manager and court monitor track the individual's participation in the treatment program and submit periodic reports to the judge concerning the individual's progress. Participants report back periodically so the judge can monitor treatment compliance, and additional status review hearings are held on an as-needed basis.[26]

To best achieve these objectives,[27] the judge needs to develop enhanced interpersonal skills and awareness of a variety of psychological techniques to persuade the individual to accept treatment and motivate him or her to participate effectively in it,[28] and must be able to build trust and manage risk.[29] These skills include the ability to convey empathy and respect, communicate effectively with the individual, listen to what the individual has to say (thereby fulfilling the individual's need for voice and validation), earn the individual's trust and confidence, and engage in motivational interviewing and various other techniques designed to encourage the individual to accept treatment

---

24 See Shauhin Talesh, *Mental Health Court Judges as Dynamic Risk Managers: A New Conceptualization of the Role of Judges*, 57 DEPAUL L. REV. 93, 96 (2007).

> [W]ith the assistance of team members—including the public defender, prosecutor, and behavioral and mental health specialists—the judge performs the following three tasks: (1) he conducts a risk assessment in which he evaluates the defendant's potential to harm himself and the public; (2) he evaluates and implements a treatment plan designed to manage and reallocate the defendant's risk; and (3) he monitors the risk over a period of time, often requiring frequent return visits by the defendant. (Id.)

25 On the often-conflicting roles of case managers in MHCs, see Castellano, *supra* note 18, at 490–91. On how caseworkers, in other contexts, transform "traditional courtroom justice," see URSULA CASTELLANO, OUTSOURCING JUSTICE: THE ROLE OF NONPROFIT CASEWORKERS IN PRETRIAL RELEASE PROGRAMS 9 (2011).

26 Susan Stefan and Bruce J. Winick, *A Dialogue on Mental Health Courts*, 11 PSYCHOL. PUB. POL'Y & L. 507, 520–21 (2005). On how the adoption of a consumer-participation model in MHCs can improve mental health court participants' capacity for voluntary participation, see McDaniel M. Kelly, *Rehabilitation through Empowerment: Adopting the Consumer-Participation Model for Treatment Planning in Mental Health Courts*, 66 CASE W. RES. L. REV. 581, 584 (2015).

27 Castellano, *supra* note 10, at 400.

28 Winick, *supra* note 23, at 126 (citing Carrie Petrucci, *Respect as a Component in the Judge–Defendant Interaction in a Specialized Domestic Violence Court that Utilizes Therapeutic Jurisprudence*, 38 CRIM. L. BULL. 263 (2002)).

29 Fisler, *supra* note 20, at 587. On the significance of trust in the context of youth and family courts, see generally Karni Perlman, *It Takes Two for TJ: Correlation between Bench and Bar Attitudes towards Therapeutic Jurisprudence—An Israeli Perspective*, 33 T. JEFFERSON L. REV. 351 (2008).

and comply with it.[30] Such judges must be culturally competent and able to "unpack" the testimony of persons not from the mainstream culture.[31] These courts provide "nuanced" approaches[32] and may signal a "fundamental shift" in the criminal justice system.[33]

Because MHCs can divert persons with mental disabilities out of the criminal justice system (where they are likely to be treated poorly), MHCs make it less likely that the person with mental disabilities will suffer at the hands of others because of that status.[34] Sanist biases may be reduced by the establishment of MHCs, staffed by a "sensitive" judiciary.[35] A study of Judge Ginger Lerner-Wren's MHC concluded that participants in that court self-reported coercion levels lower than almost any comparable measure of perceived coercion previously reported in the literature.[36] The actual, real-life experiences of the

---

30 For a thoughtful critique of MHCs, see Johnston, *supra* note 20. On the legislature's role in ensuring the success of such courts, see Sheila Moheb, *Jamming the Revolving Door: Legislative Setbacks for Mental Health Court Systems in Virginia*, 14 RICH. J.L. & PUB. INT. 29, 38–41 (2010).

31 See Michael L. Perlin and Naomi M. Weinstein, *"Said I, 'But You Have No Choice'": Why a Lawyer Must Ethically Honor a Client's Decision about Mental Health Treatment even if It Is Not What S/he Would Have Chosen*, 15 CARDOZO PUBLIC L., POL'Y & ETHICS J. 73, 100 (2016–17) ("Cultural competence is a key component in providing effective representation and resolving any ethical dilemmas . . . in mental disability law"); see also, e.g., Ruby Dhand, *Creating a Cultural Analysis Tool for the Implementation of Ontario's Civil Mental Health Laws*, 45 INT'L J.L. & PSYCHIATRY 25, 32 (2016) (recommending cultural and other intersectional factors be probed during the commitment hearing processes). See generally Michael L. Perlin and Valerie R. McClain, *"Where Souls Are Forgotten": Cultural Competencies, Forensic Evaluations and International Human Rights*, 15 PSYCHOL. PUB. POL'Y & L. 257 (2009); Casey Schutte, *Mandating Cultural Competence Training for Dependency Attorneys*, 52 FAM. CT. REV. 564 (2014).

32 Patricia C. McManus, *A Therapeutic Jurisprudential Approach to Guardianship of Persons with Mild Cognitive Impairment*, 36 SETON HALL L. REV. 591, 598 (2006).

33 Harvard Law Review Ass'n, *Mental Health Courts and the Trend toward a Rehabilitative Justice System*, 121 HARV. L. REV. 1168, 1176–77 (2008).

34 Terry Carney, David Tait, Duncan Chappell and Fleur Beaupert, *Mental Health Tribunals: "TJ" Implications of Weighing Fairness, Freedom, Protection and Treatment*, 17 J. JUD. ADMIN. 46, 54 (2007); Risdon Slate, *From the Jailhouse to Capitol Hill: Impacting Mental Health Court Legislation and Defining What Constitutes a Mental Health Court*, 49 CRIME & DELINQ. 6, 6 (2003).

35 Sana Loue, *The Involuntary Civil Commitment of Mentally Ill Persons in the United States and Romania*, 23 J. LEGAL MED. 211, 235 n.120 (2002). On sanism in the context of MHCs, see Perlin, *Gates of Eden, supra* note 9, at 204–15, and Perlin, *Cast His Robe, supra* note 9, at 31–32. See *supra* 2.1.

36 Norman G. Poythress, John Petrila, Annette McGaha and Roger Boothroyd, *Perceived Coercion and Procedural Justice in the Broward Mental Health Court*, 25 INT'L J.L. & PSYCHIATRY 517, 529 (2002); see also David Tait, *The Ritual Environment of the Mental Health Tribunal Hearing: Inquiries and Reflections*, 10 PSYCHIATRY PSYCHOL. & L. 91, 94–95 (2003). Successful judges in MHCs will typically demonstrate a sort of "charismatic authority," "an essential element of judges'

litigants in cases before Judge Lerner-Wren demonstrate that an MHC *can* be a non-coercive, dignified experience that provides procedural justice and TJ to those before it.[37] In such courts, defendants participate more actively and directly than in typical criminal courts, often speaking directly with the judge instead of sitting silently while their defense attorney speaks for them.[38] Treatment courts that provide the most time and attention from the presiding judge have been shown to be more successful.[39]

Professor Ursula Castellano has thoughtfully and insightfully argued that, for MHCs to be successful, the presiding judge need practice "the politics of benchcraft,"[40] rising "to the larger challenges embedded in the alternative courtroom."[41] Such judges "selectively apply, blend and transform" elements from the treatment and legal spheres to adjudicate cases therapeutically and to "generate more effective solutions."[42]

Studies of the MHCs conclude that such courts actually often work as they are intended to.[43] Participants in Judge Lerner-Wren's MHC had

---

ability to achieve the complex tasks of building trust and managing risk among chronic reoffenders." Castellano, *supra* note 10, at 402; see also Fisler, *supra* note 20 (discussing backgrounds of the first problem-solving court judges in New York). See generally Talesh, *supra* note 24.

37 See Judith Kaye, *Lecture*, 81 St. John's L. Rev. 743, 748 (2007) (describing MHCs as follows: "mental health courts, which . . . divert defendants from jail to treatment, reconnect them, where possible, with family and friends who care whether they live or die, . . . [and] restore their greatest loss—their sense of human dignity") (author former Chief Judge of New York Court of Appeals).

38 See Ginger Lerner-Wren, *Broward's Mental Health Court: An Innovative Approach to the Mentally Disabled in the Criminal Justice System*, in Future Trends in State Courts 1999–2000 (National Center for State Courts 2000); see also Boothroyd et al., *supra* note 21, at 57; Castellano, *supra* note 10, at 401 ("[A] hallmark feature . . . is that judges speak directly to offenders with empathy and enthusiasm"). Of course, judges' work in these courts contrasts sharply with the sort of "assembly-line justice" that they were pressured to administer when they worked in traditional courts. Id. See generally Candace McCoy, *The Politics of Problem-Solving: An Overview of the Origins and Developments of Therapeutic Courts*, 40 Am. Crim. L. Rev. 1513 (2003).

39 Emily Buss, *Developmental Jurisprudence*, 88 Temp. L. Rev. 741, 750 (2016) (citing Shelli B. Rossman and Janine M. Zweig, *What Have We Learned from the Multi-Site Adult Drug Court Evaluation? Implications for Policy, Practice, and Future Research*, in 4 The Multi-Site Adult Drug Court Evaluation: The Impact of Drug Courts 251, 259–60 (Shelli B. Rossman et al. eds., 2013)).

40 Castellano, *supra* note 10, at 403. She defines this, in part, as "learning to finesse elements of treatment and law into new professional practices." Id.

41 Id. at 417.

42 Id. Professor Castellano, in her study of four separate MHCs, found that the judges she observed were "deeply involved in investigating problems, collecting personal client information, and actively consulting with treatment professionals and law enforcement offices." Id. at 405.

43 These findings are not universal. I am concerned about the operationalization of the courts in

significantly lower arrest rates after enrollment in treatment programs than before enrollment and lower post-enrollment arrest rates than comparison groups; in fact, MHCs evaluated in a multi-site study[44] "were more successful at reducing recidivism—recidivism rates of 25% versus 10%–15%"—than were drug courts.[45] Research also suggests that mental health court participation increases access to and utilization of mental health care,[46] reduces the use of crisis or high-intensity services and reduces substance use.[47] A recent relevant study—authored by a sitting trial judge—has thus concluded that "[p]roblem-solving treatment courts are the best way to supervise criminal defendants in the community who present with high needs and a high risk to re-offend absent intervention."[48]

---

some jurisdictions. See Johnston and Flynn, *supra* note 14, at 693 (empirical study of MHCs in Erie County, PA, concluding that anticipated treatment court sentences—for all grades of offense—typically exceed county court sentences by more than a year).

44 Greg Goodale, Lisa Callahan and Henry J. Steadman, *What Can We Say about Mental Health Courts Today?* 64 PSYCHIATRIC SERVICES 298, 299 (2013) (citing, inter alia, Henry J. Steadman, Allison Redlich, Lisa Callahan, Pamela Clark Robbins and Roumen Vesselinov, *Effect of Mental Health Courts on Arrests and Jail Days: A Multisite Study*, 68 ARCHIVES GEN. PSYCHIATRY 167, 167–72 (2011)).

45 Id. See PERLIN AND CUCOLO, *supra* note 7, § 1-2.2.3 n.194 (citing, inter alia, Allison Redlich and Woojae Han, *Examining the Links between Therapeutic Jurisprudence and Mental Health Court Completion*, 38 LAW & HUM. BEHAV. 109, 109 (2014) (increased levels of procedural justice and perceived voluntariness led to decreased rates of new arrests in mental health court populations)); Evan Lowder, Sarah Desmarais and Daniel J. Baucom, *Recidivism Following Mental Health Court Exit: Between and Within-Group Comparisons*, 40 LAW & HUM. BEHAV. 118, 118 (2016) (MHCs are particularly effective for high-risk participants; time spent in such courts has positive effects on recidivism). These statistics are constant when *juvenile* MHCs are studied. See Donna M.L. Heretick and Joseph A. Russell, *The Impact of Juvenile Mental Health Court on Recidivism among Youth*, 3 J. JUV. JUST. 1 (2013).

46 See, e.g., Boothroyd et al., *supra* note 21, at 68; Andrea M. Odegaard, *Therapeutic Jurisprudence: The Impact of Mental Health Courts on the Criminal Justice System*, 83 N.D. L. REV. 225, 231 (2007). See generally Woojae Han and Allison Redlich, *The Impact of Community Treatment on Recidivism among Mental Health Court Participants*, 67 PSYCHIATRIC SERVICES 384 (2016) (noting that data showed increases in the receipt of community treatment among MHC participants and decreases in recidivism).

47 Kellie Canada, John Halloran and Clark M. Peters, *The Emergence of Mental Health Courts in the United States: Intersecting Innovation between Psychiatric Care and the Law*, 5 MENTAL HEALTH L. & POL'Y J. 31, 57 (2016) (citing, inter alia, Kelly Frailing, *How Mental Health Courts Function: Outcomes and Observations*, 33 INT'L J.L. & PSYCHIATRY 207, 212 (2010)).

48 Kerry Meyer, *Hennepin County Criminal Mental Health Court: Experiences in a Large Metropolitan Mental Health Court*, 42 MITCHELL HAMLINE L. REV. 485, 521 (2016). On how MHCs in some states can vary radically from county to county, see Monte Staton and Arthur Lurigio, *Mental Health Courts in Illinois: Comparing and Contrasting Program Models, Sanction Applications, Information Sharing, and Professional Roles*, 79 FED. PROB. 21 (2015). The potential power of coercion remains a dormant issue. See, e.g., Stacey M. Faraci, *Slip Slidin' Away?*

7.2.2   From the perspective of procedural justice

Consider the context of procedural justice[49] that asserts that "people's evaluations of the resolution of a dispute (including matters resolved by the judicial system) are influenced more by their perception of the fairness of the process employed than by their belief regarding whether the 'right' outcome was reached."[50] The question to be asked is: whether the criminal justice system treats defendants fairly and respectfully regardless of the substantive outcome reached?[51]

When those affected by decisionmaking processes perceive the process to be just, "they are much more likely to accept the outcomes of the process, even when the outcomes are adverse."[52] Professor Tom Tyler's groundbreaking research teaches that individuals with mental disabilities, like all other citizens, are affected by such process values as participation, dignity and trust, and that experiencing arbitrariness in procedure leads to "social malaise and decreases people's willingness to be integrated into the polity, accepting its authorities and following its rules."[53]

Will Our Nation's Mental Health Court Experiment Diminish the Rights of the Mentally Ill? 22 QUINNIPIAC L. REV. 811, 853 (2004) (mental health court defendants "endure much more liberty restrictions and privacy intrusions"; labeling the "sentence 'treatment,' rather than 'punishment,'" allows the court to exert more coercion over the participant than would otherwise be available).

49 The following section is partially adapted from PERLIN, A PRESCRIPTION FOR DIGNITY, *supra* note 16, ch. 6.

50 Hafemeister, Garner and Bath, *supra* note 16, at 200 (referencing, in part, Tom R. Tyler, *Procedural Justice and the Courts*, 44 CT. REV. 26, 26 (2007)); see also Larry Heuer, *What's Just about the Criminal Justice System? A Psychological Perspective*, 13 J.L. & POL'Y 209, 213 (2005) ("[P]rocedural fairness concerns, rather than outcomes, are the best predictors of people's trust and confidence in the courts").

51 Erin A. Conway, *Ineffective Assistance of Counsel: How Illinois Has Used the "Prejudice" Prong of* Strickland *to Lower the Floor on Performance When Defendants Plead Guilty*, 105 NW. U. L. REV. 1707, 1732 (2011).

52 Hafemeister, Garner and Bath, *supra* note 16, at 200 (quoting, in part, Michael M. O'Hear, *Explaining Sentences*, 36 FLA. ST. U. L. REV. 459, 478 (2009)). This applies as well to psychiatric hospital decisionmaking. See Bruce J. Winick, *A Therapeutic Jurisprudence Approach to Dealing with Coercion in the Mental Health System*, 15 PSYCHIATRY PSYCHOL. & L. 25, 39 (2008) (discussing the importance of the "degree of respect" shown to patients by treatment providers).

53 Tom Tyler, *The Psychological Consequences of Judicial Procedures: Implications for Civil Commitment Hearings*, 46 S.M.U. L. REV. 433, 443 (1992) (as discussed in Michael L. Perlin and Deborah A. Dorfman, *"Is It More Than Dodging Lions and Wastin' Time?": Adequacy of Counsel, Questions of Competence, and the Judicial Process in Individual Right to Refuse Treatment Cases*, 2 PSYCHOLOGY, PUB. POL'Y & L. 114, 119 (1996); see also Vidis Donnelly, Aideen Lynch, Damian Mohan and Harry G. Kennedy, *Working Alliances, Interpersonal Trust and Perceived Coercion in Mental Health Review Hearings*, 5 INT'L J. MENTAL HEALTH 29, 29 (2011) (hearings lacking in

Procedural justice differences between traditional civil commitment courts—dark, "greased runways" with disinterested judges and lawyers[54]—and modern MHCs—dignity-enforcing and coercion-avoiding—could not be starker.[55] Brian McKenna and his colleagues note "the clinical and ethical importance of procedural justice principles in the enactment of civil commitment," stressing that "these principles involve allowing patients to have their say, listening to them seriously, providing patients with information and treating them with concern, fairness and respect."[56] Over 40 years ago, John Ensminger and Thomas Liguori wrote that the civil commitment process had great therapeutic potential, stressing that such hearings optimally give patients an opportunity to present and hear evidence in a meaningful court procedure.[57] The traditional civil commitment court does not give patients the opportunities highlighted by McKenna and his colleagues or by Ensminger and Liguori; however, the well-functioning mental health court does.[58]

---

procedural justice worsened working alliances between patients and physicians and diminished interpersonal trust) (cases heard in Ireland); Bruce J. Winick, *Therapeutic Jurisprudence and the Civil Commitment Hearing*, 10 J. CONTEMP. LEGAL ISSUES 37, 44 (1999) (increasing a patient's "sense of participation, dignity, and trust" during commitment proceedings will "increase his or her acceptance of the outcome of the hearing").

54 Although state laws promise dignity in such proceedings, see e.g., COLO. REV. STAT. ANN. § 27-65-101 (West 2016) as discussed in People v. *In Interest of* Vivekanathan, 338 P.3d 1017, 1025 (Colo. Ct. App. 2013), this promise is often not met.

55 See Michael L. Perlin, *Therapeutic Jurisprudence in Action*, INT'L SOC'Y FOR THERAPEUTIC JURIS. (Sept. 5, 2015), accessed October 6, 2020 at https://mainstreamtj.wordpress.com/2015/09/05/therapeutic-jurisprudence-in-action/ (discussing my experiences observing top-flight problem-solving courts in New Zealand and concluding that "I have never, in such a short period of time, had the honor to observe such examples of therapeutic jurisprudence in action"), topic discussed further in Michael L. Perlin and Alison J. Lynch, *"Mr. Bad Example": Why Lawyers Need to Embrace Therapeutic Jurisprudence to Root out Sanism in the Representation of Persons with Mental Disabilities*, 16 WYO. L. REV. 299, 314–15 (2016).

56 Brian G. McKenna, Alexander I.F. Simpson and John H. Coverdale, *What Is the Role of Procedural Justice in Civil Commitment?* 34 AUSTL. & N.Z. J. PSYCHIATRY 671, 675 (2000). Judges rarely listen to patients in traditional civil commitment courts. For a rare judicial exception, see Rennie v. Klein, 476 F. Supp. 1294, 1306 (D.N.J. 1979) (citing Theodore Van Putten and R.A. May, *Subjective Response as a Predictor of Outcome in Pharmacotherapy*, 35 ARCHIVES GEN. PSYCHIATRY 477, 480 (1978) ("Schizophrenics have been asked every question except, 'How does the medication agree with you?' Their response is worth listening to"), *modified*, 653 F.2d 836 (3d Cir. 1983), *vacated and remanded*, 458 U.S. 1119 (1982). See generally *supra* 5.2.3.1.1.

57 John J. Ensminger and Thomas D. Liguori, *The Therapeutic Significance of the Civil Commitment Hearing: An Unexplored Potential*, 6 J. PSYCHIATRY & L. 5 (1978), reprinted in THERAPEUTIC JURISPRUDENCE: THE LAW AS A THERAPEUTIC AGENT 245, 251–58 (David Wexler ed., 1990).

58 On the significance of dignity values in civil commitment hearings, see Deborah A. Dorfman, *Effectively Implementing Title I of the Americans with Disabilities Act for Mentally Disabled*

7.2.3   From the perspective of therapeutic jurisprudence

Consider next the context of TJ.[59] TJ presents a model for assessing the impact of case law and legislation, recognizing that, as a therapeutic agent, the law can have therapeutic or anti-therapeutic consequences. "The ultimate aim of therapeutic jurisprudence is to determine whether legal rules, procedures, and lawyer roles can or should be reshaped to enhance their therapeutic potential while not subordinating due process principles."[60]

Consider first how civil commitment courts are the antithesis of TJ, in stark contrast to the TJ-modeling MHCs of the sort presided over by Judge Wren (and others, e.g., Judge Matthew D'Emic in Brooklyn[61] and Judge Michael Finkle in Seattle[62]). MHCs—when structured properly and when chaired by a judge who "buys into" the TJ model—are perfect exemplars of the practical utility of TJ.[63] As one commentator has noted, TJ "has expanded the role of courts to include a rehabilitative process."[64]

The promotion and creation of such courts are consistent with TJ's aims and aspirations,[65] especially where litigants are given the "voice"

Persons: A Therapeutic Jurisprudence Analysis, 8 J.L. & HEALTH 105, 121 (1994), and Tyler, *supra* note 53, at 444–45. It is more likely that those in a well-functioning juvenile mental health court will be consulted about decisions made about them. See Voula Marinos, *Methodologies for the Study of TJ Processes or Procedural Justice within the Operation of TJ-Related Courts: A Conversation* (Oct. 15, 2016) (unpublished manuscript presented at the annual Therapeutic Jurisprudence Workshop at Osgoode Hall Law Sch., York University, Toronto).

59 See generally *supra* 2.5.

60 Perlin, *Cast His Robe, supra* note 9, at 7–8 (footnotes omitted).

61 See generally Matthew J. D'Emic, *Mental Health Courts: Bridging Two Worlds*, 31 TOURO L. REV. 369 (2015) (hereinafter D'Emic, *Bridging*); Matthew J. D'Emic, *The Promise of Mental Health Courts*, 22 CRIM. JUST 24 (2007).

62 See generally Anne Harper and Michael J. Finkle, *Mental Health Courts, Judicial Leadership and Effective Court Intervention*, 51 JUDGES' J. 4 (2012).

63 See generally Kate Diesfeld and Brian McKenna, *The Therapeutic Intent of the New Zealand Mental Health Review Tribunal*, 13 PSYCHIATRY PSYCHOL. & L. 100 (2006); Kate Diesfeld and Brian McKenna, *The Unintended Impact of the Therapeutic Intentions of the New Zealand Mental Health Review Tribunal? Therapeutic Jurisprudence Perspectives*, 14 J.L. & MED. 566 (2007); Jelena Popovic, *Court Process and Therapeutic Jurisprudence: Have We Thrown the Baby out with the Bathwater?* 1 ELAW J. 60 (2006) (Australia).

64 Odegaard, *supra* note 46, at 258.

65 See Leroy Kondo, *Advocacy of the Establishment of Mental Health Specialty Courts in the Provision of Therapeutic Justice for Mentally Ill Offenders*, 24 SEATTLE U. L. REV. 373, 446–47 (2000).

that TJ demands.[66] They are grounded[67] and rooted[68] in TJ; they reflect TJ "theory in practice";[69] and they acknowledge that a defendant's appearance in such a court comes at a "painful and crucial point in life."[70]

Next, consider the need for dignity in the legal process in cases involving persons with mental disabilities.[71] One of the central principles of TJ is a commitment to dignity.[72] With colleagues, I have concluded that "[t]he *perception* of receiving a fair hearing is therapeutic because it contributes to the individual's sense of dignity and conveys that he or she is being taken seriously."[73] Professors Jonathan Simon and Stephen Rosenbaum embrace TJ as a modality of analysis and focus specifically on this issue of voice: "When procedures give people an opportunity to exercise voice, their words are given respect, decisions are explained to them, their views taken into account, and they substantively feel less coercion."[74] With my colleague Naomi Weinstein, I have argued that "attorneys must embrace the principles and tenets of TJ as a means of best ensuring the dignity of their clients and of maximizing the likelihood that voice, validation and voluntariness[75] will be

---

66 Nicola Ferencz and James McGuire, *Mental Health Review Tribunals in the UK: Applying a Therapeutic Jurisprudence Perspective*, 37 CT. REV. 48, 51 (2000).

67 James L. Nolan, Jr., *Redefining Criminal Courts: Problem-Solving and the Meaning of Justice*, 40 AM. CRIM. L. REV. 1541, 1541 (2003).

68 John Cummings, *The Cost of Crazy: How Therapeutic Jurisprudence and Mental Health Courts Lower Incarceration Costs, Reduce Recidivism, and Improve Public Safety*, 56 LOY. L. REV. 279, 280–81 (2010).

69 Michael Codben and Ron Albers, *Beyond the Squabble: Putting the Tenderloin Community Justice Center in Context*, 7 HASTINGS RACE & POVERTY L.J. 53, 56 (2010).

70 D'Emic, *Bridging, supra* note 61, at 376.

71 See *supra* 2.5; see also, e.g., Heather Ellis Cucolo and Michael L. Perlin, *Promoting Dignity and Preventing Shame and Humiliation by Improving the Quality and Education of Attorneys in Sexually Violent Predator (SVP) Civil Commitment Cases*, 28 U. FLA. J.L. & PUB. POL'Y 291 (2017); Michael L. Perlin and Naomi Weinstein, *"Friend to the Martyr, a Friend to the Woman of Shame": Thinking about the Law, Shame and Humiliation*, 24 S. CAL. REV. L. & SOC. JUST. 1 (2014); Perlin and Lynch, *To Wander off in Shame, supra* note 11.

72 See generally BRUCE J. WINICK, CIVIL COMMITMENT: A THERAPEUTIC JURISPRUDENCE MODEL 161 (2005). Dignity inquiries permeate the criminal justice system, especially as the concept applies to persons with mental disabilities.

73 Michael L. Perlin, Keri K. Gould and Deborah A. Dorfman, *Therapeutic Jurisprudence and the Civil Rights of Institutionalized Mentally Disabled Persons: Hopeless Oxymoron or Path to Redemption?* 1 PSYCHOL. PUB. POL'Y & L. 80, 114 (1995) (emphasis added).

74 Jonathan Simon and Stephen A. Rosenbaum, *Dignifying Madness: Rethinking Commitment Law in an Age of Mass Incarceration*, 70 U. MIAMI L. REV. 1, 51 (2015).

75 See Amy D. Ronner, *Songs of Validation, Voice, and Voluntary Participation: Therapeutic Jurisprudence, Miranda and Juveniles*, 71 U. CIN. L. REV. 89, 94–95 (2002). As discussed above,

enhanced."[76] The modern mental health court model is the single, best way to provide such dignity.[77]

7.3   International human rights law

Any consideration of contemporary mental disability law must include an inquiry into its relationship to international human rights law, especially the Convention on the Rights of Persons with Disabilities (CRPD).[78] This Convention "radically changes the scope of international human rights law as it applies to all persons with disabilities, and in no area is this more significant than in the area of mental disability law,"[79] as it "finally empowered the 'world's largest minority' to claim their rights, and to participate in [the world] on an equal basis with others who have achieved specific treaty recognition and protection."[80]

The "most revolutionary international human rights document ever created that applies to persons with disabilities," it furthers the human rights approach, and recognizes the right of people with disabilities to equality in almost every aspect of life.[81] It firmly endorses a social model of disability—a clear and direct repudiation of the medical

---

a "voluntary" status in mental health commitment is not always truly voluntary. On ways that hospital staff can routinely manipulate disparity in bargaining to coerce patients into accepting voluntary commitment status (thus avoiding court hearings), see Susan Reed and Dan Lewis, *The Negotiation of Voluntary Admission in Chicago's State Mental Hospitals*, 18 J. PSYCHIATRY & L. 137, 143–48 (1990); see also Joel Haycock, David Finkelman and Helene Presskreischer, *Mediating the Gap: Thinking about Alternatives to the Current Practice of Civil Commitment*, 20 NEW ENG. J. ON CRIM. & CIV. CONFINEMENT 265, 278 (1994) ("[The patient's lawyers], in collusion with the care-givers, disempower him or her and effectively thwart the establishment of a voluntary treatment compact between the patient and mental health professionals"). See *supra* 4.7.2.

76 Perlin and Weinstein, *supra* note 31, at 115.

77 See generally David Yamada, *Dignity, "Rankism," and Hierarchy in the Workplace: Creating a "Dignitarian" Agenda for American Employment Law*, 28 BERKELEY J. EMP. & LAB. L. 305 (2007).

78 G.A. Res. 61/106, U.N. Doc. A/RES/61/106 (Jan. 24, 2007).

79 Michael L. Perlin, *"Striking for the Guardians and Protectors of the Mind": The Convention on the Rights of Persons with Disabilities and the Future of Guardianship Law*, 117 PENN ST. L. REV. 1159, 1163 (2013).

80 Michael L. Perlin, *"Your Old Road Is/ Rapidly Agin'": International Human Rights Standards and Their Impact on Forensic Psychologists, the Practice of Forensic Psychology, and the Conditions of Institutionalization of Persons with Mental Disabilities*, 17 WASH. U. GLOBAL STUDIES L. REV. 79, 91 (2018).

81 Id.

model that traditionally was part and parcel of mental disability law,[82] and "sketches the full range of human rights that apply to all human beings."[83] It provides a framework for ensuring that mental health laws "fully recognize the rights of those with mental illness."[84] As the author and a colleague have previously written, the "CRPD can be, and should be, a blueprint for advocates representing persons traumatized as a result of their mental disabilities."[85]

The United States has signed, but has not ratified, the CRPD.[86] Under such circumstances, "a state's obligations under it are controlled by the Vienna Convention on the Law of Treaties . . . which requires signatories 'to refrain from acts which would defeat [the Disability Convention's] object and purpose.'"[87] Domestic courts have cited the CRPD approvingly in cases involving guardianship matters, and, in one such case, Surrogate Judge Glen noted that the CRPD was "entitled to 'persuasive weight' in interpreting our own laws and constitutional protections."[88] In short, the CRPD must be taken seriously in the United States by all domestic courts.[89]

Article 1 of the CRPD outlines its purpose: to "promote, protect and ensure the full and equal enjoyment of all human rights and

---

82 See generally Michael L. Perlin, *"Abandoned Love": The Impact of* Wyatt v. Stickney *on the Intersection between International Human Rights and Domestic Mental Disability Law*, 35 LAW & PSYCHOL. REV. 121, 138–41 (2011).

83 Janet E. Lord and Michael A. Stein, *Social Rights and the Relational Value of the Rights to Participate in Sport, Recreation, and Play*, 27 B.U. INT'L L.J. 249, 256 (2009). It describes the social model of disability as a condition arising from "interaction with various barriers [that] may hinder [the individual's] full and effective participation in society on an equal basis with others" instead of inherent limitations. CRPD, Art. 1; see also, e.g., Perlin, *supra* note 79, at 1174.

84 Bernadette McSherry, *International Trends in Mental Health Laws: Introduction*, 26 LAW CONTEXT: A SOCIO-LEGAL J. 1, 8 (2008).

85 Mehgan Gallagher and Michael L. Perlin, *"The Pain I Rise Above": How International Human Rights Can Best Realize the Needs of Persons with Trauma-Related Mental Disabilities*, 29 FLA. J. INT'L L. 271, 278–79 (2018).

86 See Michelle Diament, *Obama Urges Senate to Ratify Disability Treaty*, DISABILITY SCOOP (May 18, 2012), accessed October 6, 2020 at https://www.disabilityscoop.com/2012/05/18/obama-urges-senate-treaty/15654/.

87 *In re* Mark C.H., 906 N.Y.S.2d 419, 433 (Surr. Ct. 2010) (alteration in original) (citing Vienna Convention on the Law of Treaties, Art. 18, May 23, 1969, 1155 U.N.T.S. 331); see also, e.g., *In re* Guardianship of Dameris L., 956 N.Y.S.2d 848, 854 (Surr. Ct. 2012) (holding that substantive-due-process requirement of principle of LRA applies to guardianships sought for mentally disabled persons). See Dlugacz and Wimmer, *supra* note 7, at 362–63.

88 *Dameris L.*, 956 N.Y.S.2d at 855.

89 Perlin, *supra* note 79, at 1160; Gallagher and Perlin, *supra* note 85, at 280.

fundamental freedoms by all persons with disabilities, and to promote respect for their inherent dignity."[90] The definition is all-inclusive, and includes "those who have long-term physical, mental, intellectual or sensory impairments which in interaction with various barriers may hinder their full and effective participation in society on an equal basis with others."[91] It further calls for non-discrimination and "full and effective participation and inclusion in society."[92]

Article 12 declares that persons with disabilities have equal recognition before the law,[93] Article 13 proclaims that persons with disabilities shall have equal access to justice on an equal basis with others[94] and Article 14 states that all persons with disabilities shall enjoy the right to liberty and security of person, and that nations must ensure that people with disabilities are not deprived of their liberty unlawfully or arbitrarily.[95] The ratification of the Convention illustrates "profound shifts both in the conception of human rights and the implementation of human rights in public policy domains."[96]

Other sections of the CRPD make clear that persons with disabilities have the same human rights as all other persons, and, importantly, many track—either consciously or unconsciously—the holdings of the decisions in *Wyatt v. Stickney*[97] and its supplemental standards. Thus, other articles call for "[r]espect for inherent dignity" and

---

90 CRPD, Art. 1. See, e.g., Leslie Salzman, *Guardianship for Persons with Mental Illness: A Legal and Appropriate Alternative?* 4 St. Louis U. J. Health L. & Pol'y 279, 283–84 (2011) ("The CRPD is predicated on the obligation to respect each person's inherent dignity, autonomy, and independence, including the freedom to make one's own choices").

91 CRPD, Art. 1.

92 Id., Art. 3.

93 Id., Art. 12.

94 Id., Art. 13. This includes the provision of accommodations for persons with disabilities "in order to facilitate their effective role as direct and indirect participants . . . in all legal proceeding. . . ." Id. As discussed elsewhere (see *supra* Chapter 3), access to adequate and dedicated counsel is one of the most critical issues in bringing life to international human rights law within a mental disability law context. See Michael L. Perlin, *International Human Rights Law and Comparative Mental Disability Law: The Universal Factors*, 34 Syracuse J. Int'l & Com. L. 333, 342 (2007).

95 CRPD, Art. 14.

96 Penelope Weller, *Human Rights and Social Justice: The Convention on the Rights of Persons with Disabilities and the Quiet Revolution in International Law*, 4 Pub. Space: J. L. & Soc. Just. 74, 90 (2009).

97 344 F. Supp. 373 (M.D. Ala. 1972), *aff'd in part, rev'd in part*, 344 F. Supp. 387 (M.D. Ala. 1972), *aff'd in part, rev'd in part sub nom.* Wyatt v. Aderholt, 503 F.2d 1305 (5th Cir. 1974). See generally *supra* 5.1.3 et seq.

"nondiscrimination";[98] "[f]reedom from torture or cruel, inhuman or degrading treatment or punishment";[99] "[f]reedom from exploitation, violence and abuse";[100] a right to protection of the "integrity of the person";[101] the right to community living;[102] the right to health and the nondiscriminatory provision of services;[103] and the right to rehabilitation.[104]

It is vital to keep in mind that these provisions apply not just to persons in the *civil* mental health system (the focus of this book to this point) but also to those in the *forensic* system (those charged with or convicted of crime).[105] Consider these findings by Human Rights Watch with regard to persons with mental disabilities in prison settings:

> Corrections officials at times needlessly and punitively deluge them with chemical sprays; shock them with electric stun devices; strap them to chairs and beds for days on end; break their jaws, noses, ribs; or leave them with lacerations, second degree burns, deep bruises, and damaged internal organs. The violence can traumatize already vulnerable men and women, aggravating their symptoms and making future mental health treatment more difficult.[106]

In a recent article on restoration of competency practices, Professor Susan McMahon focuses on the status of such individuals in *jail*

---

98 CRPD, Art. 3.

99 Id., Art. 15.

100 Id., Art. 16.

101 Id., Art. 17.

102 Id., Art. 19.

103 Id., Art. 25.

104 Id., Art. 26.

105 See *infra* chapters 8–11. It is also important to always keep in mind that there is a significant *blurring* between the civil and forensic/criminal mental disability law systems, and that that blurring increases with time. See, e.g., Michael L. Perlin, Deborah A. Dorfman and Naomi M. Weinstein, *"On Desolation Row": The Blurring of the Borders between Civil and Criminal Mental Disability Law, and What It Means for All of Us*, 24 Tex. J. on Civ. Libs. & Civ. Rts. 59 (2018), discussing four areas of "negative blurring"—the proliferation of assisted outpatient treatment (AOT) statutes (see *supra* 4.7.3), the expansion of sexually violent predator acts, the sanctioning in some jurisdictions of the imprisonment of insanity acquittees in prison facilities, and the provision of no meaningful continuity of care, resulting in large numbers of persons continually "shuttling" between jails (or prisons) and mental hospital—and one area of "positive" blurring, the proliferation of mental health courts, see *supra* 7.2 *et seq.*

106 Human Rights Watch, *Callous and Cruel* (2015), accessed October 6, 2020 at https://www.hrw.org/report/2015/05/12/callous-and-cruel/use-force-against-inmates-mental-disabilities-us-jails-and.

settings: "Some defendants with mental health conditions have it far worse. Unable to follow the strict rules and regulations of a jail environment, they are punished and placed in solitary confinement at much higher rates than the general population."[107]

In short, when seeking to navigate the criminal justice system, this navigation must be done with an eye toward the international human rights system as well.[108]

---

107 Susan McMahon, *Reforming Competence Restoration Statutes: An Outpatient Model*, 107 GEO. L.J. 601, 614 (2019).

108 Perlin and Gallagher, *supra* note 1, at 18.

8   Criminal incompetencies

8.1   Introduction[1]

Any consideration of criminal incompetencies must begin by acknowledging the multiple embedded inquiries. It is essential to consider incompetency to stand trial, competency to plead guilty and competency to waive counsel.

8.2   Incompetency to stand trial

The concept of incompetency to stand trial is a constant element in Anglo-American law. Few principles are as strongly entrenched in our criminal jurisprudence as the doctrine that an "incompetent" defendant may not be put to trial.

The primary purpose is to "safeguard the accuracy of adjudication."[2] Over a century ago, a state supreme court suggested, "It would be inhumane, and to a certain extent a denial of a trial on the merits, to require one who has been disabled by the act of God from intelligently making his defense to plead or to be tried for his life or liberty."[3]

For multiple reasons, it became black letter law that the "trial and conviction of a person mentally and physically incapable of making a defense violates certain immutable principles of justice which inhere in the very idea of a free government."[4]

---

1 See MICHAEL L. PERLIN AND HEATHER ELLIS CUCOLO, MENTAL DISABILITY LAW: CIVIL AND CRIMINAL ch. 13 (3d ed. 2016) (2019 update). For discussion of competency at all pre- and post-trial stages, including, inter alia, questions related to confessions, searches and appeals, see id., §§ 13-2.5 to 13-2.6.8. Competency at sentencing is discussed *infra* 10.3.

2 Claudine Walker Ausness, *The Identification of Incompetent Defendants: Separating Those Unfit for Adversary Combat from Those Who Are Fit*, 66 KY. L.J. 666, 668 (1978).

3 Jordan v. State, 135 S.W. 327, 328 (Tenn. 1911).

4 Sanders v. Allen, 100 F.2d 717, 720 (D.C. Cir. 1938).

- An incompetent defendant might alone have exculpatory information that he or she is incapable of transmitting to counsel;[5]
- To try an incompetent defendant has been likened to permitting an adversary contest "in which the defendant, like a small boy being beaten by a bully, is unable to dodge or return the blows";[6]
- The trial of an incompetent transforms the adversary process "from a reasoned interaction between an individual and his community" into "an invective against an insensible object";[7] and
- "It seems essential to the philosophy of punishment that the defendant knows why he is being punished, and such comprehension is to a great extent dependent on involvement with the trial itself."[8]

The rationale is clear. It is fundamentally unfair, per *Dusky v. United States*,[9] to put a defendant to trial who may not have "sufficient present ability to consult with his lawyer with a reasonable degree of rational understanding [or] a rational as well as a factual understanding of the proceedings against him."[10] To this end, the defendant must be able to "appraise and assess the proceedings."[11] A defendant must have the ability to communicate, the capacity to reason "from a simple premise to a simple conclusion," the ability to "recall and relate facts concerning his actions" and the ability "to comprehend instructions and advice, and make decisions based on well-explained alternatives."[12]

Incompetency is a *status*, not a defense.[13] Incompetency is in no way a concession of factual guilt (as is the invocation of the insanity defense).[14] The American Bar Association Standards for Criminal

---

5 E.g., United States v. Chisolm, 149 F. 284, 287 (S.D. Ala. 1906).

6 Ausness, *supra* note 2, at 669.

7 Note, *Incompetency to Stand Trial*, 81 Harv. L. Rev. 454, 458 (1967).

8 Id. See Michael L. Perlin, *"God Said to Abraham/Kill Me a Son": Why the Insanity Defense and the Incompetency Status Are Compatible with and Required by the Convention on the Rights of Persons with Disabilities and Basic Principles of Therapeutic Jurisprudence*, 54 Am. Crim. L. Rev. 477, 488 (2017).

9 362 U.S. 402 (1960).

10 Id. at 402. See Peter R. Silten and Richard Tullis, *Mental Competency in Criminal Proceedings*, 28 Hastings L.J. 1053, 1062–64 (1977).

11 Ausness, *supra* note 2, at 672.

12 Michael L. Perlin and Alison J. Lynch, *"My Brain Is So Wired": Neuroimaging's Role in Competency Cases Involving Persons with Mental Disabilities*, 27 B.U. Pub. Int. L.J. 73, 78 n.28 (2018).

13 American Bar Association, Standards for Criminal Justice, Criminal Justice Mental Health Standards, ch. 7, pt. IV (2015) (ABA Standards).

14 Perlin and Lynch, *supra* note 12, at 76.

Justice underscore that the status of incompetence to stand trial "has no bearing on guilt or innocence."[15]

Dusky—which was commonly seen as confusing and less than helpful[16]—was supplemented by *Drope v. Missouri*[17] to require that the defendant be able to "assist in his defense."[18] The *Drope* court ruled:

> [E]vidence of a defendant's irrational behavior, his demeanor at trial, and any prior medical opinion on competence to stand trial are all relevant in determining whether further inquiry is required, but . . . even one of these factors standing alone may, in some circumstances, be sufficient. There are, of course, no fixed or immutable signs which invariably indicate the need for further inquiry to determine fitness to proceed; the question is often a difficult one in which a wide range of manifestations and subtle nuances are implicated. That they are difficult to evaluate is suggested by the varying opinions trained psychiatrists can entertain on the same facts.[19]

A New York court has listed six factors to be considered in determinations of incompetency:

> [W]hether the defendant: (1) is oriented as to time and place; (2) is able to perceive, recall, and relate; (3) has an understanding of the process of the trial and the roles of judge, jury, prosecutor, and defense attorney; (4) can establish a working relationship with his attorney; (5) has sufficient intelligence and judgment to listen to the advice of counsel and, based on that advice, appreciate (without necessarily adopting) the fact that one course of conduct may be more beneficial to him than another; and (6) is sufficiently stable to enable him to withstand the stresses of the trial without suffering a serious prolonged or permanent breakdown.[20]

8.2.1   Constitutional standards

The conviction of one not competent to stand trial violates due process.[21] If there is a "bona fide doubt" as to the defendant's competence,

---

15 ABA STANDARDS, *supra* note 13.
16 See Gerald Bennett, *A Guided Tour through Selected ABA Standards Relating to Incompetence to Stand Trial*, 53 GEO. WASH. L. REV. 375, 378–79 (1985).
17 420 U.S. 162 (1972).
18 Id. at 171.
19 Id. at 180.
20 People v. Picozzi, 482 N.Y.S.2d 335, 337 (A.D. 1984), *appeal denied*, 64 N.Y.2d 1137 (1985).
21 See Pate v. Robinson, 383 U.S. 375, 385 (1966).

the trial judge must raise the issue *sua sponte*, and weigh it at a suitable hearing accompanied by procedures "sufficient to permit a trier of fact reasonably to assess an accused's competency against prevailing medi-- cal and legal standards."[22]

The fact that a defendant is psychotic does not mean that he or she is necessarily incompetent to stand trial.[23] Thus, courts have found that defendants with most serious mental illnesses were not necessarily incompetent to stand trial.[24] Nonetheless, a defendant must have "a modicum of intelligence" so as to assist counsel, and must be able to "comprehend his predicament."[25]

8.2.2 Burden of proof

The Supreme Court has held that a state statute placing the burden of proof in an incompetency proceeding on the defendant does not violate due process,[26] but subsequently held that the placement of the burden on a defendant by clear and convincing evidence *did* violate due process.[27]

Prior to the Court's decisions in *Medina v. California* and *Cooper v. Oklahoma*, there had been a relatively significant statutory split in the jurisdictions over the issue of the burden of proof at a hearing to determine competency to stand trial; in some jurisdictions the burden was on the defendant, in others on the state, and in yet others, on the moving party.[28]

8.2.2.1 *Medina v. California*

In *Medina*, the Court found that allocating the burden to the defendant—per the California statute in question in that case—did not "offend some principle of justice so rooted in the traditions and

---

22 See Holmes v. King, 709 F.2d 965, 967 (5th Cir. 1983) (quoting Fulford v. Maggio, 692 F.2d 354, 361 (5th Cir. 1982), *rev'd on other grounds*, 462 U.S. 111 (1983)).

23 See, e.g., Ronald Roesch, Stephen D. Hart and Patricia A. Zapf, *Conceptualizing and Assessing Competency to Stand Trial: Implications and Applications of the MacArthur Treatment Competence Model*, 2 PSYCHOL. PUB. POL'Y & L. 96, 101 (1996).

24 See PERLIN AND CUCOLO, *supra* note 1, § 13-1.2.2.

25 See, e.g., People v. Francabandera, 354 N.Y.S.2d 609, 614 (Ct. App. 1974).

26 See Medina v. California, 505 U.S. 437 (1992).

27 See Cooper v. Oklahoma, 517 U.S. 348 (1996).

28 See PERLIN AND CUCOLO, *supra* note 1, § 13-1.3.1.1.

conscience of our people as to be ranked as fundamental."[29] While the defendant has a constitutional right not to be tried while legally incompetent, as long as the state makes available to the defendant "access to procedures for making a competency evaluation," it need not assume the burden of proof on the incompetency to stand trial question.[30] Although an impaired defendant might be limited in his or her ability to assist counsel in demonstrating incompetence, that inability, by itself, might constitute probative evidence of incompetence, noting further that defense counsel will often have "the best informed view" of the defendant's ability to participate in his or her defense.[31]

Justice O'Connor concurred (on behalf of herself and Justice Souter), expressing concern that defendants will feign incompetence, and that placement of the burden on the defendant may have a prophylactic effect by ensuring that the greatest amount of available information as to the defendant's mental condition is before the court.[32] Justice Blackmun dissented (on behalf of himself and Justice Stevens). He stressed language in *Drope v. Missouri* that the right to be tried while competent is "fundamental" to the adversary system of justice,[33] and added that the right to be tried while competent was the "foundational right" for the effective exercise of all other criminal trial process rights.[34] The fact that, in cases where the evidence is inconclusive, a defendant may still be subjected to trial, he added, was a development that might introduce a "systematic and unacceptably high risk" that persons will be tried and convicted "who are unable to follow or participate in the proceedings determining their fate."[35]

8.2.2.2   Cooper v. Oklahoma

The Supreme Court again returned to this question in *Cooper v. Oklahoma*, ruling that a statute placing the burden of proof on the defendant to disprove competence to stand trial by clear and convincing evidence was unconstitutional.[36] The court concluded that it was persuaded "both by traditional and modern practice" that the state

---

29 505 U.S. at 446, quoting Patterson v. New York, 432 U.S. 197, 202 (1977).

30 Id. at 449.

31 Id. at 450.

32 Id. at 455 (O'Connor, J., concurring).

33 420 U.S. at 172.

34 *Medina*, 505 U.S. at 457 (Blackmun, J., dissenting).

35 Id. at 464.

36 517 U.S. 348, 356 (1996).

could not put to trial a defendant who may have demonstrated that it was more likely than not that he or she was incompetent.[37]

The heightened standard "offends a principle of justice that is deeply 'rooted in the traditions and conscience of our people'";[38] focusing on the need for fundamental fairness, the *Oklahoma* rule imposed "a significant risk of an erroneous determination that the defendant is competent,"[39] a risk carrying "dire consequences."[40]

8.2.3   Expert testimony—the evaluation

Competency evaluations are typically, although perhaps unnecessarily,[41] performed in maximum security hospitals to which defendants have been committed for specified time periods. The concern over the deprivation of rights for pretrial detainees, waiting in jail for court-ordered competency services, has been vigorously litigated. In *Trueblood v. Washington State Dep't of Social and Health Services*,[42] the Ninth Circuit upheld the district court's conclusions regarding the constitutional rights of class members, "agree[ing] that DSHS [Washington State Department of Social and Health Services] must conduct competency evaluations within a reasonable time following a court's order," and affirming that a permanent injunction "remains an appropriate vehicle for monitoring and ensuring that class members' constitutional rights are protected."[43] The case was returned to the district court to reconsider "what constitutes a reasonable time in which to conduct the evaluations."[44] In an important clarification of the harms suffered by incompetent persons in jail, the district court wrote:

> For class members who are found incompetent, each additional day spent in jail waiting is an additional day spent without access to desperately needed medication and treatment, incarcerated in a place that cannot provide the environment or type of care needed by incompetent class members. Each

---

37 Id. at 355.

38 Id. at 362, quoting *Medina*, 505 U.S. at 445.

39 *Cooper*, 517 U.S. at 363.

40 Id. at 364.

41 See Michael L. Perlin, *"For the Misdemeanor Outlaw": The Impact of the ADA on the Institutionalization of Criminal Defendants with Mental Disabilities*, 52 ALABAMA L. REV. 193 (2000).

42 822 F.3d 1037 (9th Cir. 2016).

43 Id. at 1040, 1046.

44 Trueblood v. Washington State Dep't of Social and Health Services, 2016 U.S. Dist. LEXIS 108637 (W.D. Wash. 2016).

additional day spent in jail increases the risk of suicide and of other types of self harm, and increases the risk that a class member will be victimized by other inmates. . . . For class members suffering from mental illness, each additional day spent incarcerated—especially in solitary confinement— makes that class member's mental illness more habitual and harder to cure, resulting in longer restoration periods or in the inability to ever restore that person to competency. Longer restoration treatment periods increase the cost to the state and therefore to the public of treating that individual, and longer restoration periods stymie the efficient use of restoration bed space. (*internal citations omitted*)[45]

Courts have frequently considered both the quality and scope of expert evaluations in this aspect of the proceedings. In one case, where the defendant's original expert evaluation focused solely on his proffered delusional compulsion defense, the Eleventh Circuit affirmed a habeas corpus grant. As this evaluation lacked an assessment of his competency to stand trial, it was not an appropriate basis upon which to support a competency finding.[46]

8.2.4 Medicating defendants

One of the most perplexing substantive and procedural problems in the area of competency to stand trial is the question of what has been characterized as "synthetic" or "artificial" competency: whether an incompetent defendant can be medicated against his or her will so as to make him or her competent to stand trial.[47]

8.2.4.1 *Sell v. United States*

In *Sell v. United States*, the Supreme Court held that the federal government may involuntarily administer antipsychotic drugs to render a mentally ill defendant competent to stand trial only if the treatment is medically appropriate, substantially unlikely to have side effects that may undermine the trial's fairness, and necessary to significantly further important governmental trial-related interests.[48]

---

45 Id. at **42–43.

46 Ford v. Gaither, 953 F.2d 1296 (11th Cir. 1992).

47 For the history of the development of this doctrine, including an extensive discussion of the cases of United States v. Charters, 863 F.2d 302 (4th Cir. 1988), *cert. denied*, 494 U.S. 1016 (1990), *vacating* 829 F.2d 479 (4th Cir. 1987), see PERLIN AND CUCOLO, *supra* note 1, § 8-7.3.1.

48 539 U.S. 166, 179 (2003).

The defendant had been found incompetent to stand trial and ordered hospitalized for up to four months to determine whether there was "substantial probability" that he would attain competency.[49] Two months into the hospitalization, the hospital recommended that Sell take antipsychotic medication, and Sell refused.[50] Following a hearing, the magistrate found that Sell was a danger to himself and others at the hospital, and that "the government has shown in as strong a manner as possible, that anti-psychotic medications are the only way to render the defendant not dangerous and competent to stand trial."[51]

The district court affirmed the magistrate's order, holding that the medication represented the "only viable hope of rendering defendant competent to stand trial" and appeared "necessary to serve the government's compelling interest in obtaining an adjudication of defendant's guilt or innocence of numerous and serious charges."[52] The Eighth Circuit also affirmed.[53]

The Supreme Court vacated and remanded. Reaching the merits, the Court recognized that under *Washington v. Harper*[54] and *Riggins v. Nevada*,[55] Sell had a liberty interest in avoiding the involuntary administration of antipsychotic drugs, and this interest was protected by the Fifth Amendment's due process clause against all but "essential" or "overriding" state interests.[56] The Court held:

> These two cases, *Harper* and *Riggins*, indicate that the Constitution permits the government involuntarily to administer antipsychotic drugs to a mentally ill defendant facing serious criminal charges in order to render that defendant competent to stand trial, but only if the treatment is medically appropriate, is substantially unlikely to have side effects that may undermine the fairness of the trial, and, taking account of less intrusive alternatives, is necessary significantly to further important governmental trial-related interests.[57]

---

49 Id. at 170.

50 Id. at 171.

51 Id. at 173.

52 Id. at 174.

53 Id.

54 494 U.S. 210 (1990). See *infra* 10.4.3.

55 504 U.S. 127 (1992). See *infra* 9.5.4.

56 *Sell*, 539 U.S. at 179.

57 Id. On the significance of each of these issues, see, e.g., Susan McMahon, *It Doesn't Pass the Sell*

"The inquiry into whether medication is permissible, say, to render an individual nondangerous is usually more 'objective and manageable' than the inquiry into whether medication is permissible to render a defendant competent," and closer to the court's familiar role in assessing dangerousness for the purposes of involuntary civil commitment.[58] Importantly, the Court stressed—much more clearly than it did in *Riggins*[59]—the need to engage in a "least restrictive alternative" analysis in every such case. The words "intrusive" and "restrictive" are in the opinion well over a dozen times, and the significance of that use of language should not be underestimated.

8.2.4.2   *In the aftermath of Sell*

The Ninth Circuit, in *United States v. Weber*, applied *Sell* principles to a case that involved subjecting a defendant—under supervised court release following a conviction for possession of child pornography— to penile plethysmograph testing as a release condition. The Court vacated and remanded, on the grounds that the trial court failed to make an individualized determination of whether such testing was necessary to accomplish its goals and that it failed to make an individualized determination as to whether *this* defendant should be subject to such testing. In doing so, it relied on *Sell* for the proposition that, when a condition of release "implicates a particularly significant liberty interest of the defendant, then the district court must support its decision on the record" with evidence that the condition "involves no greater deprivation of liberty than is reasonably necessary."[60]

On the related question of whether *Sell* applies to other stages of the proceedings beyond trial competency, consider *United States v. Baldovinos*.[61] There, the Fourth Circuit, while conceding that it was plain error for the government to involuntarily medicate the defendant without consideration of the *Sell* factors for the purposes of making him competent to be sentenced, nonetheless affirmed the defendant's conviction and sentence (because, it concluded, that the medication error did not seriously affect the fairness or integrity of the proceedings).[62]

Test: Focusing on "the Facts of the Individual Case" in Involuntary Medication Inquiries, 50 Aм. Crim. L. Rev. 387 (2013).

58 Id. (quoting *Riggins*, 504 U.S. at 140 (Kennedy, J., concurring)).

59 See *infra* 9.5.4.

60 451 F.3d 552, 558 (9th Cir. 2006).

61 434 F.3d 233 (4th Cir. 2006), *cert. denied*, 546 U.S. 1203 (2006).

62 Id. at 243. On competency and sentencing, see *infra* 10.3.

8.2.5 Disposition of cases of individuals found incompetent to stand trial

Until the Supreme Court's 1972 decision in *Jackson v. Indiana*,[63] a finding of incompetency was frequently the equivalent of a life sentence to a maximum security forensic psychiatric institution.[64] *Jackson*, which applied the due process clause to incompetency commitment decisionmaking, declared such automatic lifelong commitments unconstitutional.[65] Before *Jackson*, by way of example, in Massachusetts, more incompetent defendants left Bridgewater Hospital—the facility to which persons found incompetent to stand trial (IST) were regularly committed—by dying than by all other avenues combined.[66]

Jackson was a severely intellectually disabled, deaf and mute person "with a mental level of a pre-school child" who could neither read nor write.[67] The Court held that long-term, indeterminate commitment of such an individual, based solely on his or her incompetence to stand trial, violates the Constitution.[68] It found (1) a violation of the equal protection clause in subjecting an IST defendant to a more lenient commitment standard and to a more stringent standard of release than generally applicable to those who have never been charged with offenses, "thus condemning him in effect to permanent institutionalization,"[69] and (2) a violation of the due process clause in committing an individual for more than the "reasonable period of time" necessary to determine "whether there is a substantial chance of his attaining the capacity to stand trial in the foreseeable future."[70]

---

63 406 U.S. 715 (1972); see *supra* 4.2.5.

64 See Michael L. Perlin, Keri K. Gould and Deborah A. Dorfman, *Therapeutic Jurisprudence and the Civil Rights of Institutionalized Mentally Disabled Persons: Hopeless Oxymoron or Path to Redemption?* 1 Psychol. Pub. Pol'y & L. 80, 85 (1995).

65 406 U.S. at 731–32.

66 E.g., Steven L. Engelberg, *Pretrial Criminal Commitment to Mental Institutions: The Procedure in Massachusetts and Suggested Reform*, 17 Cath. U. L. Rev. 163 (1967) (one defendant institutionalized 63 years).

67 *Jackson*, 406 U.S. at 717. See *supra* 4.2.5 n.53, for a discussion of the relevant facts of the *Jackson* case.

68 Id. at 720.

69 Id. at 730.

70 Id. at 733. If it were to be determined that the defendant would *not* regain his or her competence within such a "foreseeable time," then the state "must either institute the customary civil commitment proceeding that would be required to commit indefinitely any other citizen, or release the defendant." Id. at 738. While the Court did not set a finite time limit on the "reasonable length of time" in which such a determination should be made, it noted that Jackson's three-and-one-half-

Compliance with *Jackson* has never been a rousing success. Nearly four decades after the *Jackson* decision, many jurisdictions have not yet implemented it in full.[71] As Professors Morris and Meloy wrote over 25 years ago:

> Although more than twenty years have passed since the Court decided *Jackson*, the question [of whether the court that ordered the incompetent defendant's treatment is statutorily obligated to review periodically the defendant's progress toward attaining competence] has not been answered by the statutes of thirty-two states and the District of Columbia. Of this number, twenty jurisdictions do not address the issue at all.[72]

8.3 Competency to plead guilty

The issue of assessing the competence of guilty pleas entered by mentally disabled defendants presents "one of the most difficult doctrinal and practical problems faced by the criminal justice system."[73] Courts originally split on the significant question of whether the standard to plead guilty is the same as, higher than, or otherwise different from, the traditional standard for competency to stand trial articulated in *Dusky v. United States*.[74]

The majority view maintained there was no substantial difference, and that the same test applies in assessing the validity of a guilty plea.[75] This position was challenged, however, by a series of cases that suggested a different test: "A defendant is not competent to plead guilty if a mental [disability] has substantially impaired his ability to make a reasoned choice among the alternatives presented to him and to understand the consequences of his plea."[76] Such a test has been employed by those courts that find it necessary for judges to "assess a defendant's

---

year period of confinement "sufficiently establishe[d] the lack of a substantial probability that he will ever be able to participate fully in a trial." Id. at 738–30.

71 See *supra* 3.2.6, nn.67–69 (citing research sources).

72 See Grant Morris and J. Reid Meloy, *Out of Mind? Out of Sight: The Uncivil Commitment of Permanently Incompetent Criminal Defendants*, 27 U.C. DAVIS L. REV. 1, 8 (1993).

73 James Ellis and Ruth Luckasson, *Mentally Retarded Criminal Defendants*, 53 GEO. WASH. L. REV. 414, 460 (1985).

74 362 U.S. 402 (1960); see *supra* 8.2.

75 See, e.g., Malinauskas v. United States, 505 F.2d 649 (5th Cir. 1974).

76 E.g., Seiling v. Eyman, 478 F.2d 211, 215 (9th Cir. 1973).

competency *with specific reference to the gravity of the decisions* with which the defendant is faced."[77]

The Supreme Court ended the controversy by holding, in *Godinez v. Moran*, that the standard for pleading guilty was no higher than for standing trial.[78] It rejected the notion that competence to plead guilty must be measured by a higher (or even different) standard from that used in incompetency to stand trial cases, reasoning that a defendant who was found competent to stand trial would have to make a variety of decisions requiring choices: whether to testify, whether to seek a jury trial, whether to cross-examine his or her accusers and, in some cases, whether to raise an affirmative defense.[79] While the decision to plead guilty is a "profound one," "it is no more complicated than the sum total of decisions that a defendant may be called upon to make during the course of a trial."[80] Finally, the court reaffirmed that any waiver of constitutional rights must be "knowing and voluntary."[81]

It concluded on this point:

> Requiring that a criminal defendant be competent has a modest aim: It seeks to ensure that he has the capacity to understand the proceedings and to assist counsel. While psychiatrists and scholars may find it useful to classify the various kinds and degrees of competence, and while States are free to adopt competency standards that are more elaborate than the *Dusky* formulation, the Due Process Clause does not impose these additional requirements.[82]

Justice Blackmun dissented (for himself and Justice Stevens), focusing squarely on what he saw as the likely potential that the defendant's decision to plead guilty was the product of "medication and mental illness."[83] He reviewed the expert testimony as to the defendant's state

---

77 Id. at 215 (emphasis added).

78 509 U.S. 389 (1993).

79 Id. at 398.

80 Id.

81 Id. at 400, quoting Parke v. Raley, 506 U.S. 20, 29 (1992).

82 Id. at 403. Justices Kennedy and Scalia concurred, noting their concern with those aspects of the opinion that compared the decisions made by a defendant who pleads guilty with those made by one who goes to trial, and expressing their "serious doubts" that there would be a heightened competency standard under the due process clause if these decisions were *not* equivalent. Id.

83 Id. at 410.

of depression, a colloquy between the defendant and the trial judge in which the court was informed that the defendant was being given medication, the trial judge's failure to inquire further and discover the psychoactive properties of the drugs in question, the defendant's subsequent testimony as to the "numbing" effect of the drugs, and the "mechanical character" and "ambiguity" of the defendant's answers to the court's questions at the plea stage.[84]

On the question of the multiple meanings of competency, Justice Blackmun added:

> [T]he majority cannot isolate the term "competent" and apply it in a vacuum, divorced from its specific context. A person who is "competent" to play basketball is not thereby "competent" to play the violin. The majority's monolithic approach to competency is true to neither life nor the law. Competency for one purpose does not necessarily translate to competency for another purpose.[85]

He concluded:

> To try, convict and punish one so helpless to defend himself contravenes fundamental principles of fairness and impugns the integrity of our criminal justice system. I cannot condone the decision to accept, without further inquiry, the self-destructive "choice" of a person who was so deeply medicated and who might well have been severely mentally ill.[86]

8.4   Competency to waive counsel

Since the US Supreme Court's ruling in *Faretta v. California*, that a defendant has a federal constitutional right to represent him or her self if he or she voluntarily elects to do so,[87] courts began to focus on the question of whether a defendant has "the *mental capacity to waive the right to counsel* with a realization of the probable risks and consequences of his action."[88] Again, in *Godinez v. Moran*, the Supreme Court ruled that the standard for waiving counsel is the same as for

---

84 Id. at 410–11.

85 Id. at 413.

86 Id. at 414.

87 422 U.S. 806, 835 (1975).

88 E.g., People v. Clark, 213 Cal. Rptr. 837, 840 (App. 1985), *rev. denied* (1985) (emphasis in original).

being found competent to stand trial.[89] It found there was "no reason" to believe that the decision to waive counsel requires an "appreciably higher level of mental functioning than the decision to waive other constitutional rights," rejecting the defendant's arguments that a self-representing defendant must have "greater powers of comprehension, judgment, and reason, than would be necessary to stand trial with the aid of an attorney."[90]

This argument, the Court concluded, rested on a "flawed premise: the competence that is required of a defendant seeking to waive his right to counsel is the competence to *waive the right*, not the competence to represent himself."[91] Relying on its decision in *Faretta*, it found that a defendant's ability to represent himself "has no bearing upon his competence to choose self-representation."[92] Justice Blackmun again dissented.[93]

8.4.1 *Indiana v. Edwards*

The Supreme Court subsequently held in *Indiana v. Edwards* that the Constitution permits states to insist upon representation by counsel for those who are competent enough to stand trial but who still suffer from severe mental illness to the point where they are not competent to conduct trial proceedings by themselves.[94] At the least, *Edwards* carves out an important exception to the law as stated in *Godinez*.

After multiple competency evaluations, Edwards proceeded to trial represented by counsel. The jury convicted him of charges of criminal recklessness and theft but failed to reach a verdict on other charges, of attempted murder and battery.[95] When the state announced that it was going to retry Edwards on the charges on which the initial jury was hung, Edwards again asked the court to permit him to represent himself. Referring to the lengthy record of psychiatric reports, the trial court noted that Edwards still suffered from schizophrenia and concluded that "[w]ith these findings, he's competent to stand trial but I'm not going to find he's competent to defend himself." Edwards was then

---

89 509 U.S. at 398.
90 Id.
91 Id. at 399 (emphasis in original).
92 Id.
93 Id. at 411–12.
94 554 U.S. 164 (2008).
95 Id. at 169.

represented by appointed counsel at his retrial, and was convicted by a jury on both counts.[96]

After Indiana state courts ordered a new trial, finding that the trial court's refusal to permit him to represent himself at his retrial deprived him of his constitutional right of self-representation, the Supreme Court vacated and remanded. It concluded that as *Faretta* "did not consider the question of mental competency"[97] (noting that other post-*Faretta* cases made it clear that "the right of self-representation is not absolute"),[98] it characterized *Godinez* as presenting "a question closer to that at issue here."[99]

The Court held that the Constitution permits a state to limit a defendant's self-representation right by insisting upon representation by counsel at trial—"on the ground that the defendant lacks the mental capacity to conduct his trial defense unless represented."[100] It "caution[ed] against the use of a single mental competency standard for deciding both (1) whether a defendant who is represented by counsel can proceed to trial and (2) whether a defendant who goes to trial must be permitted to represent himself."[101] Here it turned to behavioral science and to concepts of procedural justice in explaining its rationale:

> Mental illness itself is not a unitary concept. It varies in degree. It can vary over time. It interferes with an individual's functioning at different times in different ways. The history of this case . . . illustrates the complexity of the problem. In certain instances, an individual may well be able to satisfy *Dusky*'s mental competence standard, for he will be able to work with counsel at trial, yet at the same time he may be unable to carry out the basic tasks needed to present his own defense without the help of counsel.[102]

Next, it looked at concerns related to issues of dignity,[103] underscoring that, in the case of a defendant with an "uncertain mental state, the

---

96 Id.

97 Id. at 171.

98 Id., citing Martinez v. Court of Appeal, 528 U.S. 152, 163 (2000) (no right of self-representation on direct appeal in a criminal case).

99 *Edwards*, 554 U.S. at 171.

100 Id.

101 Id. at 175.

102 Id. at 175–76.

103 See Michael L. Perlin, *"Dignity Was the First to Leave"*: Godinez v. Moran, *Colin Ferguson, and the Trial of Mentally Disabled Criminal Defendants*, 14 BEHAV. SCI. & L. 61 (1996).

spectacle that could well result from his self-representation at trial is at least as likely to prove humiliating as ennobling."[104] Not only must proceedings *be* fair, they must "*appear* fair to all who observe them."[105] The Constitution thus permits states "to insist upon representation by counsel for those competent enough to stand trial under *Dusky* but who still suffer from severe mental illness to the point where they are not competent to conduct trial proceedings by themselves."[106]

Justice Scalia dissented (for himself and Justice Thomas), taking the position that:

> The Court today concludes that a State may nonetheless strip a mentally ill defendant of the right to represent himself when that would be fairer. In my view the Constitution does not permit a State to substitute its own perception of fairness for the defendant's right to make his own case before the jury—a specific right long understood as essential to a fair trial.[107]

---

104 *Edwards,* 554 U.S. at 176.

105 Id. at 177.

106 Id. at 178. On how *Edwards* "underscored dignity's important role in the law," see Heather Ellis Cucolo and Michael L. Perlin, *Promoting Dignity and Preventing Shame and Humiliation by Improving the Quality and Education of Attorneys in Sexually Violent Predator (SVP) Civil Commitment Cases,* 28 FLA. J. L. & PUB. POL'Y 291, 313 (2017).

107 *Edwards,* 554 U.S. at 180.

9   The insanity defense

9.1   Introduction[1]

Insanity defense issues have concerned courts and legislatures for thousands of years. Although the Supreme Court has recently ruled that abolition of the defense does not necessarily violate due process, it is still the law in almost all US jurisdictions. Given the controversy that surrounds it, its symbolic values must be considered carefully. Beyond this, questions of post-acquittal commitment and hospital discharge, as well as the omnipresence of myths about the defense's use must be kept in mind.[2]

9.2   Overview and historical background[3]

No area of our legal system has engendered more intense debate than the role of the insanity defense in the criminal justice process. On one hand, it reflects "the fundamental moral principles of our criminal law," resting on "assumptions that are older than the Republic."[4] On the other, it has been floridly rebuked by an Attorney General of the United States as the major stumbling block in the restoration of "the effectiveness of Federal law enforcement," and as tilting the "balance between the forces of law and the forces of lawlessness."[5] The defense is rarely pled,[6] but nonetheless, it continues to serve as a "surrogate for

---

1 See MICHAEL L. PERLIN AND HEATHER ELLIS CUCOLO, MENTAL DISABILITY LAW: CIVIL AND CRIMINAL ch. 14 (3d ed. 2016) (2019 update).

2 On questions related to "special populations" (juveniles and defendants with intellectual, physiological and genetic disabilities), see id., § 14-1.8 *et seq.* On questions related to cultural and syndrome defenses, see id., §14-1.9 *et seq.*

3 See MICHAEL L. PERLIN, THE JURISPRUDENCE OF THE INSANITY DEFENSE (1994).

4 United States v. Lyons, 739 F.2d 994, 995 (5th Cir. 1984) (Rubin, J., dissenting).

5 *The Insanity Defense Hearings before the Senate Comm. on the Judiciary*, 97th Cong., 2d Sess. 27 (1982) (testimony of William French Smith).

6 See, e.g., Joseph H. Rodriguez, Laura M. LeWinn and Michael L. Perlin, *The Insanity Defense*

resolution of the most profound issues in criminal justice."[7] It remains "the raw nerve at the cutting edge of law and psychiatry."[8]

The insanity defense has been "a major component of the Anglo-American common law for over 700 years,"[9] and its forerunners can be traced back over 3,000 years.[10] Its "modern" roots can be traced to a 1505 case, the first recorded jury verdict of insanity.[11]

9.3   The development of insanity tests

9.3.1   Before *M'Naghten*

It is important to consider the different substantive insanity defense tests which have evolved over the past century and a half. Thus, in *Rex v. Arnold*,[12] the court charged the jury in this manner:

> *it must be a man that is totally deprived of his understanding and memory, and doth not know what he is doing, no more than an infant, than a brute, or a wild beast, such a one is never the object of punishment. . . .*[13]

Subsequently, in 1800 in the case of James Hadfield, the court modified this standard:

---

under Siege: *Legislative Assaults and Legal Rejoinders*, 14 RUTGERS L.J. 397, 401 (1983) (in New Jersey, in fiscal 1982, of 32,500 cases studied, the insanity defense was pled in 50 cases and successful in only 15).

7 LINCOLN CAPLAN, THE INSANITY DEFENSE AND THE TRIAL OF JOHN W. HINCKLEY, JR. 127 (1984).

8 Michael L. Perlin, *The Things We Do for Love: John Hinckley's Trial and the Future of the Insanity Defense in the Federal Courts*, 30 N.Y.L. SCH. L. REV. 857, 863 (1985).

9 See 2 HENRY BRACTON, DE LEGIBUS ET CONSUETUDINIBUS ANGLIAE 424 (Longman, Thorne trans. 1968) ("The insanity defense has been in existence since at least the twelfth century").

10 Rudolph J. Gerber, *Is the Insanity Test Insane?* 20 AM. J. JURIS. 111 (1975). The defense is rooted in Talmudic, Greek and Roman history, was articulated in the sixth century Code of Justinian and in the ninth century "Dooms of Alfred." See Jacques Quen, *Anglo-American Criminal Insanity: An Historical Perspective*, 10 J. HIST. BEHAV. SCI. 313 (1974) (Talmudic roots); Barbara Weiner, *Not Guilty by Reason of Insanity: A Sane Approach*, 56 CHICAGO-KENT L. REV. 1057, 1058 (1980) (Greek roots); THEODORE F.T. PLUNKETT, A CONCISE HISTORY OF THE COMMON LAW 261–62 (5th ed. 1956) (Roman roots); Weiner, *supra* at 1058 (Justinian code); NIGEL WALKER, CRIME AND INSANITY IN ENGLAND 219 (1968) (Dooms of Alfred).

11 See WALKER, *supra* note 10, at 25–26 (citing YEARBOOKS OF HENRY VIII, 21 Michaelmas Term, plea 16 (1505)).

12 16 How. St. Tr. 694 (1724). This was the "first of the historically significant" insanity defense trials. See Quen, *supra* note 10, at 316.

13 *Arnold*, 16 How. St. Tr. at 765 (emphasis added).

that a man could know right from wrong, could understand the nature of the act he was about to commit, could manifest a clear design and foresight and cunning in planning and executing it, but if his mental condition produced or was the cause of a criminal act he should not be held legally responsible for it.[14]

This trend continued in the case of *Regina v. Oxford*, in which Lord Chief Justice Denman's charge to the jury combined portions of what would later be known as the "irresistible impulse" test and the "product" test.[15]

9.3.2 *M'Naghten*'s case

The most significant case in British insanity defense arose out of the shooting by Daniel M'Naghten of Edward Drummond, the secretary of the man he mistook for his intended victim: Prime Minister Robert Peel.[16] Following the admission of unanimous forensic expert testimony that M'Naghten was insane,[17] and after being informed that an insanity acquittal would lead to the defendant's commitment to a psychiatric hospital,[18] the jury found M'Naghten NGRI.[19]

Infuriated, Queen Victoria questioned why the law was of "no avail," since "everybody is morally convinced that [the] malefactor . . . [was] perfectly conscious and aware of what he did,"[20] and demanded that the legislature "lay down the rule"[21] so as to protect the public

---

14 Hadfield's Case, 27 How. St. Tr. 1281, 1313–14 (K.B. 1800).

15 173 Eng. Rep. 941 (N.P. 1840); see *infra* 9.3.3 and 9.3.4.

16 8 Eng. Rep. 718, 719–20 (H.L. 1843). See generally RICHARD MORAN, KNOWING RIGHT FROM WRONG: THE INSANITY DEFENSE OF DANIEL MCNAUGHTAN (1981). This political element was also present in the other major forerunner cases. In *Arnold*, the defendant had shot and wounded a British Lord, see Julian Eule, *The Presumption of Sanity: Bursting the Bubble*, 25 UCLA L. REV. 637, 643 (1978); in *Hadfield*, the defendant attempted to assassinate King George III, see Richard Moran, *The Origin of Insanity as a Special Verdict: The Trial for Treason of James Hadfield (1800)*, 19 LAW AND SOCIETY REV. 487 (1985); and in *Oxford*, the defendant attempted to assassinate Queen Victoria, see Frank R. Freemon, *The Origin of the Medical Expert Witness: The Insanity of Edward Oxford*, 22 J. LEGAL MED. 349 (2001).

17 See MORAN, *supra* note 16, at 18.

18 Id. at 19.

19 Id.

20 Id. at 20 (quoting Queen Victoria's Letters, Royal Archives RA 14/8).

21 Donald H.J. Hermann and Yvonne S. Sor, *Convicting or Confining? Alternative Directions in Insanity Law Reform: Guilty but Mentally Ill versus New Rules for Release of Insanity Acquittees*, 1983 B.Y.U. L. REV. 499, 510 (quoting 1 BENSON, THE LETTERS OF QUEEN VICTORIA, 1837–1861 587 (1907)).

"from the wrath of madmen who they feared could now kill with impunity."[22]

In response, the House of Lords asked the Supreme Court of Judicature to answer five questions regarding the insanity law; the answers to two of these five became the *M'Naghten* test:

> [T]he jurors ought to be told in all cases that every man is presumed to be sane, and to possess a sufficient degree of reason to be responsible for his crimes, until the contrary be proved to their satisfaction; and that to establish a defence on the ground of insanity, it must be clearly proved that, at the time of the committing of the act, the party accused was labouring under such a defect of reason, from disease of the mind, as not to know the nature and quality of the act he was doing; or, if he did know it, that he did not know he was doing what was wrong.[23]

This "rigid" test[24] has been criticized severely as bearing "little relation to the truths of mental life,"[25] reflecting "antiquated and outworn medical and ethical concepts,"[26] criticisms that were launched as soon as the case was decided.[27] Nevertheless, American courts quickly adopted the *M'Naghten* formulation, codifying it as the standard test, "with little modification," in virtually all jurisdictions until the middle of the twentieth century.[28]

9.3.3 Irresistible impulse

Partially responding to a major criticism of *M'Naghten*—that it concentrated inappropriately on the defendant's cognitive powers and ignores the "affective and volitional components of behavior"[29]—several courts developed what became known as the "irresistible impulse" test, allowing for the acquittal of a defendant if his (or her) mental disorder caused him (or her) to experience an "irresistible and uncontrollable

---

22 Id.

23 *M'Naghten's Case*, 8 Eng. Rep. at 722.

24 Perlin, *supra* note 8, at 862.

25 Benjamin Cardozo, *What Medicine Can Do for Law*, in Law and Literature and Other Essays and Addresses 70, 106 (Karl Menninger ed., 1931).

26 William A. White, Twentieth Century Psychiatry 493 (1936).

27 Isaac Ray, A Treatise on the Medical Jurisprudence of Insanity 42–43 (Winfred Overhholser ed., 1962) (first published in mid-nineteenth century).

28 Weiner, *supra* note 10, at 1060.

29 Hermann and Sor, *supra* note 21, at 515.

impulse to commit the offense, even if he remained able to understand the nature of the offense and its wrongfulness."[30]

9.3.4   Durham v. United States—the "product test"

Dr. Isaac Ray's criticisms of the *M'Naghten* decision helped lead to the "product" test: "if the [crime] was the offspring or product of mental disease in the defendant, he was not guilty by reason of insanity."[31] This test, although applauded by legal and medical commentators,[32] was not accepted in any jurisdiction other than New Hampshire until 1954, when it was adopted by the District of Columbia in *Durham v. United States*.[33] *Durham* rejected both *M'Naghten* and the irresistible impulse tests, on the theory that the mind of man was a functional unit, and that a far broader test would be appropriate.[34]

It held that an accused would not be criminally responsible if his or her "unlawful act was the product of mental disease or mental defect."[35] This test would provide for the broadest range of psychiatric expert testimony.[36] However, a wide range of criticisms—among them, that it failed to provide helpful guidelines to jurors,[37] and that it was too heavily dependent upon expertise[38]—resulted in the DC Court of Appeals modifying *Durham*,[39] and then ultimately dismantling it, concluding, in

---

30 See George Dix, *Criminal Responsibility and Mental Impairment in American Criminal Law: Responses to the Hinckley Acquittal in Historical Perspective*, in 1 LAW AND MENTAL HEALTH: INTERNATIONAL PERSPECTIVES 1, 7 (David Weisstub ed., 1986). This doctrine was adopted in an 1886 Alabama state Supreme Court case, *Parsons v. State*, 2 So. 854, 866–67 (Ala. 1886), and subsequently—at its high-water mark—in approximately 18 jurisdictions, ABRAHAM GOLDSTEIN, THE INSANITY DEFENSE 241–42 n.1 (1967).

31 State v. Pike, 49 N.H. 399, 442 (1870) (Doe, J., dissenting), overruled on other grounds in Hardy v. Merrill, 56 N.H. 227 (1875).

32 PETER W. LOW, JOHN CALVIN JEFFRIES AND RICHARD J. BONNIE, THE TRIAL OF JOHN W. HINCKLEY, JR.: A CASE STUDY IN THE INSANITY DEFENSE 17 (1986).

33 214 F.2d 862 (D.C. Cir. 1954), overruled in United States v. Brawner, 471 F.2d 969, 981 (D.C. Cir. 1972).

34 Id. at 870–71 (discussing criticisms of *M'Naghten* test).

35 Id. at 874–75.

36 Id. at 876.

37 HERBERT FINGARETTE, THE MEANING OF CRIMINAL INSANITY 30 (1972).

38 Hermann and Sor, *supra* note 21, at 520.

39 See, e.g., McDonald v. United States, 312 F.2d 847, 851 (D.C. Cir. 1962), clarifying that "mental disease and defect" include "any abnormal condition of the mind which substantially affects mental or emotional processes or substantially impairs behavior control."

United States v. Brawner,[40] that it was impossible to place appropriate limitations on psychiatric testimony within a framework requiring a determination of causation.

9.3.5   American Law Institute-Model Penal Code test

The American Law Institute (ALI) couched the substantive insanity defense standard of its Model Penal Code (MPC) in language which focused on *volitional* issues as well as *cognitive* ones. Under this standard, a defendant would not be responsible for his (or her) criminal conduct if, as a result of mental disease or defect, he (or she) "lack[ed] substantial capacity either to appreciate the criminality of his conduct or to conform his conduct to the requirements of law."[41]

This test differed significantly from *M'Naghten*. *First*, its use of "substantial" responded to case law that had required "a showing of *total* impairment for exculpation from criminal responsibility."[42] *Second*, the substitution of the word "appreciate" for the word "know" showed that a defendant "must be emotionally as well as intellectually aware of the significance of his conduct."[43] *Third*, it "capture[d] both the cognitive and affective aspects of impaired mental understanding."[44] *Fourth*, its use of the word "wrongfulness" rather than "criminality" reflected a focus on "an impaired moral sense rather than an impaired sense of legal wrong."[45]

This test was subsequently adopted by over half of the states[46] and, in some form, by all but one of the federal circuits,[47] including, as noted, the DC Circuit, once the home of *Durham*.[48]

---

40 471 F.2d 969, 973 (D.C. Cir. 1972). In *Brawner*, the Court of Appeals adopted the American Law Institute-Model Penal Code (ALI-MPC) test.

41 MODEL PENAL CODE § 4.01(1) (Tent. Draft No. 4 1955).

42 Hermann and Sor, *supra* note 21, at 522 (emphasis added).

43 GOLDSTEIN, *supra* note 30, at 87.

44 Hermann and Sor, *supra* note 21, at 522.

45 Id.

46 See Barbara Weiner, *Mental Disability and Criminal Law*, in THE MENTALLY DISABLED AND THE LAW 693, 712 (Samuel Jan Brakel, John Parry and Barbara Weiner eds., 3d ed. 1985).

47 Cases are collected in Kathryn J. Fritz, *The Proposed Federal Insanity Defense: Should the Quality of Mercy Suffer for the Sake of Safety?* 22 AM. CRIM. L. REV. 49, 55–56 nn.42, 46 (1984).

48 Omitted from this book is a discussion of the diminished capacity defense. See generally PERLIN AND CUCOLO, *supra* note 1, § 14-1.2.6.

9.3.6 Federal legislative developments

In the federal system, the substantive insanity defense had traditionally been the result of circuit case law.[49] However, after John Hinckley was found NGRI in the shooting of then-President Ronald Reagan, the Insanity Defense Reform Act of 1984[50] was enacted, having the effect of "returning the insanity defense in federal jurisdictions to *status quo ante* 1843: the year of . . . *M'Naghten*."[51] In addition to discarding the ALI-MPC test, the bill made changes in the law in other material ways:[52]

(1) It shifted the burden of proof to defendants, by a quantum of clear and convincing evidence;[53]
(2) It established strict procedures for the hospitalization and release of defendants found NGRI;[54] and
(4) It severely limited the scope of expert testimony in insanity cases.[55]

9.3.7 State legislative developments

The Hinckley verdict precipitated further reevaluation of the defense's future in at least 23 states.[56] In 15 of 16 that changed post-acquittal

---

49 See Fritz, *supra* note 47.

50 18 U.S.C. § 17.

51 Perlin, *supra* note 8, at 862; PERLIN, *supra* note 3, at 25.

52 On how the federal law "was a scientific step backwards," see Melinda Carrido, *Revisiting the Insanity Defense: A Case for Resurrecting the Volitional Prong of the Insanity Defense in Light of Neuroscientific Advances*, 41 Sw. L. REV. 309, 320 (2012).

53 See 18 U.S.C. § 17(b). Prior to this, all federal courts previously had placed the burden on the prosecution. For a representative pre-*Hinckley* case, see United States v. Andrew, 666 F.2d 915 (5th Cir. 1982) and cases cited id. at 918.

54 See James Ellis, *The Consequences of the Insanity Defense: Proposals to Reform Post-Acquittal Commitment Laws*, 35 CATH. U.L. REV. 961, 991 (1986).

55 See FED. R. EVID. 704 (1984):

> (a) Except as provided in subdivision (b), testimony in the form of opinion or inference otherwise admissible is not objectionable because it embraces an ultimate issue to be decided by the trier of fact.
> (b) No expert witness testifying with respect to the mental state or condition of a defendant in a criminal case may state an opinion or inference as to whether the defendant did or did not have the mental state or condition constituting an element of the crime charged or of a defense thereto. Such ultimate issues are matters for the trier of fact alone.

56 Linda Fentiman, *"Guilty but Mentally Ill": The Real Verdict Is Guilty*, 26 B. C. L. REV. 601, 604 nn.18–19 (1985).

procedures, commitment terms were lengthened, court supervision tightened or burden of proof altered, by shifting burden from state to defendant and/or reducing quantum from "beyond a reasonable doubt" to "preponderance of the evidence" or "clear and convincing evidence." In six of eight that changed substantive tests, definitions were restricted, either by changing from ALI-MPC or *M'Naghten* plus irresistible impulse to *M'Naghten*, or by restricting insanity defense testimony to *mens rea* evidence.[57]

9.3.8 "Guilty but mentally ill"

The most significant recent development in state insanity defense formulations has been the adoption in over a dozen jurisdictions of the hybrid "guilty but mentally ill" (GBMI) verdict.[58] This verdict received its initial incentive in 1975 in Michigan, following outcry over a state supreme court decision which prohibited automatic commitment of insanity acquittees.[59] It was intended to "protect the public from violence inflicted by persons with mental ailments who slipped through the cracks of the criminal justice system."[60] A defendant would be found GBMI if he or she were guilty of the offense in question, and was mentally ill but not legally insane at the time of the offense.[61] The rationale in support of such legislation was that it would reduce insanity acquittals, and assure treatment of those who were GBMI within a correctional setting.[62]

Most analyses have been critical, rejecting it as "conceptually flawed and procedurally problematic,"[63] as "not only superfluous [but] dangerous"[64] and as not accomplishing a different result than a guilty verdict.[65] Empirically, it was found to not offer significant public pro-

---

57 Lisa Callahan, Connie Mayer and Henry J. Steadman, *Insanity Defense Reform in the United States Post-*Hinckley, 11 MENT. & PHYS. DIS. L. REP. 54 (1987); in eight jurisdictions, a GBMI verdict—see *infra* 9.3.8—was added.

58 See Clark v. Arizona, 548 U.S. 735, 752 n.19 (2006) (listing jurisdictions), discussed *infra* 9.4.1.

59 People v. McQuillan, 221 N.W.2d 569 (Mich. 1974).

60 People v. Seefeld, 95 Mich. App. 197, 290 N.W.2d 123, 124 (1980).

61 MICH. STAT. ANN. § 768.36.

62 See Ames Robey, *Guilty but Mentally Ill*, 6 BULL. AM. ACAD. PSYCHIATRY & L. 374, 379–80 (1978).

63 Bradley McGraw, Dina Farthing-Capowich and Ingo Keilitz, *The "Guilty but Mentally Ill" Plea and Verdict: Current State of the Knowledge*, 30 VILL. L. REV. 117, 121 (1985).

64 Rodriguez, LeWinn and Perlin, *supra* note 6, at 411.

65 Hermann and Sor, *supra* note 21, at 578–81.

tection.[66] Perhaps most importantly, findings show that, in practice, the GBMI defendant is not ensured treatment "beyond that available to other offenders."[67] As a result, the GBMI verdict has become "deceptive and hollow."[68]

9.4   At the US Supreme Court

9.4.1   *Clark v. Arizona*

In *Clark*,[69] the Court concluded that due process did not prohibit the use of an insanity test couched solely in terms of the capacity to tell whether an act charged as a crime was right or wrong, nor did it prohibit restriction of consideration of defense evidence to evidence that bears on the defendant's *mens rea* (guilty mind):[70]

> [C]ognitive incapacity is itself enough to demonstrate moral incapacity. Cognitive incapacity, in other words, is a sufficient condition for establishing a defense of insanity, albeit not a necessary one. As a defendant can therefore make out moral incapacity by demonstrating cognitive incapacity, evidence bearing on whether the defendant knew the nature and quality of his actions is both relevant and admissible. In practical terms, if a defendant did not know what he was doing when he acted, he could not have known that he was performing the wrongful act charged as a crime.[71]

It should be noted that the decision in *Clark* spawned some of the most caustic commentary in decades responding to a Court decision in this area of law and policy.[72]

---

66 Christopher Slobogin, *The Guilty but Mentally Ill Verdict: An Idea Whose Time Should Not Have Come*, 53 GEO. WASH. L. REV. 494, 510–12 (1985).

67 McGraw, Farthing-Capowich and Keilitz, *supra* note 63, at 187.

68 PERLIN, *supra* note 3, at 95. See, e.g., People v. Marshall, 448 N.E.2d 969, 980 (Ill. App. 1983) (GBMI verdict does not provide a right to treatment for such offenders beyond the constitutional right to minimally adequate medical care available to all prisoners).

69 548 U.S. 735 (2006).

70 Id. at 742, construing Arizona's "guilty except insane" law, see ARIZ. REV. STAT. ANN. § 131105(A) (3).

71 Id. at 752. Justice Kennedy dissented for himself, Justice Stevens and Justice Ginsburg, criticizing the basis of the Court's distinction between incapacity evidence and *mens rea* evidence as "razor-thin." Id. at 787. Justice Breyer also dissented. Id. at 779.

72 See, e.g., Henry Fradella, *How* Clark v. Arizona *Imprisoned Another Schizophrenic while Signaling the Demise of Clinical Forensic Psychology in Criminal Courts*, 10 N.Y. CITY L. REV. 127 (2006); Susan Rozelle, *Fear and Loathing in Insanity Law: Explaining the Otherwise Inexplicable* Clark v. Arizona, 58 CASE W. RES. L. REV. 19 (2007).

9.4.2 Kahler v. Kansas

Several states have abolished the insanity defense, retaining a limited *mens rea* defense.[73] Nevada's attempts at abolition were struck down as unconstitutional, a sharply divided state Supreme Court finding that legal insanity was a "fundamental principle" entitled to due process protections.[74] In its most recent term, however, the Supreme Court ruled that such abolition—in the case of a Kansas statute that retained a *mens rea* exception[75]—did not violate the due process clause.[76]

Noting initially that state rules about criminal liability violate due process only if they "offend … some principle of justice so rooted in the traditions and conscience of our people as to be ranked as fundamental,"[77] the Court concluded that "crafting [insanity defense] doctrines involves balancing and rebalancing over time complex and oft-competing ideas about 'social policy' and 'moral culpability'—about the criminal law's 'practical effectiveness' and its 'ethical foundations.'"[78] Under Kansas law, mental illness is a defense to culpability if it prevented a defendant from forming the requisite criminal intent; a defendant is permitted to offer whatever evidence of mental health he or she deems relevant at sentencing; and a judge has discretion to replace a defendant's prison term with commitment to a mental health facility.[79] The Court's review of historical sources "reveal no settled consensus favoring Kahler's preferred right-from-wrong rule [the *M'Naghten* test]."[80]

It thus rejected the notion that any particular test of insanity developed into a "constitutional baseline,"[81] preferring to allow the balance between criminal culpability and mental illness to "remain open to revision as new medical knowledge emerges and societal norms evolve."[82]

---

73 See, e.g., UTAH CODE ANN. § 76-2-305; IDAHO CODE § 18-207; MONT. CODE ANN. §§ 46-14-101 *et seq.*

74 State v. Finger, 27 P.3d 66 (Nev. 2001).

75 See KAN. STAT. ANN. § 21-5209.

76 Kahler v. Kansas, 140 S. Ct. 1021 (2020).

77 Leland v. Oregon, 343 U.S. 790, 798 (1952).

78 *Kahler*, 140 S. Ct. at 1028, quoting, in part, Powell v. Texas, 392 U.S. 514, 538 (1968).

79 Id. at 1029.

80 Id. at 1030.

81 Id.

82 Id. at 1037.

Justice Breyer's dissent (for himself, Justices Ginsburg and Sotomayor) responded in this manner:

> But here, Kansas has not simply redefined the insanity defense. Rather, it has eliminated the core of a defense that has existed for centuries: that the defendant, *due to mental illness*, lacked the mental capacity necessary for his conduct to be considered morally blameworthy. Seven hundred years of Anglo-American legal history, together with basic principles long inherent in the nature of the criminal law itself, convince me that Kansas' law "offends . . . principle[s] of justice so rooted in the traditions and conscience of our people as to be ranked as fundamental."[83]

9.5   Procedural issues[84]

9.5.1   Defendant's right not to plead insanity defense

The results of a "successful" insanity defense may include heightened stigma and public enmity, acknowledgment of the commission of the underlying act, nearly universal automatic post-acquittal commitment (often to an inadequate, dangerous or substandard facility) and extensive post-hospitalization supervision. As a result, the defendant may wish to refuse to invoke the defense.[85]

Most recent cases have found that a trial judge may not force the defense upon a competent-to-stand-trial defendant if the defendant "intelligently and voluntarily" decides to forgo that defense.[86] On the other hand, if the defendant does not have "the capacity to reject the defense,"[87] the court retains the discretion to raise it *sua sponte*. Per the lead case of *Frendak v. United States*:

> [W]henever the evidence suggests a substantial question of the defendant's sanity at the time of the crime, the trial judge must conduct an inquiry

---

83 Id. at 1038.

84 Other procedural issues—notice, privilege against self-incrimination, informing the jury of the consequences of an NGRI verdict, bifurcated trials, jury questions, summations—are discussed in PERLIN AND CUCOLO, *supra* note 1, § 14-1.3.1, § 14-1.3.3, §§ 14-1.3.4 *et seq.*, § 14-1.3.5, § 14-1.3.6.5 and § 14-1.3.6.6. Issues as to expert testimony are discussed *infra* 10.1.

85 On the related question of whether a defendant is competent to enter an NGRI plea, see Coolbroth v. District Ct. of Seventeenth Judicial Dist., 766 P.2d 670 (Colo. 1988) (due process prohibits any determination of sanity until such time as the defendant is restored to competency).

86 E.g., Frendak v. United States, 408 A.2d 364, 380–81 (D.C. App. 1979).

87 Id. at 378.

designed to assure that the defendant has been fully informed of the alternatives available, comprehends the consequences of failing to assert the defense, and freely chooses to raise or waive the defense. . . .

If the judge finds that the defendant is capable of making a voluntary and intelligent decision to forgo an insanity defense, the judge must respect the defendant's decision and permit the jury's verdict to stand. . . . If, on the other hand, the judge is convinced that the defendant can not or has not made such a voluntary and intelligent waiver, the judge has the discretion to raise that defense *sua sponte*.[88]

In endorsing this test, a New Jersey appellate court cautioned that the hearing "should not be converted into a second competency hearing."[89] Rather, once defendant's competency to stand trial is established, the inquiry on the "insanity waiver" hearing should be limited to determining:

> defendant's awareness of his rights and available alternatives, his comprehension of the consequences of failing to assert the defense and the freeness of the decision to waive the defense, and should avoid an incursion into the area of mental capacity, which might develop into an irreconcilable conflict with the finding of competency to stand trial.[90]

Related to this question are other issues involving a defendant's right to make fundamental choices about his or her defense. In 2018, the Supreme Court held, in *McCoy v. Louisiana*, that fundamental principles afford criminal defendants the right to define the fundamental purpose of their defense at trial, even if most other accused persons in similar circumstances would pursue a different objective and adopt a different approach.[91] In light of this holding, courts began to reevaluate whether a person's Sixth Amendment rights were violated when counsel was permitted to present an insanity defense against their client's objection. Thus, in *United States v. Read*,[92] the Ninth Circuit held that the defendant's Sixth Amendment rights were violated when the trial judge permitted counsel to present an insanity defense against Read's clear objection.[93]

---

88 Id. at 380–81.

89 State v. Khan, 417 A.2d 585, 591 (N.J. App. Div. 1980), overruled on other grounds, State v. Handy, 73 A.3d 421 (N.J. 2013).

90 Id.

91 138 S. Ct. 1500, 1505–06 (2018).

92 918 F.3d 712 (9th Cir. 2019).

93 Id. at 719.

9.5.2   Procedures after an NGRI finding

In *Jones v. United States*,[94] the Supreme Court clarified that it was constitutional to create different retention/release rules for persons found NGRI than to civil patients.[95] The facts of *Jones* were straightforward. Jones was arrested on a charge of attempted petty larceny of a jacket from a department store, a misdemeanor under local law, punishable by a maximum one-year prison sentence. He was found NGRI following a bench trial and, pursuant to local statute, was ordered committed to a mental hospital.[96]

His appeal from denial of release was rejected, the District of Columbia Court of Appeals reasoning that abbreviated post-commitment procedures were appropriate "because of the predictive value of the initial determination of insanity and dangerousness at the criminal trial."[97] Eventually, the Supreme Court affirmed.

First, it sanctioned automatic commitment based on an insanity acquittal. As an insanity acquittal establishes beyond a reasonable doubt the fact that the defendant committed a criminal act, this provides "concrete evidence" as to the patient's dangerousness that is generally "as persuasive as any predictions about dangerousness" made regularly in involuntary civil commitment proceedings.[98]

The Court refused to distinguish between acts of violence and crimes such as the one with which Jones was charged, quoting from a District of Columbia Circuit Court of Appeals opinion (written by Chief Justice Burger when he sat on that court):

> [T]o describe the theft of watches and jewelry as "non-dangerous" is to confuse danger with violence. Larceny is usually less violent than murder or assault, but in terms of public policy the purpose of the statute is the same as to both.[99]

---

94 463 U.S. 354 (1983).

95 See *supra* 4.5.1, discussing Addington v. Texas, 441 U.S. 418 (1979) (burden on state by at least clear and convincing evidence).

96 463 U.S. at 359–60.

97 Id. at 373. The defendant had sought a hearing like those available to persons facing civil commitment, including a jury determination as to whether the hospital had proven, by clear and convincing evidence, that he was still mentally ill and dangerous. Id. at 360–61.

98 Id., at 364–65.

99 Id. at 365 n.14, quoting Overholser v. O'Beirne, 302 F.2d 852, 861 (D.C. Cir. 1961).

On the question of whether the patient's mental illness continued, the Court found that it was reasonable "to conclude that someone whose mental illness was sufficient to lead him to commit a criminal act is likely to remain ill and in need of treatment."[100] "Insanity acquittees," the court found, "constitute a special class that should be treated differently from other candidates for commitment."[101] Finally, the Court rejected the patient's argument that his release was compelled because he had already been institutionalized for a longer period of time than had he received the maximum sentence for the misdemeanor involved.[102]

Dissenting for himself and Justices Marshall and Blackmun, Justice Brennan charged that the court "pos[ed] the wrong question," and restated the issue: "whether the fact that an individual has been found 'not guilty by reason of insanity,' by itself, provides a constitutionally adequate basis for involuntary, indefinite commitment to psychiatric hospitalization."[103] He concluded that indefinite commitment "without the due process protections adopted in *Addington* and *O'Connor v. Donaldson*[104] is not reasonably related to any of the Government's purported interests in confining insanity acquittees for psychiatric treatment."[105] Justice Stevens also dissented, finding that the patient was "presumptively entitled to his freedom after he had been incarcerated for a period of one year."[106]

9.5.3   *Foucha v. Louisiana*

Although it had been taken for granted that an insanity acquittee must be released from confinement if he or she is no longer mentally ill or dangerous, that principle was given new content in *Foucha v. Louisiana*.[107] *Foucha* considered the continued post-insanity commit-

---

100   Id. at 366.

101   Id. at 370.

102   Id. at 368–69. *Jones* implicitly rejected the rationale and holding of State v. Krol, 344 A.2d 289, 297 (N.J. 1975), that had found "that the fact that the person to be committed has previously engaged in criminal acts is not a constitutionally acceptable basis for imposing upon him a substantially different standard or procedure for involuntary commitment," and that "labels [of] 'criminal commitment' and 'civil commitment' are of no constitutional significance."). See *supra* 4.2.5.1.2.

103   Id. at 370–71.

104   422 U.S. 563 (1975); see *supra* 4.2.5.1.3.

105   *Jones*, 463 U.S. at 386.

106   Id. at 387.

107   504 U.S. 71 (1992).

once no longer insane = must be released

ment of a defendant who had been found to be no longer mentally ill, but was still considered dangerous. The Court found that, since the basis for holding Foucha in a hospital as an insanity acquittee had disappeared, the state could no longer hold him on that basis,[108] relying on its opinion in *O'Connor*[109] for the proposition that, once the basis for a constitutionally permissible commitment disappeared, an individual could no longer be institutionalized.[110]

9.5.4   The right to refuse medication: *Riggins v. Nevada*

In *Riggins v. Nevada*,[111] the Court considered whether the involuntary administration of antipsychotic drugs to a defendant during the pendency of his trial violated his right to a fair trial by impeding his ability to consult with counsel, by interfering with the content of his own testimony or by negatively affecting his capacity to follow the proceedings?

After Riggins was arrested and jailed pending trial, he told a jail psychiatrist that he was "hearing voices in his head and having trouble sleeping," and informed him that, in the past, he had been prescribed the antipsychotic drug Mellaril. The psychiatrist then prescribed Mellaril, and subsequently increased the dosage to 800 mgs per day, an unusually large amount.[112] About ten weeks later, after Riggins' dosage had been reduced to 450 mgs, he was found competent to stand trial.[113]

The defendant then unsuccessfully sought a court order that would have terminated the administration of antipsychotic drugs during the pendency of the trial, on the theory that, as the defendant was proffering an insanity defense, he had a right to have the jury see him in "his

---

108 Id. at 77.

109 422 U.S. 563, 574–75 (1975).

110 It rejected the state's argument that Foucha's anti-personality diagnosis was a sufficient rationale for continued institutionalization. First, in Louisiana, antisocial personality disorder is not viewed as a "mental illness." *Foucha*, 504 U.S. at 78. Second, relying on Jackson v. Indiana, 406 U.S. 715 (1972), see *supra* 8.2.5, the Court found that if he could no longer be held as an insanity acquittee, he was entitled to constitutionally adequate procedures to establish permissible grounds for his confinement. *Foucha*, 504 U.S. at 79. Finally, stressing the "fundamental nature" of the individual's "right to liberty," the court concluded that Foucha—who had never been convicted of a crime—could not be punished. Id.

111 504 U.S. 127 (1992).

112 See id. at 137 (800 mgs within the "toxic range"); see also id. at 143 (Kennedy, J., concurring) (expert testified that 800 mgs was a sufficient dosage with which to "tranquilize an elephant").

113 Id. at 130–31.

true mental state."[114] He presented an insanity defense at trial, testifying that "voices in his head" had told him that killing the victim would be justifiable homicide. He was found guilty and sentenced to death.

On appeal, the Supreme Court reversed. While it presumed that the administration of the drugs was "medically appropriate,"[115] it weighed whether that administration, nevertheless, deprived the defendant of a fair trial. In answering this question, it turned first to the conclusion in *Washington v. Harper* that "the forcible injection of medication into a nonconsenting person's body represents a substantial interference with that person's liberty," and focused on *Harper*'s discussion of such drugs' side effects.[116] As *Harper* had found forced drugging of a convicted prisoner impermissible absent a finding of "overriding justification," a pretrial detainee (such as Riggins) would be entitled to "at least as much protection."[117]

The Court did not set down a bright-line test articulating the state's burden in sustaining forced drugging of a detainee at trial, but it found this burden would be met had the state demonstrated either (1) medical appropriateness and, considering less intrusive alternatives, "essential for the sake of Riggins' own safety or the safety of others," or (2) a lack of less intrusive means by which to obtain an adjudication of the defendant's guilt or innocence.[118]

It noted that the error below may well have impaired the defendant's trial rights, affecting not just his outward appearance, but also "the content of his testimony . . . , his ability to follow the proceedings, or the substance of his communication with counsel." It concluded that allowing the defendant to present expert testimony to *explain* the side effects could not possibly be curative of the possibility that the defendant's own testimony, his interaction with counsel or his trial comprehension were compromised by the drugs, and even with this testimonial assistance, an "unacceptable risk of prejudice remained."[119]

---

114 Id.

115 Id. at 133.

116 Id. at 134, quoting *Harper*, 494 U.S. 210, 229–30 (1990). See *infra* 10.4.3.

117 *Riggins*, 504 U.S. at 135.

118 Id. at 135–36.

119 Id. at 137–38.

Justice Kennedy concurred, taking a stronger anti-drugging position. Focusing extensively on the potential of side effects, he wrote that he would not allow the use of antipsychotic medication to make a defendant competent to stand trial "absent an *extraordinary* showing" on the state's part, and noted further that he doubted this showing could be made "given our present understanding of the properties of these drugs."[120] He concentrated on side effects' potential impact on defendant's fair trial rights—by altering his demeanor in a way that "will prejudice his reactions and presentation in the courtroom," and by rendering him "unable or unwilling" to assist counsel.[121]

If the medication inhibits his capacity to react to the proceedings and to demonstrate "remorse or compassion," the prejudice suffered by the defendant can be especially acute at the sentencing stage.[122] If the defendant cannot be tried without his behavior and demeanor being substantially affected by involuntary treatment, "the Constitution requires that society bear this cost in order to preserve the integrity of the trial process."[123]

9.6   Empirical data and myths[124]

The empirical research reveals that at least nine myths about the use of the insanity defense and its consequences have arisen and been perpetuated, but are all "unequivocally disproven by the facts."[125] Valid and reliable research unanimously agrees that juror attitudes in insanity defense cases reflect bias,[126] and research has both validated the

---

120 Id. at 139.

121 Id. at 142.

122 Id. at 144, citing William Geimer and Jonathan Amsterdam, *Why Jurors Vote Life or Death: Operative Factors in Ten Florida Death Penalty Cases*, 15 AM. J. CRIM. L. 1, 51–53 (1987–88) (assessment of remorse may be a dispositive factor to jurors in death penalty cases).

123 *Riggins*, 504 U.S. at 145. Justice Thomas dissented, suggesting the opinion might lead to reversals in cases involving "penicillin or aspirin." Id. at 155.

124 See generally Michael L. Perlin, *The Insanity Defense: Nine Myths That Will Not Go Away*, in THE INSANITY DEFENSE: MULTIDISCIPLINARY VIEWS ON ITS HISTORY, TRENDS, AND CONTROVERSIES 3 (Mark D. White ed., 2017).

125 Michael L. Perlin, *Whose Plea Is It Anyway? Insanity Defense Myths and Realities*, 79 PHILA. MED. 5, 6 (1983).

126 E.g., Jennifer Skeem, Jennifer Eno Louden and Jennee Evans, *Venirepersons's Attitudes toward the Insanity Defense: Developing, Refining, and Validating a Scale*, 28 LAW & HUM. BEHAV. 623 (2004); Jennifer Louden and Jennifer Skeem, *Constructing Insanity: Jurors' Prototypes, Attitudes, and Legal Decision-Making*, 25 BEHAV. SCI. & L. 449 (2007).

mythic nature of each of these erroneous beliefs[127] and has supported the findings of distortion and infection.[128]

9.6.1   Myth #1: *The insanity defense is overused*

There is no disputing the empirical analyses.[129] The general public,[130] the lawyers[131] and legislators[132] "dramatically"[133] and "grossly"[134] overestimate both the frequency and the success rate of the insanity plea. This error has "undoubtedly . . . abetted" "bizarre depictions,"[135] "distortion[s]"[136] and inaccuracies[137] in media portrayals of persons with mental illness who are charged with crimes.

9.6.2   Myth #2: *Use of the insanity defense is limited to murder cases*

In one jurisdiction, less than one-third of the successful insanity pleas entered over an eight-year period were reached in cases involving a victim's death.[138] Importantly, individuals who plead insanity in such cases are no more likely to receive an NGRI verdict than are persons charged with other crimes.[139]

---

127 See Tarika Daftary-Kapur, Jennifer L. Groscup, Maureen O'Connor, Frank Coffaro and Michele Galietta, *Measuring Knowledge of the Insanity Defense: Scale Construction and Validation*, 29 BEHAV. SCI. & L. 40 (2011).

128 E.g., State v. Moore, 525 So. 2d 870 (Fla. 1988) (reversible error where trial judge failed to excuse juror who said his beliefs about insanity defense would probably prevent him from following court's instructions).

129 See Valerie Hans, *An Analysis of Public Attitudes toward the Insanity Defense*, 24 CRIMINOLOGY 393 (1986).

130 Richard A. Pasewark, Mark L. Pantle and Henry J. Steadman, *The Insanity Plea in New York State, 1965–1976*, 51 N.Y. ST. B.J. 186 (1979).

131 Richard A. Pasewark and Paul L. Craig, *Insanity Plea: Defense Attorneys; Views*, 8 J. PSYCHIATRY & L. 413, 415, 436–40 (1980).

132 Richard A. Pasewark and Mark Pantle, *Insanity Plea: Legislators' View*, 136 AM. J. PSYCHIATRY 222–23 (1979) (in response to survey, one state's legislators estimated that 4,400 defendants pled insanity and that 1,800 were found NGRI in a sample time period; in reality, 102 defendants asserted the defense, and only one was successful).

133 Pasewark, Pantle and Steadman, *supra* note 130, at 186.

134 Pasewark and Pantle, *supra* note 132, at 223.

135 Henry Steadman and Joseph Cocozza, *Selective Reporting and the Public's Misconceptions of the Criminally Insane*, 41 PUB. OPIN. Q. 523, 532 (1977–78).

136 Id. at 523.

137 Id. at 532.

138 Rodriguez, LeWinn and Perlin, *supra* note 6, at 402.

139 Henry Steadman, Lydia Keitner, Jeraldine Braff and Thomas M. Arvanites, *Factors Associated with a Successful Insanity Plea*, 140 AM. J. PSYCHIATRY 401, 402–03 (1983).

9.6.3   Myth #3: *There is no risk to the defendant who pleads insanity*

Defendants who asserted an insanity defense at trial, but were ultimately found guilty of their charges, served significantly longer sentences than defendants tried on similar charges who did not assert the insanity defense.[140] These findings are consistent if the universe is limited to homicide cases.[141]

9.6.4   Myth #4: *NGRI acquittees are quickly released from custody*

Actually, NGRI acquittees spend about *double* the amount of time that defendants convicted of similar charges spend in prison settings; often, they face a lifetime of post-release judicial oversight.[142] Most importantly, the *less* serious the offense, the longer the gap between the amount of time that an insanity acquittee serves and the amount of time that a convicted defendant serves. For example, a California study showed that those found NGRI of *nonviolent* crimes were confined for periods over *nine times* as long.[143]

In one jurisdiction, only 15 percent of insanity acquittees had, within eight years, been released from all restraints,[144] 35 percent remained in full custody, and 47 percent were under partial court restraint following conditional release.[145]

9.6.5   Myth #5: *NGRI acquittees spend much less time in custody than do defendants convicted of the same offenses*

NGRI acquittees spend almost *double* the amount of time that defendants convicted of similar charges spend in prison settings;[146] often, they face a lifetime of post-release judicial oversight.[147]

---

140 Rodriguez, LeWinn and Perlin, *supra* note 6, at 401–02.

141 Id. at 402 n.32.

142 Michael L. Perlin, *Unpacking the Myths: The Symbolism Mythology of Insanity Defense Jurisprudence*, 40 Case W. Res. L. Rev. 599, 651 (1989–90).

143 Michael L. Perlin, *"For the Misdemeanor Outlaw": The Impact of the ADA on the Institutionalization of Criminal Defendants with Mental Disabilities*, 52 Ala. L. Rev. 193, 210 (2000).

144 Rodriguez, LeWinn and Perlin, *supra* note 6, at 403.

145 Id.

146 Id. at 403–04.

147 Id.

9.6.6   Myth #6: *Most insanity defense trials feature "battles of the experts"*[148]

Much of the public assumes—drawing on "Action news" depictions of controversial cases involving the insanity defense—that *all* insanity defense cases involve a "battle of the experts" who "will say whatever they are being paid to say," especially if they are experts testifying on behalf of the defense.[149] The empirical reality is contrary. In a survey from Hawaii, there was congruence on the question of insanity in over 90 percent of all cases, and in Oregon, the prosecutor's expert agreed with the defense expert in 80 percent of such cases.[150] These findings have been consistent with other research over the past 60+ years.[151]

9.6.7   Myth #7: *Criminal defense attorneys overuse the insanity defense as a means of "beating the rap"*

This is simply not so. First, the level of representation made available in many jurisdictions to the population in question is significantly substandard, and the case law is replete with examples of lawyers who have totally "missed" the evidence that an insanity defense would be the appropriate defense strategy; this has been clear for decades.[152] Second, *some* attorneys proffer an insanity defense for independent strategic reasons: as a plea-bargaining chip or as a vehicle by which they can obtain mental health treatment for their clients.[153] Third, juror bias exists independently of what defense lawyers do, and is "not induced by attorneys."[154]

---

148 See PERLIN, *supra* note 3, at 112–13.

149 Ronald L. Moore, *Learning about Forensics: What You Don't Know Can Hurt You, and Your Client*, ASPATORE, 2012 WL 5077959 (2012).

150 Jeffrey L. Rogers, Joseph D. Bloom and Spero M. Manson, *Insanity Defense: Contested or Conceded?* 141 AM. J. PSYCHIATRY 885 (1984).

151 David C. Acheson, *McDonald v. United States: The Durham Rule Redefined*, 51 GEO. L.J. 580, 589 (1963).

152 See, e.g., Michael L. Perlin, Talia R. Harmon and Sarah Chatt, *"A World of Steel-Eyed Death": An Empirical Evaluation of the Failure of the Strickland Standard to Ensure Adequate Counsel to Defendants with Mental Disabilities Facing the Death Penalty*, 53 U. MICH. J. L. REF. 261 (2020) (discussing cases).

153 Pasewark and Craig, *supra* note 131.

154 J. Alexander Tanford and Sarah Tanford, *Better Trials through Science: A Defense of Psychologist-Lawyer Collaboration*, 66 N.C. L. REV. 741, 748–49 (1988).

9.6.8   Myth #8: *The insanity defense is a "rich man's" defense*

Prominent US Senators have characterized the defense as a "rich man's defense,"[155] a "textbook parody of empirical and behavioral reality."[156] Actually, the defense is disproportionately used in cases involving indigent defendants.[157] But, because of exaggerated media attention in high-profile cases, this myth persists.[158]

9.6.9   Myth #9: *Criminal defendants who plead insanity are usually faking*

This is the oldest of the insanity defense myths, and the one that has bedeviled American jurisprudence since the mid-nineteenth century.[159] It continues to be reflected contemporaneously on a regular basis in prosecutorial summations,[160] especially where the defendant's outward, *physical* appearance does not comport with "ordinary common sense" characterizations of "insanity."[161] Judges declare themselves unable to determine whether pleas of insanity are real or feigned.[162]

The empirical data is radically different. In an eight-year study of 141 individuals found NGRI in one jurisdiction, independent experts

---

155 PERLIN, *supra* note 3, at 18 (citing Senate hearings).

156 Id. at 19.

157 See *Hearings on Bills to Amend Title 18 to Limit the Insanity Defense before the S. Judiciary Comm.*, 97th Cong., 2d Sess. 80 (1982) (testimony of Dr. Henry Steadman); see also PERLIN, *supra* note 3, at 18–19 (criticizing as unfounded the proposition that the insanity defense is a "rich man's ploy").

158 Michael L. Perlin, *"His Brain Has Been Mismanaged with Great Skill": How Will Jurors Respond to Neuroimaging Testimony in Insanity Defense Cases?* 42 AKRON L. REV. 885, 903 (2009).

159 See RAY, *supra* note 27, § 247, at 243; HENRY L. CLINTON, DEFENSE OF INSANITY IN CRIMINAL CASES: ARGUMENT OF HENRY L. CLINTON 6 (1873).

160 For a case example, see People v. Lundell, 538 N.E.2d 186, *app'l denied*, 545 N.E.2d 122 (Ill. 1989) (prosecutor's closing statement that defendant had fabricated insanity defense with aid of his counsel was reversible error).

161 On the question of whether or not defendant's insanity comports with "ordinary common sense," see People v. Tylkowski, 524 N.E.2d 1112, *app'l denied*, 530 N.E.2d 260 (Ill. 1988); see generally Michael L. Perlin, *"She Breaks Just Like a Little Girl": Neonaticide, the Insanity Defense, and the Irrelevance of "Ordinary Common Sense,"* 10 WM. & MARY J. WOMEN & L. 1 (2003).

162 See, e.g., People v. Marshall, 61 Cal.Rptr.2d 84, 100 (1997) (court "in no position to appraise a defendant's conduct in the trial court as indicating insanity, a calculated attempt to feign insanity and delay the proceedings, or sheer temper").

agreed that 115 had schizophrenia (including 38 of the 46 cases involving a victim's death), and in only 3 of the 141 cases was the diagnostician unwilling or unable to specify the nature of the patient's mental illness.[163]

---

163   Rodriguez, LeWinn and Perlin, *supra* note 6, at 404; the most comprehensive multi-state survey reveals that 84 percent of those acquitted by reason of insanity carried a diagnosis either of schizophrenia or other major mental disorder. Lisa Callahan, Henry J. Steadman, Margaret A. McGreevy and Pamela Clark Robbins, *The Volume and Characteristics of Insanity Defense Pleas: An Eight State Study*, 19 BULL. AM. ACAD. PSYCHIATRY & L. 331, 336 (1991).

10 Access to experts, sentencing, and correctional treatment issues

10.1 Introduction[1]

One of the most critical issues in all aspects of forensic mental disability law is that of access to experts. In its most recent term, the Supreme Court took note of the way that the balance between criminal culpability and mental illness must "remain open to revision as new medical knowledge emerges and societal norms evolve."[2] The role of experts in helping judges and jurors understand this balance is essential. It is also clear that few criminal trial process issues are as volatile as the appropriate role of psychiatric testimony at the sentencing stage. Finally, it is vital to consider how the rules of the right to refuse medication and the right to treatment apply to those in correctional facilities. This chapter will consider each of these issues.[3]

10.2 Access to experts

The use of partisan experts in insanity defense trials had been "well established" for over 300 years[4] as being of the "utmost importance" to the trial's outcome,[5] serving at least three purposes:

[F]irst, it supplies the court with facts concerning the offender's illness; second, it presents informed opinion concerning the nature of that illness;

---

1 See MICHAEL L. PERLIN AND HEATHER ELLIS CUCOLO, MENTAL DISABILITY LAW: CIVIL AND CRIMINAL chs 15 and 16 (3d ed. 2016) (2019 update).

2 Kahler v. Kansas, 120 S. Ct. 1028, 1037 (2020). See *supra* 9.4.2.

3 On other trial process issues (e.g., privilege against self-incrimination and confessions), see PERLIN AND CUCOLO, *supra* note 1, §§ 15-2 to 15-2.3.6 and 15-3 to 15-3.4. On issues involving persons with mental disability on probation and parole, see id., §§ 16-3 to 16-3.2. On other issues involving prisoners with mental disabilities, see id., §§ 16-4 to 16-4.3.1.

4 MANFRED S. GUTTMACHER, THE MIND OF THE MURDERER 112 (1960).

5 ISAAC RAY, A TREATISE ON THE MEDICAL JURISPRUDENCE OF INSANITY § 27, at 48 (1838) (1962).

and third, it furnishes a basis for deciding whether the illness made the patient legally insane at the time of the crime under that jurisdiction's standards of insanity.[6]

As a result, an indigent defendant's access to independent medical evidence became "inextricably intertwined with his very ability to obtain a fundamentally fair trial."[7] The absence of such a witness "goes to the very trustworthiness of the criminal justice process."[8]

10.2.1 Ake v. Oklahoma

In *Ake v. Oklahoma*,[9] a death penalty case, the Supreme Court ruled that an indigent criminal defendant who makes a threshold showing that insanity is likely to be a significant factor at trial is constitutionally entitled to a psychiatrist's assistance.[10] The Court had "long recognized that when a State brings its judicial power to bear on an indigent defendant in a criminal proceeding, it must take steps to insure that the defendant has a fair opportunity to present his defense."[11] This principle, grounded in the guarantee of "fundamental fairness," derives from the belief "that justice cannot be equal when, simply as a result of his poverty, a defendant is denied the opportunity to participate meaningfully in a judicial proceeding in which his liberty is at stake."[12]

"Meaningful access to justice" is the theme of the relevant cases; "mere access to the courthouse doors does not by itself assure a proper functioning of the adversary process."[13] A criminal trial is "fundamentally unfair if the State proceeds against an indigent defendant without making certain that he has access to the raw materials integral to the

---

6 Seymour Halleck, *The Role of the Psychiatrist in the Criminal Justice System*, in PSYCHIATRY 1982 ANNUAL REVIEW 386, 391 (1982).

7 Michael L. Perlin, *The Supreme Court, the Mentally Disabled Criminal Defendant, Psychiatric Testimony in Death Penalty Cases, and the Power of Symbolism: Dulling the* Ake *in* Barefoot's *Achilles Heel*, 3 N.Y.L. SCH. HUMAN RTS. ANN. 91, 126 (1985).

8 See United States v. Theriault, 440 F.2d 713, 717 (5th Cir. 1971), *cert. denied*, 411 U.S. 984 (1973) (Wisdom, J., concurring).

9 470 U.S. 68 (1985).

10 See generally Heather Ellis Cucolo and Michael L. Perlin, *"Far from the Turbulent Space": Considering the Adequacy of Counsel in the Representation of Individuals Accused of Being Sexually Violent Predators*, 18 U. PA. J. L. & SOC. CHANGE 125, 159–60 (2015).

11 *Ake*, 470 U.S. at 76.

12 Id.

13 Id. at 77.

building of an effective defense."[14] The Court considered the "pivotal role" psychiatry has come to play in criminal proceedings, reflecting the "reality . . . that when the State has made the defendant's mental condition relevant to his criminal culpability and to the punishment he might suffer, the assistance of a psychiatrist may well be crucial to the defendant's ability to marshal his defense."[15]

The Court then set out the psychiatrist's role in such cases:

[P]sychiatrists gather facts, both through professional examination, interviews, and elsewhere, that they will share with the judge or jury; they analyze the information gathered and from it draw plausible conclusions about the defendant's mental condition, and about the effects of any disorder on behavior; and they offer opinions about how the defendant's mental condition might have affected his behavior at the time in question. . . . [P]sychiatrists can identify the "elusive and often deceptive" symptoms of insanity, . . . and tell the jury why their observations are relevant. Further, where permitted by evidentiary rules, psychiatrists can translate a medical diagnosis into language that will assist the trier of fact, and therefore offer evidence in a form that has meaning for the task at hand. . . . [P]sychiatrists ideally assist lay jurors, who generally have no training in psychiatric matters, to make a sensible and educated determination about the medical condition of the defendant at the time of the offense.[16]

Courts have generally read Ake narrowly, and have refused to require appointment of an expert unless it is "absolutely essential to the defense."[17] By way of examples, courts have split on whether there is a right to an expert *psychologist* to perform psychological testing under Ake,[18] and have also, without citing Ake, rejected an application for the right to the appointment of a social psychologist to aid in jury

---

14 Id.

15 Id. at 80. See also Michael L. Perlin, "And I See through Your Brain". Access to Experts, Competency to Consent, and the Impact of Antipsychotic Medications in Neuroimaging Cases in the Criminal Trial Process, [2009] STAN. TECH. L. REV. 4, **14–16.

16 Ake, 470 U.S. at 80–81.

17 Perlin, supra note 15, at *21.

18 Compare Jones v. State, 375 S.E.2d 648 (Ga. Ct. App. 1988) (rejecting defendant's request for additional psychological evaluation; limiting Ake to *psychiatrists*) and Hough v. State, 524 N.E.2d 1287 (Ind. 1988) (no right under Ake to appointment of social psychologist to help in jury selection), with Funk v. Commonwealth, 379 S.E.2d 371 (Va. Ct. App. 1989) (rejecting defendant's argument that psychiatric assistance is *mandated* under Ake; no error to appoint clinical *psychologist*) and King v. State, 877 S.W.2d 583 (Ark. 1994) (appointment of psychologist sufficient under state statute).

selection.[19] *Ake*, on the other hand, was relied on so as to require the appointment of a pathologist in a criminal case.[20] On the perhaps-closer question of the requirement of the appointment of a DNA expert, after an intermediate appellate court in Virginia relied on *Ake* to require the appointment of such an expert, that decision was subsequently vacated, with no discussion of *Ake* in the subsequent opinion.[21]

10.2.2 *McWilliams v. Dunn*

More recently, in *McWilliams v. Dunn*,[22] the Supreme Court elaborated upon *Ake*. There, a case in which it had been alleged that the defendant had been malingering, the Court built on its *Ake* holding to explain that the defendant had the right to an expert to "translate these data [medical records, other doctors' reports] into a legal strategy."[23]

This expert could have appropriately explained that the defendant's "purported malingering was not necessarily inconsistent with mental illness."[24] The court underscored that "unless a defendant is 'assure[d]' the assistance of someone who can effectively perform these functions, he has not received the 'minimum' to which *Ake* entitles him."[25] The state failed to comply with *Ake*, as neither the neuropsychologist who had examined defendant nor any other expert helped defense evaluate neuropsychologist's report or capital murder defendant's extensive medical records[26] and "translate such data into legal strategy."[27]

---

19 Hough v. State, 560 N.E.2d 511 (Ind. Sup. Ct.), *on reh'g* (1990).

20 Wallace v. State, 553 N.E.2d 456 (Ind. 1990), *cert. denied*, 500 U.S. 948 (1991).

21 See, e.g., Husske v. Commonwealth, 448 S.E.2d 331 (Va. Ct. App. 1994) (state required to appoint DNA expert under *Ake*), *vacated*, 462 S.E.2d 120 (Va. Ct. App. 1995) (*Ake* issue not discussed), *aff'd*, 476 S.E.2d 920 (Va. 1996), *cert. denied*, 519 U.S. 1154 (1997). For a consideration of the application of *Ake* to DNA and other non-psychiatric evidence, see Paul Giannelli, Ake v. Oklahoma: *The Right to Expert Assistance in a Post-Daubert, Post-DNA World*, 89 CORNELL L. REV. 1305, 1418–19 (2004), concluding that "*Ake's* rationale extends to nonpsychiatric experts."

22 137 S. Ct. 1790 (2017).

23 Id. at 1800.

24 Id.

25 Id. at 1794.

26 Id. at 1796.

27 Id. at 1800. Dissenting for himself and three others, Justice Alito characterized the majority decision as "an inexcusable departure from sound practice." Id. at 1811. The next term, in Ayestas v. Davis, 138 S. Ct. 1080 (2018), the Court ruled that the lower courts applied too stringent a standard in rejecting defendant's request for funding so that he could develop arguments that his trial counsel's failure to investigate petitioner's mental health and alcohol and drug abuse rose to the level of ineffectiveness of counsel case turning primarily on interpretation of 18 U.S.C. §

Ake and *McWilliams* implicitly raise another question: might there be, in some circumstances, the right to an *additional* expert: to explain to jurors why their "ordinary common sense"[28]—abetted by heuristic reasoning[29]—is fatally flawed in such areas as the recidivism rate of sex offenders,[30] the rates of success and disposition of cases involving defendants who plead insanity[31] and the significance of mental disability as a mitigation factor in death penalty cases?[32] In such cases, where "junk science" has a remarkable hold over fact-finders,[33] perhaps this *additional* expert will make it less likely that that phenomenon will contaminate the legal process.[34]

10.3   Sentencing[35]

In response to criticisms of indeterminate sentencing, Congress passed the 1984 Sentencing Reform Act[36] to seek to bring a measure of regularity and uniformity in federal sentencing. A Sentencing Commission was created and was mandated to promulgate Sentencing Guidelines in accordance with the Act.[37] The constitutionality of these Guidelines—a binding set of rules that courts must use in imposing sentences[38]—was initially upheld by the Supreme Court in *Mistretta v. United States*.[39]

3599(f), providing that district court "may authorize" funding for "investigative, expert, or other services . . . reasonably necessary for the representation of the defendant".

28 See *supra* 2.4.

29 See *supra* 2.3.

30 See PERLIN AND CUCOLO, *supra* note 1, ch. 5.

31 See *supra* 9.6.1.

32 See *infra* 11.3.

33 See e.g., Michael L. Perlin and Alison J. Lynch, *"Mr. Bad Example": Why Lawyers Need to Embrace Therapeutic Jurisprudence to Root out Sanism in the Representation of Persons with Mental Disabilities*, 16 WYO. L. REV. 299, 312 (2016): "Scientific discovery moves faster than the law, and it is critical to make sure that the legal system is given an opportunity to catch up, rather than risk allowing 'junk science' to influence how a defendant is treated."

34 See Michael L. Perlin, *"Deceived Me into Thinking/I Had Something to Protect": A Therapeutic Jurisprudence Analysis of When Multiple Experts Are Necessary in Cases in which Fact-Finders Rely on Heuristic Reasoning and "Ordinary Common Sense,"* 13 L.J. SOC'L JUST. 88 (2020).

35 This section is largely adapted from Michael L. Perlin, *"I Expected It to Happen/I Knew He'd Lost Control": The Impact of PTSD on Criminal Sentencing after the Promulgation of DSM-5*, [2015] UTAH L. REV. 881.

36 See 18 U.S.C. §§ 3551; 28 U.S.C. §§ 991–98 (1988).

37 See 28 U.S.C. § 994(a)(1).

38 See id. Under the Act, a series of permissible sentencing ranges is created for each federal criminal offense. See 28 U.S.C. § 994(b)(2).

39 488 U.S. 361 (1989).

Under the Guidelines, a sentencing court initially was allowed to depart from the prescribed ranges where "the defendant committed a non-violent offense while suffering from significantly reduced mental capacity not resulting from voluntary use of drugs or other intoxicants."[40] There, a lower sentence "may be warranted" to reflect the extent to which the reduced mental capacity contributed to the commission of the offense, as long as the defendant's criminal history "does not indicate a need for incarceration to protect the public."[41]

Subsequently, the Guidelines were amended to bar below-range departures in cases where (1) the significantly reduced mental capacity was caused by the voluntary use of drugs or other intoxicants; (2) the facts and circumstances of the defendant's offense indicate a need to protect the public because of actual violence or a serious threat of violence; or (3) the defendant's criminal history indicates a need to incarcerate the defendant or protect the public.[42] Further, addiction to gambling would not be a reason for a downward departure.[43] Also, under the amended Guidelines:

> "Significantly reduced mental capacity" means the defendant, although convicted, has a significantly impaired ability to (A) understand the wrongfulness of the behavior comprising the offense or to exercise the power of reason, or (B) control behavior that the defendant knows is wrongful.[44]

Subsequent amendments further limited the circumstances under which a court can depart from the range of sentences prescribed in the Guidelines, limiting departures based on aberrant behavior and physical impairment,[45] and prohibiting departures based on diminished capacity in cases involving crimes against children and sexual offenses.[46] In general, the amendment prohibits departures based on factors that are not enumerated in the Guidelines or on combinations of factors which would not independently warrant a departure.[47]

---

40 U.S. SENTENCING COMM'N, 2011 FEDERAL SENTENCING GUIDELINES MANUAL § 5k2.13 (2011).

41 Id.

42 United States Sentencing Guidelines § 5K2.13 (amended 1998).

43 Id., § 5H1.4 (amended 1998).

44 Id., § 5K2.13, comment (n.1) (amended 1998).

45 Id., §§ 5K2.20, 5K2.22 (amended 2003).

46 18 U.S.C. § 3553 (b)(2) (amended 2003); United States Sentencing Guidelines § 5K2.0(b) (amended 2003).

47 18 U.S.C. § 3553 (b)(2) (amended 2003); United States Sentencing Guidelines § 5K2.0(b) (amended 2003).

Great discretion is vested in the trial courts in determining when a sentence reduction is appropriate under the Guidelines;[48] decisions not to depart from the Guidelines are generally not appealable.[49] Only if the district court misunderstood its authority to reduce the defendant's sentence will appellate courts be willing to disturb sentencing determinations.[50]

In several cases, courts invoked the Guidelines to reduce a defendant's sentence based on his or her reduced mental capacity. By way of example, in *United States v. Speight*,[51] the court found that a defendant (convicted of drug and firearm offenses) who suffered from schizophrenia and other emotional disturbances met all the criteria of the Guidelines, and that a sentence reduction was thus warranted.[52] But generally, determinations to *not* depart from the Guidelines are upheld.

However, subsequent judicial developments radically altered Sentencing Guidelines practice. First, in *Blakely v. Washington*, the Supreme Court struck down the Washington state Sentencing Guidelines as unconstitutional.[53] There, the Supreme Court applied its earlier ruling in *Apprendi v. New Jersey*,[54] holding that a defendant's right to jury trial was violated by a sentencing scheme that allowed a judge to impose a sentence above the statutory maximum based on facts neither admitted by the defendant nor found beyond a reasonable doubt by a jury. In its next term, a deeply-divided Court ruled in *United States v. Booker* and *United States v. Fanfan*[55] that the federal Sentencing Guidelines were subject to jury trial requirements of the Sixth Amendment, and that the Sixth Amendment's requirement that the jury find certain sentencing facts was incompatible with the Federal Sentencing Act, thus requiring severance of the Act's provisions that had made guidelines "mandatory."[56]

---

48 E.g., United States v. Yellow Earrings, 891 F.2d 650, 654–55 (8th Cir. 1989).

49 E.g., United States v. Ghannam, 899 F.2d 327 (4th Cir. 1990).

50 E.g., United States v. Ruklick, 919 F.2d 95 (8th Cir. 1990) (reversing trial court's refusal to depart from Guidelines in case where defendant had mental capacity of 12-year-old).

51 726 F. Supp. 861 (D.D.C. 1989).

52 Id. at 867–68.

53 542 U.S. 296 (2004).

54 530 U.S. 466 (2000).

55 543 U.S. 220 (2005).

56 Id. at 245.

Sentencing judges thus must consider (1) offense and offender characteristics; (2) the need for a sentence to reflect the basic aims of sentencing, namely, (a) "just punishment" (retribution), (b) deterrence, (c) incapacitation, (d) rehabilitation; (3) the sentences legally available; (4) the Sentencing Guidelines; (5) Sentencing Commission policy statements; (6) the need to avoid unwarranted disparities; and (7) the need for restitution.[57]

Subsequently, in *United States v. Anderson*,[58] interpreting *Booker* and vacating defendant's sentence, the court noted that the government "fail[ed] to account for the district court's consideration and discussion of Anderson's 'serious mental health issues,' presented in support of his request for a downward departure."[59] Elsewhere, courts have relied on *Booker* as authority for imposing non-guidelines sentences in cases of defendants seeking downward departures based on diminished mental capacities.[60]

It is also necessary to consider competency. It is black letter law that a court may not sentence an incompetent defendant.[61] Scholars have begun to explore the implications of competency doctrines on the resentencing of prisoners (who may have been competent when originally sentenced, but whose mental states have deteriorated while imprisoned).[62]

10.4   Treatment issues

10.4.1   Persons with mental disabilities in prisons[63]

There is no dispute that persons with mental disabilities are disproportionately represented in the criminal justice system. More individuals

---

57 18 U.S.C. § 3553(a), as discussed in United States v. Rita, 551 U.S. 338, 347–48 (2007).

58 452 F.3d 87 (1st Cir. 2006).

59 Id. at 93.

60 United States v. Pallowick, 364 F. Supp. 2d 923, 926 (E.D. Wis. 2005) ("In the present case, defendant moved for a downward departure based on his diminished mental capacity and vulnerability to abuse in prison. However, this was before *Booker* made the guidelines advisory. . . . Consistent with [defendant's] argument, I concluded that a non-guideline sentence was appropriate").

61 E.g., United States v. Collins, 949 F.2d 921 (7th Cir. 1991).

62 See Elizabeth Ford, Barry Winkler, Virginia Barber-Rioja, Christina Dell'Anno and Shelly Cohen, *Competency to Be Resentenced and the Rockefeller Drug Law Reform Act: How Does It Affect the Mentally Ill?* 37 J. Am. Acad. Psychiatry & L. Online 245 (2009).

63 On the specific issues faced by prisoners with intellectual disabilities, see Perlin and Cucolo,

with mental disabilities are now being incarcerated in penal facilities (and housed in pretrial institutions while awaiting trial) than in previous years.[64] Prisoners with mental disabilities are kept in solitary confinement disproportionately longer than other inmates.[65]

A federal court has found that Alabama's treatment of prisoners with mental disabilities was "horrendously inadequate" and in violation of the Eighth Amendment.[66] It came to this conclusion because of these violations by the state Department of Corrections:

(1)   Failing to identify prisoners with serious mental health needs and to classify their needs properly;

(2)   Failing to provide individualized treatment plans to prisoners with serious mental health needs;

(3)   Failing to provide psychotherapy by qualified and properly supervised mental health staff and with adequate frequency and sound confidentiality;

(4)   Providing insufficient out-of-cell time and treatment to those who need residential treatment; and failing to provide hospital-level care to those who need it;

(5)   Failing to identify suicide risks adequately and providing inadequate treatment and monitoring to those who are suicidal, engaging in self-harm, or otherwise undergoing a mental health crisis;

(6)   Imposing disciplinary sanctions on mentally ill prisoners for symptoms of their mental illness, and imposing disciplinary sanctions without regard for the impact of sanctions on prisoners' mental health;

(7)   Placing seriously mentally ill prisoners in segregation without extenuating circumstances and for prolonged periods of time; placing prisoners with serious mental health needs in segregation without adequate consideration of the impact of segregation

---

supra note 1, § 16-4.2. On the specific issues raised when prisoners are in so-called "super-max" facilities, see id. § 16-4.3.1.

64 See generally Michael L. Perlin, *"Wisdom Is Thrown into Jail": Using Therapeutic Jurisprudence to Remediate the Criminalization of Persons with Mental Illness*, 17 MICH. ST. U. J. MED. & L. 343 (2013).

65 See, e.g., Jessica Knowles, *"The Shameful Wall of Exclusion": How Solitary Confinement for Inmates with Mental Illness Violates the Americans with Disabilities Act*, 90 WASH. L. REV. 893, 896, 907 (2015).

66 Braggs v. Dunn, 2017 U.S. Dist. LEXIS 98755 (M.D. Ala. June 27, 2017), slip op. at 299.

on mental health; and providing inadequate treatment and monitoring in segregation.[67]

10.4.2   Right of prisoners with mental disabilities to treatment

It was estimated over a decade ago that 15 percent of male adults in prisons and jails have a mental illness, as do 31 percent of female adults,[68] a rate of two to four times that of the general population.[69] This issue grows in importance yearly.[70] Building on the Supreme Court's decision of *Estelle v. Gamble*[71] that the Eighth Amendment obligates the government to provide medical care to those whom it incarcerates, other federal courts have found a limited right to mental health care,[72] and, in at least one instance, to habilitation services in the cases of intellectually disabled offenders.[73]

In the most important recent case, the Second Circuit held that, as part of their right to adequate medical care,[74] plaintiffs—inmates at a county correctional facility—had a right to discharge planning.[75] Noting that, while under the Supreme Court's decision in *DeShaney v. Winnebago Cty. Dep't of Soc. Servs.*, there was no constitutional right to substantive services to persons in the community,[76] when a person is involuntarily held in state custody, and thus wholly dependent upon the state, the state takes on an affirmative duty to provide for his or her "safety and general well-being."[77] This "special relationship exception" imposes a

---

67 Id., slip op. at 300–01.

68 Henry Steadman, Fred C. Osher, Pamela Clark Robbins, Brian Case and Steven Samuels, *Prevalence of Serious Mental Illness among Jail Inmates*, 60 PSYCHIATRIC SERVS. 761 (2009).

69 Michael L. Perlin, *"Yonder Stands Your Orphan with His Gun": The International Human Rights and Therapeutic Jurisprudence Implications of Juvenile Punishment Schemes*, 46 TEXAS TECH L. REV. 301, 309–10 (2013).

70 Perlin, *supra* note 64.

71 429 U.S. 97, 104 (1976).

72 E.g., Bowring v. Godwin, 551 F.2d 44 (4th Cir. 1977); Inmates of Allegheny County Jail v. Pierce, 612 F.2d 754 (3d Cir. 1979).

73 Ruiz v. Estelle, 503 F. Supp. 1265, 1345 (S.D. Tex. 1980), *aff'd in part and rev'd in part*, 679 F.2d 1115 (5th Cir. 1982), *cert. denied*, 460 U.S. 1042 (1983). See also id., 679 F.2d at 1167.

74 Charles v. Orange County, 925 F.3d 73 (2d Cir. 2019). Plaintiffs were lawful permanent residents of the United States who had been detained by agents of the US Immigration and Customs Enforcement (ICE) agency and housed in the Orange County facility during the pendency of their immigration cases. Id. at 78–79.

75 Id. at 80.

76 489 U.S. 189, 196 (1989). See *supra* 6.5.

77 *Charles*, 925 F.3d at 82, quoting *DeShaney*, 489 U.S. at 199–200.

duty on the state in recognition of "the limitation which [the state] has imposed on [the person's] freedom to act on his own behalf."[78]

The Circuit read this obligation hand-in-glove with the requirements of *Gamble* that deliberate indifference to the medical needs of an incarcerated person violates the Eighth Amendment,[79] noting that these protections had also been extended to civil detainees who were housed in institutions for persons with mental disabilities.[80]

The Court reasoned that discharge planning was not so different from other measures the state takes in providing care to those in its custody as to be categorically beyond the reach of the "special relationship" exception; if "discharge planning is to occur at all, it must, by definition, occur prior to release from custody." If discharge planning is essential to providing care for mentally ill individuals, the rationale for the "special relationship" exception applies to this need no less than the need for other types of care, it found. "That the harmful consequences of a lack of discharge planning occur after release from custody does not remove discharge planning from the purview of the 'special relationship' exception."[81]

Discharge planning was, in fact, part of in-custody care:[82]

> It comports with common sense that someone with a serious mental illness would need to receive a summary of his medical records, including documents indicating his diagnosis and his prescribed medications. These aspects of a discharge plan are expected parts of what non-incarcerated patients seek, and pay for, in visiting doctors and hospitals for treatment. . . . [To] the extent Plaintiffs complain that they were not provided with documentation regarding the treatment they received while in custody, their complaint relates to the provision of in-custody medical care.[83]

---

78 *Charles*, 925 F.3d at 82, quoting *DeShaney*, 489 U.S. at 200.

79 *Charles*, 925 F.3d at 82, citing *Estelle*, 429 U.S. at 104.

80 *Charles*, 925 F.3d at 82, citing Youngberg v Romeo, 457 U.S. 307, 321–22 (1982). See *supra* 5.1.4. On a constitutional perspective on issues involving continuity of care in general, see Naomi M. Weinstein and Michael L. Perlin, *"Who's Pretending to Care for Him?": How the Endless Jail-to-Hospital-to-Street-Repeat Cycle Deprives Persons with Mental Disabilities the Right to Continuity of Care*, 8 WAKE FOREST J.L. & POL'Y 455 (2018).

81 *Charles*, 925 F.3d at 83.

82 Id.

83 Id. at 83–84 (emphasis in original).

10.4.3   Refusal of medication

Earlier sections of this work considered the doctrine of the right of incompetent defendants and the right of defendants pleading the insanity defense at trial to refuse medication.[84] The scope of the right in each case differed, and both differ from the scope of the right discussed in this section, the rights of those convicted of crime. The Supreme Court's jurisprudence on the medication refusal rights of forensic patients—those convicted of crime, those at trial pleading the insanity defense, and those awaiting trial—is doctrinally inconsistent, in large part, because of the totemic significance to the Court of the defendant's *status* in the criminal justice system, what might be referred to as "litigational side-effects."[85]

In the correctional case, *Washington v. Harper*,[86] the court—focusing on the plaintiff's status as a prisoner—found that the need to consider "prison safety and security" led it to uphold a prison regulation[87] if it were "reasonably related to legitimate penological interests," even where a fundamental interest is implicated.[88] This decision stemmed from the court's balancing the principle that inmates retained "at least some constitutional rights despite incarceration with the recognition that prison authorities are best equipped to make difficult decisions regarding prison administration."[89] Thus, the Court had little trouble finding that the regulation passed constitutional muster, given the "legitimacy and importance" of the governmental interest in combating the special dangers inherent in a prison environment made up of individuals with a "demonstrated proclivity for antiso-

---

84 See Sell v. United States, 539 U.S. 166 (2003), *supra* 8.2.4.1 (defendants incompetent to stand trial); Riggins v. Nevada, 504 U.S. 127 (1992), *supra* 9.5.4 (defendants pleading the insanity defense).

85 See Michael L. Perlin and Meredith R. Schriver, *"You Might Have Drugs at Your Command": Reconsidering the Forced Drugging of Incompetent Pre-Trial Detainees from the Perspectives of International Human Rights and Income Inequality*, 8 ALBANY GOV'T L. REV. 381, 397–98 (2015).

86 494 U.S. 210 (1990). Note that *Harper* was decided before either *Riggins* or *Sell*.

87 That regulation, Special Offender Center (SOC) Policy 600.30, provided for a pre-administration hearing before a committee composed of a psychiatrist, a psychologist and a correctional associate superintendent, and allowed for involuntary medication if the psychiatrist and at least one other committee member found that the prisoner suffered from a mental disorder either gravely disabling him or her or causing him or her to present a likelihood of serious harm to him or her self or others.

88 Id., at 222, citing Turner v. Safley, 482 U.S. 78, 89 (1987), and O'Lone v. Estate of Shabazz, 482 U.S. 342, 349 (1987).

89 Id. at 223–24.

cial, and often violent, conduct."[90] The state's obligation to treat the plaintiff medically must be considered in the context of the "needs of the institution," including the "safety of prison staffs and administrative personnel" and the "duty to take reasonable measures for the prisoners' own safety."[91] This obligation was even greater, the Court reasoned, where the prisoner was incarcerated in a facility restricted to inmates with mental illnesses.[92] The regulation was thus a "rational means of furthering the State's legitimate objectives."[93]

The Court found that inmates' interests were "adequately protected, and perhaps better served" by allowing medication decisions to be made by medical professionals rather than by a judicial officer.[94] Finding no indication that "institutional biases affected or altered" the decision before it, the court refused to presume that members of the institutional staff "lack the necessary independence to provide an inmate with a full and fair hearing" in accordance with the regulation.[95] Justice Stevens dissented, characterizing the liberty of citizens to resist the administration of "mind altering drugs" as "aris[ing] from our Nation's most basic values."[96] He had "no doubt" that the refusal of such medication was "a fundamental liberty interest deserving the highest order of protection."[97] He added: "[S]erving institutional convenience eviscerates the inmate's substantive liberty interest in the integrity of his body and mind."[98]

Harper clarified an important strand of Supreme Court jurisprudence: prison security concerns will, virtually without exception, outweigh individual autonomy interests.[99] Focus on the importance of social control in the prison environment and its concern with safety measures makes the Court's ultimate decision inevitable. Further, the decision reflects the Court's comfort with the idea that antipsychotic

---

90 Id., citing, inter alia, Hudson v. Palmer, 468 U.S. 517, 526 (1984). See also *Harper*, 494 U.S. at 227, basing holding on the "given . . . requirements of the prison environment."

91 Id., citing Hewitt v. Helms, 459 U.S. 460, 473 (1983), and *Hudson*, 468 U.S. at 526–27.

92 *Harper*, 494 U.S. at 225.

93 Id.

94 Id. at 231.

95 Id.

96 Id. at 237.

97 Id. at 241.

98 Id. at 249–50. Justice Blackmun also concurred in a brief opinion. Id. at 236–37.

99 See Laura Ryan, *Washington State Prison Procedure for the Forcible Administration of Antipsychotic Medication to Prison Inmates Does Not Violate Due Process*: Washington v. Harper, 59 U. CIN. L. REV. 1373, 1414 (1991).

medication can be used by *prison* authorities as a means of ensuring a less violent prison atmosphere, notwithstanding an individual prisoner's interest—that it concedes is "not insubstantial"—in avoiding the administration of such drugs.

11 The death penalty

11.1 Introduction[1]

Perhaps the most explosive area of criminal law and procedure as it relates to mental disability is that of the death penalty. The most important inquiries relate to findings of dangerousness, the role of mitigation, the competency of a person with mental disability to be executed and whether persons with intellectual disabilities are to be subject to capital punishment.

11.2 Testimony as to "dangerousness" at the penalty phase

In *Jurek v. Texas*,[2] the Supreme Court upheld a state statutory scheme requiring that the jury determine, beyond a reasonable doubt, whether there was a "probability that the defendant would commit criminal acts of violence that would constitute a continuing threat to society."[3] On this issue, the plurality opinion established its guidelines as to such a "dangerousness" finding:

> It is, of course, not easy to predict future behavior. The fact that such a determination is difficult, however, does not mean that it cannot be made.
>
> Indeed, prediction of future criminal conduct is an essential element in many of the decisions rendered throughout our criminal justice system. . . . The task that a jury must perform in answering the statutory question in issue is thus basically no different from the task performed countless times throughout the American system of criminal justice. What is essential is

---

1 See Michael L. Perlin and Heather Ellis Cucolo, Mental Disability Law: Civil and Criminal ch. 17 (3d ed. 2016) (2019 update).

2 See James Liebman and Michael Shepard, *Guiding Capital Sentencing Discretion beyond One "Boiler Plate": Mental Disorder as a Mitigating Factor*, 66 Geo. L.J. 757, 759 n.15 (1978) (*Sentencing Discretion*).

3 428 U.S. 262, 277 (1976).

that the jury have before it all possible relevant information about the individual defendant whose fate it must determine. Texas law clearly assures that all such evidence will be adduced.[4]

This aspect of the opinion was specifically seen as flawed by vagueness[5] and prejudicially misleading to the defendant.[6]

11.2.1   *Barefoot v. Estelle*

In *Barefoot v. Estelle*,[7] two psychiatrists testified in response to hypothetical questions at the penalty phase that the defendant "would probably commit further acts of violence and represent a continuing threat to society";[8] neither had examined the defendant.[9] The jury subsequently accepted this testimony and the death penalty was imposed.[10]

Before the Supreme Court, the defendant made three basic arguments:

- Psychiatrists, individually and as a group, are incompetent to predict with an acceptable degree of reliability that a particular criminal will commit other crimes in the future, and so represent a danger to the community.
- Psychiatrists should not be permitted to testify about future dangerousness in response to hypotheticals without having examined the defendant personally.
- Here, the testimony of the psychiatrists was so unreliable that the sentence should be set aside.[11]

---

4 Id. at 274–76.

5 See, e.g., Giles Scofield, *Due Process in the United States Supreme Court and the Death of the Texas Capital Murder Statute*, 8 AM. J. CRIM. L. 1, 32 (1980).

6 See, e.g., William Green, *Capital Punishment, Psychiatric Experts, and Predictions of Dangerousness*, 13 CAP. U. L. REV. 533, 540–42 (1984).

7 463 U.S. 880 (1983), superseded on other grounds by statute as recognized in Slack v. McDaniel, 529 U.S. 473 (2000).

8 Id. at 884. One of the psychiatrists was Dr. James Grigson, the infamous "Dr. Death," see Charles Ewing, *"Dr. Death" and the Case for an Ethical Ban on Psychological Predictions of Dangerousness in Capital Sentencing Proceedings*, 8 AM. J.L. & MED. 407, 410 (1983), who operated "at the brink of quackery." George Dix, *The Death Penalty, "Dangerousness," Psychiatric Testimony, and Professional Ethics*, 5 AM. J. CRIM. L. 151, 172 (1977).

9 *Barefoot*, 463 U.S. at 887.

10 Id. at 884–85.

11 Id.

The Court rejected the argument that psychiatrists could not reliably predict future dangerousness in this context, noting that it made "little sense" to exclude *only* psychiatrists from the "entire universe of persons who might have an opinion on this issue," and that the defendant's argument would also "call into question those other contexts in which predictions of future behavior are constantly made."[12] On the hypotheticals issue, the Court simply held that expert testimony "is commonly admitted as evidence where it might help the fact finder do its assigned job,"[13] and that the fact that the witnesses had not examined the defendant "went to the weight of their testimony, not to its admissibility."[14]

It also rejected the views presented by amicus American Psychiatric Association that:

(1)   such testimony was invalid due to "fundamentally low reliability," and
(2)   long-term predictions of future dangerousness were essentially lay determinations that should be based on "predictive statistical or actuarial information that is fundamentally nonmedical in nature."[15]

The majority also took issue with arguments raised by Justice Blackmun in dissent:

> All of these professional doubts about the usefulness of psychiatric predictions can be called to the attention of the jury. Petitioner's entire argument, as well as that of Justice Blackmun's dissent, is founded on the premise that a jury will not be able to separate the wheat from the chaff. We do not share in this low evaluation of the adversary process.[16]

Justice Blackmun dissented (for himself, and Justices Brennan and Marshall), rejecting the Court's views on the psychiatric issue:

> The Court holds that psychiatric testimony about a defendant's future dangerousness is admissible, despite the fact that such testimony is wrong

---

12 Id. at 896–98.
13 Id. at 903.
14 Id. at 904.
15 Id. at 920–23 (Blackmun, J., dissenting).
16 Id. at 899 n. 7.

two times out of three. The Court reaches this result—even in a capital case—because, it is said, the testimony is subject to cross-examination and impeachment. In the present state of psychiatric knowledge, this is too much for me. One may accept this in a routine lawsuit for money damages, but when a person's life is at stake—no matter how heinous his offense—a requirement of greater reliability should prevail. In a capital case, the specious testimony of a psychiatrist, colored in the eyes of an impressionable untouchability of a medical specialist's words, equates with death itself.[17]

Relying on the American Psychiatric Association's amicus brief, Justice Blackmun made four main points:

(1) no "single, reputable source" was cited by the majority for the proposition that psychiatric predictions of long-term violence "are wrong more often than they are right";

(2) laymen can do "at least as well and possibly better" than psychiatrists in predicting violence;

(3) it is "crystal-clear" from the literature that the state's witnesses "had no expertise whatever"; and

(4) such "baseless" testimony cannot be reconciled with the Constitution's "paramount concern for reliability in capital sentencing."[18] Because such purportedly scientific testimony was imbued with an "aura of scientific infallibility," it was capable of "shroud[ing] the evidence [, leading] the jury to accept it without critical scrutiny."[19] Justice Blackmun charged: "When the court knows full well that psychiatrists' predictions of dangerousness are specious, there can be no excuse for imposing on the defendant, on pain of his life, the heavy burden of convincing a jury of laymen of the fraud."[20]

In an earlier article, the author suggested that:

Barefoot appears to be indefensible on evidentiary grounds, on constitutional grounds and on common sense grounds. It flies in the face of virtually all of the relevant scientific literature. It is inconsistent with the development of evidence law doctrine, and it makes a mockery of earlier

---

17 Id. at 916.
18 Id. at 917–19.
19 Id.
20 Id. at 924.

Supreme Court decisions cautioning that *extra* reliability is needed in capital cases.[21]

No subsequent developments have suggested that this assessment requires any major substantive revision.

11.3   Mitigation

A consideration of the role of mental disability in the possible mitigation of sentence in death penalty cases begins with the test created by Prof. James Liebman and a colleague:[22]

(1)   whether the offender's suffering evidences expiation or inspires compassion;

(2)   whether the offender's cognitive and/or volitional impairment at the time he or she committed the crime affected his or her responsibility for his or her actions, and thereby diminished society's need for revenge;

(3)   whether the offender, subjectively analyzed, was less affected than the mentally normal offender by the deterrent threat of capital punishment at the time he or she committed the crime; and

(4)   whether the exemplary value of capitally punishing the offender, as objectively perceived by reasonable persons, would be attenuated by the difficulty those persons would have identifying with the executed offender.[23]

The initial Supreme Court cases sketched out the broad contours of the doctrine. In *Lockett v. Ohio*, the Court drew on the Eighth and Fourteenth Amendments to require that the sentencing authority, in all but the rarest kind of capital case, not be precluded from considering, as a mitigating factor, "any aspect of a defendant's character or record that defendant proffers as a basis for a sentence less than death."[24] Then, five years later, in *Eddings v. Oklahoma*,[25] the

---

21 Michael L. Perlin, *The Supreme Court, the Mentally Disabled Criminal Defendant, Psychiatric Testimony in Death Penalty Cases, and the Power of Symbolism: Dulling the* Ake *in* Barefoot's *Achilles Heel*, 3 N.Y.L. Sch. Hum. Rights Ann. 91, 111 (1985) (emphasis in original).

22 *Sentencing Discretion, supra* note 2.

23 *Id.* at 818 (gender neutral language added).

24 438 U.S. 586, 604 (1978).

25 455 U.S. 104 (1983).

Court held that the sentencing authority must consider *any* relevant mitigating evidence in sentencing a defendant. Not insignificantly, *Eddings* had been the victim of child abuse and was "emotionally disturbed," with mental and emotional development at a level below his chronological age.[26] And next, in *Penry v. Lynaugh*, the Court held that mitigating evidence of a defendant's intellectual disability and childhood abuse has relevance to his or her moral culpability beyond the scope of the "special issues" that jurors must consider in weighing punishment. Without such information, jurors cannot express their "reasoned moral response" in determining whether the death penalty is the appropriate punishment.[27]

How do jurors respond to such evidence? Research with mock jurors (and archival research in cases involving actual jurors) has revealed (1) a defendant's unsuccessful attempt to raise an insanity defense positively correlates with a death penalty verdict, (2) a mental illness defense is rated as a less effective strategy than other alternatives at the penalty phase (even including the alternative of raising no defense at all), and (3) jurors who are "death qualified"[28] are more likely to convict capital defendants who suffer from nonorganic mental disorders.[29] Further, jurors often demand that defendants conform to popular, commonsensical visual images of "looking crazy." This further "ups the ante" for defendants raising a mental status defense in a death penalty case.[30]

This dilemma is compounded further by the fact that many mental disorders of this cohort of defendants are never identified:

> Either no one looks for them, or the defendants do not consider themselves impaired, so they never request special evaluations. Even when defendants are examined, they often are unaware of what symptoms might mitigate

---

26 Id. at 107–08. See generally Michael L. Perlin, *"The Executioner's Face Is Always Well-Hidden": The Role of Counsel and the Courts in Determining Who Dies*, 41 N.Y.L. SCH. L. REV. 201, 210–11 (1996).

27 492 U.S. 302, 336–37 (1989). *Penry* had rejected defendant's claim that his mental retardation barred execution. Id. at 336.

28 See Lockhart v. McCree, 476 U.S. 162, 171–83 (1986) (upholding process of "death qualifying" jurors excluding potential jurors with "conscientious scruples" against the death penalty).

29 Michael L. Perlin, *The Sanist Lives of Jurors in Death Penalty Cases: The Puzzling Role of Mitigating Mental Disability Evidence*, 8 NOTRE DAME J. L., ETHICS & PUB. POL. 239, 246 (1994) (citing sources).

30 Id.

their sentences. Their inadequacies may make them less capable [in] assisting their attorneys in documenting types of neurological impairments that might be important for purpose of mitigation. It is thus no surprise to learn that many death row inmates exhibit signs of serious mental illness or significant mental retardation.[31]

11.4   Competency to be executed

The Supreme Court addressed this issue, first in the case of *Ford v. Wainwright*.[32] In the only portion of any of the four separate opinions to command a majority of the Court, it held that the Eighth Amendment prohibits the imposition of the death penalty on an "insane prisoner."[33] There was no majority consensus on what procedures were due; the opinion left it to the states to develop appropriate procedures that would "enforce the constitutional restriction upon its execution of sentences."[34] The "lodestar" of any such procedures "must be the overriding dual imperative of providing redress for those with substantial claims and of encouraging accuracy in the factfinding determination."[35]

There were multiple opinions in *Ford*. Most significantly, Justice O'Connor's concurrence[36] and Justice Rehnquist's dissent[37] both

---

31 Ellen Berkman, *Mental Illness as an Aggravating Circumstance in Capital Sentencing*, 89 Colum. L. Rev. 291, 298 (1989).

32 477 U.S. 399 (1986).

33 Id. at 405–10. There was no question as to the profundity of the defendant's mental illness:

> He believed that the prison guards, part of the conspiracy, had been killing people and putting the bodies in the concrete enclosures used for beds. Later, he began to believe that his women relatives were being tortured and sexually abused somewhere in the prison. This notion developed into a delusion that the people who were tormenting him at the prison had taken members of Ford's family hostage. . . . Ford [subsequently reported] that 135 of his friends and family were being held hostage in the prison, and that only he could help them. By "day 287" of the "hostage crisis," the list of hostages had expanded to include "senators, Senator Kennedy, and many other leaders." App., 53. In a letter to the Attorney General of Florida, written in 1983, Ford appeared to assume authority for the "crisis," claiming to have fired a number of prison officials. He began to refer to himself as "Pope John Paul, III," and reported having appointed nine new justices to the Florida Supreme Court. (Id. at 402)

34 Id. at 416–17. Here, the court noted that it was not suggesting that "only a full trial on the issue of sanity will suffice to protect the federal interests." Id. at 416.

35 Id. at 417.

36 Id. at 427.

37 Id. at 431.

reflected an obsessive fear[38] that defendants will raise "false"[39] or "spurious claims"[40] in desperate attempts to stave off execution. This fear—a doppelganger of the public's "outrage" over what it perceives as "abusive" insanity acquittals, thus allowing "guilty" defendants to "beat the rap"—remains the source of much tension in this area.[41]

Subsequently, courts generally interpreted *Ford* narrowly, many finding that competency to be executed depends only on three findings:

- that the prisoner is aware he or she committed the murders,
- that he or she is going to be executed, and
- that he or she is aware of the reasons the state has given for his or her execution.[42]

The Supreme Court then returned to this issue in *Panetti v. Quarterman*,[43] where the defendant (charged with capital murder in the slayings of his estranged wife's parents) had been previously hospitalized numerous times for serious psychiatric disorders.[44] Notwithstanding his "bizarre," scary, and "trance-like" behavior, he was found competent to stand trial and competent to waive counsel.[45]

After the jury rejected Panetti's insanity defense, it sentenced him to death. After exhausting state court remedies, his writ of habeas corpus was denied, the court ruling that the test for competency to be executed "requires the petitioner know no more than the fact of his impending execution and the factual predicate for the execution."[46] On appeal, the Supreme Court rejected a narrow reading of *Ford*, and reversed.

---

38 Perlin, *supra* note 26, at 216.

39 *Ford*, 477 U.S. at 429.

40 Id. at 435.

41 Perlin, *supra* note 26, at 216, quoting, in part, INGO KEILITZ AND JUNIUS P. FULTON, THE INSANITY DEFENSE AND ITS ALTERNATIVES: A GUIDE FOR POLICYMAKERS 3 (1984).

42 Panetti v Quarterman, 551 U.S. 930, 956 (2007).

43 Id.

44 Id. at 936.

45 Id. On waiver of counsel, see *supra* 8.4.1. At trial, Panetti wore a cowboy suit to court and attempted to subpoena Jesus Christ, Anne Bancroft and John F. Kennedy. See Brief for Petitioner at 11–12, Panetti v. Quarterman, 551 U.S. 930 (2007) (No. 06-6407), as quoted in John H. Blume, Sheri Lynn Johnson and Katherine E. Ensler, *Killing the Oblivious: An Empirical Study of Competency to be Executed Litigation*, 82 UMKC L. REV. 335, 339 (2014).

46 Panetti v. Dretke, 401 F. Supp. 2d 702, 711 (W.D. Tex. 2004).

First, it found that the trial court's failure to provide the defendant an adequate opportunity to submit expert evidence, in response to the report filed by the court-appointed experts, thus deprived him of his "constitutionally adequate opportunity to be heard."[47] It then found that the district court's narrow test unconstitutionally foreclosed the defendant from establishing incompetency by the means that the defendant sought to employ: by making a showing that his mental illness "obstruct[ed] a *rational understanding of the State's reason for his execution.*"[48] It was the prisoner's "severe, documented mental illness that is the source of gross delusions preventing him from comprehending the meaning and purpose of the punishment to which he has been sentenced."[49]

The Court carefully elaborated on—and clarified—*Ford*, reviewing testimony reflecting the defendant's "fixed delusion" system, and approvingly quoted expert testimony that pointed out that "an unmedicated individual suffering from schizophrenia can 'at times' hold an ordinary conversation," and that "it depends [whether the discussion concerns the individual's] fixed delusional system."[50] Further, it explained why execution of persons severely mentally disabled "serves no retributive purpose":

> [I]t might be said that capital punishment is imposed because it has the potential to make the offender recognize at last the gravity of his crime and to allow the community as a whole, including the surviving family and friends of the victim, to affirm its own judgment that the culpability of the prisoner is so serious that the ultimate penalty must be sought and imposed. The potential for a prisoner's recognition of the severity of the offense and the objective of community vindication are called in question, however, if the prisoner's mental state is so distorted by a mental illness that his awareness of the crime and punishment has little or no relation to the understanding of those concepts shared by the community as a whole.[51]

A decade after the decision, the Fifth Circuit ordered the district court to hold new hearings for a determination as to whether "this

---

47 *Panetti*, 551 U.S. at 949.

48 Id. at 956 (emphasis added).

49 Id. at 960.

50 Id. at 955.

51 Id. at 959. Justice Thomas dissented, characterizing the majority's holding as "half-baked." Id. at 978.

concededly mentally ill petitioner is competent to be executed."[52] Not insignificantly, in their initial petition for certiorari, Panetti's lawyers had told the Supreme Court that, in the two decades since *Ford* had been decided, the Fifth Circuit had yet to find a *single* death row inmate incompetent to be executed.[53]

11.4.1   Medication for the purposes of execution

Can mentally ill death row inmates be medicated to make them competent to be executed? This is an issue the Supreme Court has never addressed on the merits, and there is virtually no consensus in the lower courts.

In *Perry v. Louisiana*,[54] the Supreme Court had initially agreed to determine whether the Eighth Amendment bars states from medicating inmates on death row to become competent to be executed, but subsequently simply vacated the lower court's decision and remanded in light of *Washington v. Harper*.[55]

Subsequent cases reflect the depth of the split below. In *Singleton v. Norris*,[56] the court found that the state would not violate Eighth Amendment or due process by executing an inmate who has regained competency through forced medication as that would be part of "appropriate medical care."[57] Guided by *Harper* and *Ford*, the Court balanced the state's interest in carrying out a lawful death sentence against Singleton's interest in refusing medication, and found the state's interest to be "superior," especially since the defendant did not suffer side effects.[58] It explicitly rejected the defendant's claim that the Eighth Amendment prohibits the execution of one who is made "artificially competent."[59] In *Singleton v.*

---

52 See Panetti v. Davis, 863 F.3d 366 (5th Cir. 2017).

53 See Panetti v. Quarterman, 2006 WL 3880284, *26 (2006) (appellant's petition for certiorari), as discussed in Michael L. Perlin, *"Good and Bad, I Defined These Terms, Quite Clear No Doubt Somehow": Neuroimaging and Competency to be Executed after Panetti*, 28 BEHAV. SCI. & L. 671, 672 n.9 (2010).

54 111 S. Ct. 449 (1990), *reh. denied*, 111 S. Ct. 804 (1991).

55 494 U.S. 210 (1990). See *supra* 10.4.3. On remand, the Louisiana Supreme Court found, under *state* constitutional law, that the state was prohibited from medicating Perry to make him competent to be executed. State v. Perry, 610 So. 2d 746 (La. 1992).

56 319 F. 3d 1018 (8th Cir. 2003), *cert. denied*, 540 U.S. 832 (2003).

57 Id. at 1027.

58 Id. at 1025.

59 Id. at 1027.

State,[60] the South Carolina Supreme Court found that the state constitutional right to privacy would be violated if the state were to sanction
forced medication solely to facilitate execution.[61]

11.5   Execution of defendants with intellectual disabilities

In *Atkins v. Virginia*,[62] the US Supreme Court first found that it
violated the Eighth Amendment to subject persons with intellectual
disabilities[63] to the death penalty.[64] Since that time, it has returned
to this question multiple times, clarifying that inquiries into a defendant's intellectual disability (for purposes of determining whether he or
she is potentially subject to the death penalty) cannot be limited to a
bare numerical "reading" of an IQ score,[65] and that state rules based
on superseded medical standards created an unacceptable risk that a
person with intellectual disabilities could be executed in violation of
the Eighth Amendment.[66]

11.5.1   *Atkins v. Virginia*

The significance of *Atkins* is crystal clear from Justice Stevens' opening
paragraph:

---

60 437 S.E.2nd 53 (S.C. 1993). Notwithstanding the same name, these two cases involve different
    defendants and are totally unrelated.

61 *Singleton*, 437 S.E. 2d at 61.

62 536 U.S. 304 (2002).

63 At the time of the *Atkins* case, the phrase "mental retardation" was used. Twelve years later, in the
    case of Hall v. Florida, 134 S. Ct. 1986 (2014), the Court noted that it would use the phrase "intel-
    lectual disability" rather than "mental retardation" to conform with changes in the US Code and
    in the most recent version of the American Psychiatric Association's Diagnostic and Statistical
    Manual of Mental Disorders (DSM-5). Id. at 1990.

64 *Atkins*, 536 U.S. at 321:

> Construing and applying the Eighth Amendment in the light of our "evolving standards of
> decency," we therefore conclude that such punishment is excessive and that the Constitution
> "places a substantive restriction on the State's power to take the life" of a mentally retarded
> offender.

This decision came only 16 years after the Court had rejected similar arguments in Penry v.
Lynaugh, 492 U.S. 302 (1989).

65 *Hall*, 134 S. Ct. at 1990. See also Brumfield v. Cain, 135 S. Ct. 2269, 2281 (2015) (state postconvic-
    tion court's determination that prisoner's IQ score of 75 demonstrated that he could not possess
    subaverage intelligence reflected an unreasonable determination of the facts).

66 Moore v. Texas, 137 S. Ct. 1039, 1044 (2017) (*Moore I*).

Those mentally retarded persons who meet the law's requirements for criminal responsibility should be tried and punished when they commit crimes. Because of their disabilities in areas of reasoning, judgment, and control of their impulses, however, they do not act with the level of moral culpability that characterizes the most serious adult criminal conduct. Moreover, their impairments can jeopardize the reliability and fairness of capital proceedings against mentally retarded defendants. . . . The consensus reflected in deliberations [of the American public, legislators, scholars and judges] informs our answer to the question presented by this case: whether such executions are "cruel and unusual punishments" prohibited by the Eighth Amendment to the Federal Constitution.[67]

Atkins had been convicted of capital murder. In the penalty phase of Atkins' capital murder trial, the defense called a forensic psychologist, who had testified that Atkins was—per the language used at that time—"mildly mentally retarded."[68] After Atkins' death sentence was set aside (for other reasons), the same witness testified at the rehearing. However, the state's rebuttal witness testified that the defendant was not retarded, that he was "of average intelligence, at least" and that his appropriate diagnosis was antisocial personality disorder.[69] The jury resentenced Atkins to death, and the Virginia Supreme Court affirmed, over a dissent that characterized the state's expert's testimony "incredulous as a matter of law," and argued that the imposition of the death sentence on one "with the mental age of a child between the ages of 9 and 12 [was] excessive."[70]

The Court underscored that its inquiry should be guided by "objective factors," and that, the "clearest and most reliable objective evidence of contemporary values is the legislation enacted by the country's legislatures."[71] It stressed, on this point, the significant changes in

---

67 Atkins v. Virginia, 536 U.S. 304, 306–07 (2002).

68 Id. at 308. Atkins' IQ was 59. Id.

69 *Atkins*, 536 U.S. at 309 (testimony of Dr. Stanton Samenow). In other contexts, this witness has publicly stated that criminals are a "different breed of person," who seek to manipulate the system for their own ends. "He has abandoned sociologic, psychologic, and mental illness explanations for criminal behavior and holds the view that 'most diagnoses of mental illness [in criminals] resulted from the criminal's fabrications.'" See Ramdass v. Angelone, 187 F.3d 396, 410–11 n.1 (4th Cir. 1999) (Murnaghan, J., concurring, citing, in part, trial transcript), as discussed in Paul C. Giannelli, Ake v. Oklahoma: *The Right to Expert Assistance in a Post-*Daubert, *Post-DNA World*, 89 CORNELL L. REV. 1305, 1415 (2004).

70 State v. Atkins, 534 S.E.2d 312, 323–24 (Va. 2000).

71 *Atkins*, 536 U.S. at 312, quoting Penry v. Lynaugh, 492 U.S. 302, 331 (1989).

the 13 years since its *Penry* decision (at which time, only two states had banned the execution of this population); since that time, at least another 16 (and the federal government) enacted similar laws.[72] Here it focused on "the consistency of the direction of change," in light of the "well-known fact that anticrime legislation is far more popular than legislation providing protections for persons guilty of violent crime."[73] This about-face provided "powerful evidence that today our society views mentally retarded offenders as categorically less culpable than the average criminal,"[74] a finding leading it to conclude that "it is fair to say that a national consensus has developed against it."[75]

The judicial determination must be more nuanced than simply a reci-tation of IQ scores: mental retardation also involved, rather, "not only subaverage intellectual functioning, but also significant limitations in adaptive skills such as communication, self-care, and self-direction that became manifest before age 18."[76] Importantly, it distinguished this finding from a determination of competency to stand trial or criminal responsibility:

> Mentally retarded persons frequently know the difference between right and wrong and are competent to stand trial. Because of their impairments, however, by definition they have diminished capacities to understand and process information, to communicate, to abstract from mistakes and learn from experience, to engage in logical reasoning, to control impulses, and to understand the reactions of others. There is no evidence that they are more likely to engage in criminal conduct than others, but there is abundant evi-dence that they often act on impulse rather than pursuant to a premeditated plan, and that in group settings they are followers rather than leaders. Their deficiencies do not warrant an exemption from criminal sanctions, but they do diminish their personal culpability.[77]

Thus, the Court concluded this cohort of defendants should be "cat-egorically excluded from execution."[78] The retribution and deterrence

---

72 Id. at 313–15.

73 Id. at 315–16.

74 Id.

75 Id. The court added that this consensus "unquestionably reflects widespread judgment about the relative culpability of mentally retarded offenders, and the relationship between mental retarda-tion and the penological purposes served by the death penalty." Id. at 317.

76 Id. at 318.

77 Id. (emphasis added).

78 Id.

rationales that underlay the decision sanctioning the death penalty in *Gregg v. Georgia*[79] did not apply to mentally retarded offenders;[80] to apply it here would be nothing more than "the purposeless and needless imposition of pain and suffering," thus an unconstitutional punishment. On the question of retribution, "if the culpability of the average murderer is insufficient to justify the most extreme sanction available to the State, the lesser culpability of the mentally retarded offender surely does not merit that form of retribution."[81] On the question of deterrence, the Court again looked at earlier cases for a restatement of the proposition that "capital punishment can serve as a deterrent only when murder is the result of premeditation and deliberation,"[82] a "cold calculus" that was at the opposite end of the spectrum from the behavior of mentally retarded offenders.[83]

It feared that "reliance on mental retardation as a mitigating factor can be a two-edged sword that may enhance the likelihood that the aggravating factor of future dangerousness will be found by the jury,"[84] raising the specter that "mentally retarded defendants in the aggregate face a special risk of wrongful execution."[85] This reality led the Court to conclude that such was "excessive" and thus barred by the Constitution.[86]

There were two dissents, by the Chief Justice and Justice Scalia, the latter focusing on the "fear of faking":

> One need only read the definitions of mental retardation adopted by the American Association of Mental Retardation and the American Psychiatric Association to realize that the symptoms of this condition can readily be feigned. And . . . the capital defendant who feigns mental retardation risks nothing at all.[87]

---

79 428 U.S. 153, 183 (1976).

80 *Atkins*, 536 U.S. at 318.

81 Id. at 319.

82 Enmund v. Florida, 458 U.S. 782, 799 (1982). For a comprehensive overview of the relationship between the death penalty and deterrence in general, see Carol S. Steiker, *No, Capital Punishment Is Not Morally Required: Deterrence, Deontology, and the Death Penalty*, 58 STAN. L. REV. 751 (2005).

83 *Atkins*, 536 U.S. at 319.

84 Id. at 320–21, citing Penry v. Lynaugh, 492 U.S. 302, 323–25 (1989).

85 Id. at 321.

86 Id.

87 Id. at 353. Empirical analyses have found this fear "unfounded." See Blume, Johnson and Ensler, *supra* note 45, at 354; John H. Blume, Sheri L. Johnson, Paul Marcus and Emily C. Paavola, *A Tale*

"Nothing has changed," he concluded, in the nearly 300 years since Hale wrote his *Pleas of the Crown*:

> [Determination of a person's incapacity] is a matter of great difficulty, partly from the easiness of counterfeiting this disability . . . and partly from the variety of the degrees of this infirmity, whereof some are sufficient, and some are insufficient to excuse persons in capital offenses.[88]

11.5.2   Post-*Atkins* cases

Atkins was first clarified, modified and expanded in *Hall v. Florida*,[89] which made clear that inquiries into a defendant's intellectual disability (for these purposes) of determining whether he or she is potentially subject to the death penalty cannot be limited to a bare numerical "reading" of an IQ score.[90] Under Florida law, if a defendant's IQ was 70 or under, he or she had been deemed to be intellectually disabled; however, if his or her IQ measured at 71 or above, all further inquiries into intellectual disability—on the question of the application of *Atkins*—were barred.[91] *Hall* declared this rule unconstitutional for creating an "unacceptable risk" that persons with intellectual disabilities would be executed.[92]

In his majority opinion, Justice Kennedy reiterated a major point of *Atkins*:[93] that this population in question faced "a special risk of wrongful execution" because "they are more likely to give false confessions, are often poor witnesses, and are less able to give meaningful assistance to their counsel."[94] This led to a specific question before the Court: how was intellectual disability to be defined for purposes of executability?

Here, he turned to the "medical community's opinions" on this issue,[95] noting that that community defined intellectual disability according to

---

of Two (and Possibly Three) Atkins: *Intellectual Disability and Capital Punishment Twelve Years after the Supreme Court's Creation of a Categorical Bar*, 23 WM. & MARY BILL RTS. J. 393 (2014).

88 *Atkins*, 536 U.S. at 354, quoting 1 HALE, PLEAS OF THE CROWN 32–33 (1736).

89 134 S. Ct. 1986 (2014). See generally James Ellis, Hall v. Florida: *The Supreme Court's Guidance in Implementing* Atkins, 23 WM. & MARY BILL RTS. J. 383 (2014); Blume et al., *supra* note 87.

90 *Hall*, 134 S. Ct. at 1995.

91 Id. at 1994.

92 Id.

93 See 536 U.S. at 320–21.

94 *Hall*, 134 S. Ct. at 1993, quoting, in part, *Atkins*, 536 U.S. at 320–21.

95 Id.

three criteria: "significantly subaverage intellectual functioning, deficits in adaptive functioning (the inability to learn basic skills and adjust behavior to changing circumstances), and onset of these deficits during the developmental period."[96] The first two of these criteria were central, he said, as they had "long been" the defining characteristic of intellectual disability.[97]

Under Florida law, "significantly subaverage general intellectual functioning" was defined as "performance that is two or more standard deviations from the mean score on a standardized intelligence test."[98] Had the statute taken into account the IQ test's standard error of measurement (SEM) (reflecting, as it does, the "reality that an individual's intellectual functioning cannot be reduced to a single numerical score"),[99] it might have passed constitutional muster.[100] But, Florida ignored this standard error of measurement, creating, rather, a bright-line rule that any person with an IQ measured over 70 was not intellectually disabled, and was further barred from introducing any other evidence that would show that "his faculties are limited."[101]

This state rule thus forbade Florida sentencing courts from considering "even substantial and weighty evidence of intellectual disability as measured and made manifest by the defendant's failure or inability to adapt to his social and cultural environment, including medical histories, behavioral records, school tests and reports, and testimony regarding past behavior and family circumstances,"[102] notwithstanding the fact that the medical community accepts all of this evidence as probative of intellectual disability, whether or not an individual's score is over or below 70.[103]

---

96   Id. at 1994, citing, inter alia, *Atkins*, 536 U.S. at 308 n.3.

97   Id.

98   FLA. STAT. § 921.137(1) (2013).

99   "An individual's IQ test score on any given exam may fluctuate for a variety of reasons. These include the test-taker's health; practice from earlier tests; the environment or location of the test; the examiner's demeanor; the subjective judgment involved in scoring certain questions on the exam; and simple lucky guessing." *Hall*, 134 S. Ct. at 1995.

100 Id. at 1994.

101 Id., citing Cherry v. State, 959 So. 2d 702, 712–13 (Fla. 2007).

102 *Hall*, 134 S. Ct. at 1994.

103 Id., citing brief of amicus American Psychological Association, at 15–16.

Florida's rule thus disregarded "established medical practice"[104] in two interrelated ways:

> It takes an IQ score as final and conclusive evidence of a defendant's intellectual capacity, when experts in the field would consider other evidence. It also relies on a purportedly scientific measurement of the defendant's abilities, his IQ score, while refusing to recognize that the score is, on its own terms, imprecise.[105]

This contradicted all professional judgment. "The professionals who design, administer, and interpret IQ tests have agreed, for years now, that IQ test scores should be read not as a single fixed number but as a range."[106] The Court stressed: *"An individual's intellectual functioning cannot be reduced to a single numerical score."*[107] It was thus error to use such a test score "without necessary adjustment."[108] The Court also considered post-*Atkins* legislative developments, concluding that "every state legislature to have considered the issue after *Atkins*—save Virginia's— . . . whose law has been interpreted by its courts has taken a position contrary to that of Florida."[109] As the "vast majority" of states had rejected a strict 70 cutoff, and as the trend to recognize the significance of the SEM was "consisten[t]," this was, to the Court, "strong evidence of consensus that our society does not regard this strict cutoff as proper or humane."[110]

The Court also stressed that neither Florida nor its supporting amici could point to "a *single* medical professional who supports this cutoff," and that the state's rule went against "unanimous professional consensus."[111] Intellectual disability, Justice Kennedy underscored, "is a condition, not a number."[112] He concluded:

---

104 Id. at 1995.

105 Id.

106 Id.

107 Id. (emphasis added). Also, the Court added, "because the test itself may be flawed, or administered in a consistently flawed manner, multiple examinations may result in repeated similar scores, so that even a consistent score is not conclusive evidence of intellectual functioning." Id. at 1995–96.

108 Id. at 1996.

109 Id. at 1998.

110 Id.

111 Id. at 1999 (emphasis added).

112 Id. at 2001.

The death penalty is the gravest sentence our society may impose. Persons facing that most severe sanction must have a fair opportunity to show that the Constitution prohibits their execution. Florida's law contravenes our Nation's commitment to dignity and its duty to teach human decency as the mark of a civilized world. The States are laboratories for experimentation, but those experiments may not deny the basic dignity the Constitution protects.[113]

In his dissent, Justice Alito disagreed, arguing that the positions of professional associations "at best, represent the views of *a small professional elite*,"[114] concluding that Florida's standard was "sensible," comporting with the "longstanding belief that IQ tests are the best measure of intellectual functioning."[115]

Subsequently, the Court held in *Moore v. Texas*[116] that state rules—based on superseded medical standards[117]—created an unacceptable risk that a person with intellectual disabilities could be executed in violation of the Eighth Amendment.[118] The Court rearticulated its finding in *Hall* that adjudications of intellectual disability should be "informed by the views of medical experts,"[119] and that the *Briseno* standards were

---

113 Id.

114 Id. at 2006 (emphasis added).

115 Id. The Chief Justice, Justice Scalia and Justice Thomas joined in this dissent.

116 137 S. Ct. 1039 (2017) (*Moore I*).

117 Texas had adhered, in *Ex parte* Briseno, 135 S.W.3d 1 (Tex. Ct. Crim. App. 2004), to a standard that included seven evidentiary factors that it had articulated without any citation "to any authority, medical or judicial." *Moore I*, 137 S. Ct. at 1046. These factors had become known as the "Of Mice and Men" factors as they were, apparently, taken from John Steinbeck's novel of that name. The seven "*Briseno* factors" were these:

- "Did those who knew the person best during the developmental stage—his family, friends, teachers, employers, authorities—think he was mentally retarded at that time, and, if so, act in accordance with that determination?
- "Has the person formulated plans and carried them through or is his conduct impulsive?
- "Does his conduct show leadership or does it show that he is led around by others?
- "Is his conduct in response to external stimuli rational and appropriate, regardless of whether it is socially acceptable?
- "Does he respond coherently, rationally, and on point to oral or written questions or do his responses wander from subject to subject?
- "Can the person hide facts or lie effectively in his own or others' interests?
- "Putting aside any heinousness or gruesomeness surrounding the capital offense, did the commission of that offense require forethought, planning, and complex execution of purpose?" (*Moore I*, 137 S. Ct. at 1046 n.6, citing *Briseno*, 135 S.W.3d, at 8–9)

118 *Moore I*, 137 S. Ct. at 1044.

119 Id., quoting *Hall*, 135 S. Ct. at 2000.

"an invention . . . untied to any acknowledged source."[120] After quoting its language in *Hall* that "[t]he Eighth Amendment is not fastened to the obsolete,"[121] the Court in *Moore I* noted:

> *Hall* indicated that being informed by the medical community does not demand adherence to everything stated in the latest medical guide. But neither does our precedent license disregard of current medical standards.[122]

The state court erred, the Supreme Court concluded, by mistakenly "overemphasiz[ing the defendant's] perceived adaptive strengths," rather than focusing on his "adaptive deficits."[123] Further the lower court's "attachment" to the *Briseno* factors "further impeded its assessment of Moore's adaptive functioning" as they "advanced lay perceptions of intellectual disabilities," noting that the medical profession "has endeavored to counter [such] lay stereotypes."[124] Although the Texas court had said it would "abandon reliance on the *Briseno* evidentiary factors,"[125] the Supreme Court concluded that "it seems to have used many of those factors in reaching its conclusion."[126] The state court continued—in spite of the Court's admonition in *Moore I*—to rely on "lay stereotypes of the intellectually disabled."[127]

Some important strains emerge from the post-*Atkins* opinions in *Hall* and *Moore*. The focus on dignity in *Hall*—mentioned at least eight times—is of major significance.[128] This followed up its focus on dignitarian values in *Atkins*, in which it cited *Trop v. Dulles*[129] for the proposition that "the basic concept underlying the Eighth Amendment is nothing less than the dignity of man. . . . The Amendment must draw its meaning from the evolving standards of decency that mark the

---

120 *Moore I*, 137 S. Ct. at 1044.

121 Id. at 1048, quoting *Hall*, 134 S. Ct. at 1992.

122 *Moore I*, 137 S. Ct. at 1049.

123 Id. at 1050.

124 Id. at 1051–52.

125 *Ex parte* Moore, 548 S.W. 3d 552, 560 (Tex. Ct. Crim. App. 2018), *rev'd and remanded*, 139 S. Ct. 666 (2019).

126 Moore v. Texas, 138 S. Ct. 666, 671 (2019) (*Moore II*).

127 *Moore I*, 137 S. Ct. at 1052.

128 See generally Kevin Barry, *The Death Penalty & the Dignity Clauses*, 102 Iowa L. Rev. 383 (2017).

129 356 U.S. 86, 100–01 (1958).

progress of a maturing society."[130] Its strong focus in *Hall* underscores its commitment to these principles.[131]

Moore is significant for multiple reasons. First, it clarifies that the Court takes very seriously the potential peril of subjecting a person with intellectual disability to execution. Second, it reaffirms the Court's embrace of the most up-to-date professional standards in support of its constitutional discourse. Third, its focus on the way the *Briseno* factors "advanced lay perceptions of intellectual disabilities" and how the medical profession "has endeavored to counter [such] lay stereotypes"[132] tells us that the Court truly does take these issues seriously.

---

130 Atkins v. Virginia, 536 U.S. 304, 311–12 (2002).

131 Consider Justice Alito's curious dissent in *Hall*. His charge that the professional associations relied upon by the majority reflect nothing but a "small, professional elite," *Hall*, 134 S. Ct. at 2005, flies in the face of reality. At this point in time, there is not a shred of expert support that suggests that a strict numerical cutoff can or should be the "be all and end all" of assessing intellectual disability. Yet, he adheres to his rejection of *all* professional opinion (supported by *all* the valid and reliable research).

132 *Moore I*, 137 S. Ct. at 1052; *Moore II*, 139 S. Ct. at 672.

Bibliography

Books

Michael L. Perlin, Mental Disability and the Death Penalty: The Shame of the States (2013).

Michael L. Perlin, The Hidden Prejudice: Mental Disability on Trial (2000).

Michael L. Perlin, The Jurisprudence of the Insanity Defense (1994).

Michael L. Perlin and Heather Ellis Cucolo, Mental Disability Law: Civil and Criminal (3d ed. 2016) (2019 update).

Michael L. Perlin and Alison J. Lynch, Sexuality, Disability and the Law: Beyond the Last Frontier? (2016).

Bruce J. Winick, Civil Commitment: A Therapeutic Jurisprudence Model (2005).

Articles and book chapters

Morton Birnbaum, *The Right to Treatment*, 46 A.B.A. J. 499 (1960).

Henry A. Dlugacz and Christopher Wimmer, *The Ethics of Representing Clients with Limited Competency in Guardianship Proceedings*, 4 St. Louis U. J. Health L. & Pol'y 331 (2011).

Ginger Lerner-Wren, *Mental Health Courts: Serving Justice and Promoting Recovery*, 19 Annals Health L. 577 (2010).

John Monahan, *Clinical and Actuarial Predictions of Violence*, in 1 Modern Scientific Evidence: The Law and Science of Expert Testimony § 7.2.2-1[2], at 317 (David Faigman et al. eds., 1997).

Grant Morris and J. Reid Meloy, *Out of Mind? Out of Sight: The Uncivil Commitment of Permanently Incompetent Criminal Defendants*, 27 U.C. Davis L. Rev. 1, 8 (1993).

Michael L. Perlin, *"Half-Wracked Prejudice Leaped Forth": Sanism, Pretextuality, and Why and How Mental Disability Law Developed as It Did*, 10 J. Contemp. Leg. Iss. 3 (1999).

Michael L. Perlin, *"I Expected It to Happen/I Knew He'd Lost Control": The Impact of PTSD on Criminal Sentencing after the Promulgation of DSM-5*, [2015] Utah L. Rev. 881.

Michael L. Perlin, *The Insanity Defense: Nine Myths That Will Not Go Away*, in The Insanity Defense: Multidisciplinary Views on Its History, Trends, and Controversies 3 (Mark D. White ed., 2017).

Michael L. Perlin, *"Who Will Judge the Many When the Game is Through?": Considering the Profound Differences between Mental Health Courts and "Traditional" Involuntary Civil Commitment Courts*, 41 SEATTLE U. L. REV. 937 (2018).

Michael L. Perlin and Mehgan Gallagher, *"Temptation's Page Flies out the Door": Navigating Complex Systems of Disability and the Law from a Therapeutic Jurisprudence Perspective*, 25 BUFFALO HUM. RTS. L. REV. 1 (2018–19).

Michael L. Perlin, Deborah A. Dorfman and Naomi M. Weinstein, *"On Desolation Row": The Blurring of the Borders between Civil and Criminal Mental Disability Law, and What It Means for All of Us*, 24 TEX. J. ON CIV. LIBS. & CIV. RTS. 59 (2018).

Michael L. Perlin, Talia Roitberg Harmon and Sarah Chatt, *"A World of Steel-Eyed Death": An Empirical Evaluation of the Failure of the Strickland Standard to Ensure Adequate Counsel to Defendants with Mental Disabilities Facing the Death Penalty*, 53 U. MICH. J. L. REF. 261 (2020).

Joseph H. Rodriguez, Laura M. LeWinn and Michael L. Perlin, *The Insanity Defense under Siege: Legislative Assaults and Legal Rejoinders*, 14 RUTGERS L.J. 397 (1983).

Amy D. Ronner, *Songs of Validation, Voice, and Voluntary Participation: Therapeutic Jurisprudence, Miranda and Juveniles*, 71 U. CIN. L. REV. 89 (2002).

David B. Wexler, *Therapeutic Jurisprudence and Changing Concepts of Legal Scholarship*, 11 BEHAV. SCI. & L. 17 (1993).

Bruce Winick, *Restructuring Competency to Stand Trial*, 32 UCLA L. REV. 921 (1985).

Bruce Winick, *Therapeutic Jurisprudence and Problem Solving Courts*, 30 FORDHAM URBAN L.J. 1055 (2003).

Index

Titles in the **Elgar Advanced Introductions** series include: